Zora Neale Hurston and a History of Southern Life

In the series

Critical Perspectives on the Past

edited by Susan Porter Benson, Stephen Brier, and Roy Rosenzweig

Lisa M. Fine, *The Story of Reo Joe: Work, Kin, and Community in Autotown, U.S.A.*

Van Gosse and Richard Moser, eds., *The World the Sixties Made: Politics and Culture in Recent America*

Joanne Meyerowitz, ed., *History and September 11th*

John McMillian and Paul Buhle, eds., *The New Left Revisited*

David M. Scobey, *Empire City: The Making and Meaning of the New York City Landscape*

Gerda Lerner, *Fireweed: A Political Autobiography*

Allida M. Black, ed., *Modern American Queer History*

Eric Sandweiss, *St. Louis: The Evolution of an American Urban Landscape*

Sam Wineburg, *Historical Thinking and Other Unnatural Acts: Charting the Future of Teaching the Past*

Sharon Hartman Strom, *Political Woman: Florence Luscomb and the Legacy of Radical Reform*

Michael Adas, ed., *Agricultural and Pastoral Societies in Ancient and Classical History*

Jack Metzgar, *Striking Steel: Solidarity Remembered*

Janis Appier, *Policing Women: The Sexual Politics of Law Enforcement and the LAPD*

Allen Hunter, ed., *Rethinking the Cold War*

Eric Foner, ed., *The New American History, Revised and Expanded Edition*

Collette A. Hyman, *Staging Strikes: Workers' Theatre and the American Labor Movement*

Zora Neale Hurston and a History of Southern Life

Tiffany Ruby Patterson

 Temple University Press
Philadelphia

For

Esther Houston Patterson

(1926–2002)

*A wounded healer who fought her way to life
and taught us how to live and love.*

*Thank you for your spirit, your love, and for making me
resilient and free.*

For

Turner Patterson

(1918–)

*Thank you for your quiet love, your certain loyalty,
and your sense of humor.*

*You kept your promise: neither I nor my siblings or
mother ever wore patches. I love you for that.*

Temple University Press
1601 North Broad Street
Philadelphia PA 19122
www.temple.edu/tempress

Copyright © 2005 by Temple University
All rights reserved
Published 2005
Printed in the United States of America

Excerpts from Hurston's works used with the permission of the Zora Neale Hurston Trust.

⊗ The paper used in this publication meets the requirements of the American National Standard for Information Sciences–Permanence of Paper for Printed Library Materials, ANSI Z39.48-1992

Library of Congress Cataloging-in-Publication Data

Patterson, Tiffany Ruby
     Zora Neale Hurston and a history of southern life / Tiffany Ruby Patterson.
          p.   cm. — (Critical perspectives on the past)
     Includes bibliographical references and index.
     ISBN 1-59213-289-8 (cloth : alk. paper) — ISBN 1-59213-290-1 (pbk. : alk. paper)
          1. Hurston, Zora Neale—Characters—African Americans.   2. African Americans—Southern States—Historiography.   3. Hurston, Zora Neale—Knowledge—Southern States.   4. Literature and folklore—Southern States.   5. Literature and history—Southern States.   6. Southern States—In literature.   7. African Americans in literature.   I. Title.   II. Series.

PS3515.U789Z797 2005
813'.52—dc22   2004058855

2   4   6   8   9   7   5   3   1

Contents

Photo gallery follows page 112

Acknowledgments

THE DEBTS that I have accumulated in producing this book can never be repaid with a few words on a few pages. Now that it is done, the dozens of people who have assisted me, who have supported me through years of doubt and anguish, come into focus. I can thank only a few of them here, but they are all forever in my heart. A number of people read portions of the manuscript, challenged my ideas in conversation, or stimulated my development with their own work. They include Kristy Anderson, Pamela Bordelon, John Bracey, Elsa Barkley Brown, Sundiata Cha-Jua, Nahum Chandler, Karen Fields, Donnette Francis, Thomas Glave, Sean Green, Kenneth Hamilton, Gwendolyn Midlo Hall, Obrey Hendricks, Darlene Clark Hine, Robin D. G. Kelley, Jeffrey Kerr-Ritchie, Clayton King, Agustín Lao, Ricardo Laremont, Earl Lewis, Maria Lugones, Elias Mandela, Akbar Muhammed, Hector Myers, Nell Irvin Painter, Donald Quataert, Aníbal Quijano, Arnold Rampersad, Barbara Ransby, João Reis, David Roediger, Julie Saville, Nayan Shah, Tracey Sharpley-Whiting, Kathryn Kish Sklar, Judy Tanzer, Darryl Thomas, Dale Tomich, Joe Trotter, Cheryl Wall, Cornel West, Michael West, Ivy Wilson, Leo Wilton, and Lisa Yun.

The work of historians depends on documents. Some are easily accessible and others buried in unlikely places. A marvelous group of scholars searched out some of these documents for me, sometimes taking time away from their own work to do so. Elsa

Barkley Brown took time away from her work to find materials at Fisk University. Jessie Carney Smith also sent materials from Fisk. Kenneth Hamilton kept an eye out for materials from the Booker T. Washington Papers, and Kristy Anderson allowed me to sift through her considerable files on Hurston. Keith Bollum shared materials on Loughman, and Dr. Edward Etheridge sent materials from the Polk County Historical Association. Tana Porter of the Orange County Regional History Center was gracious enough to find materials and send them to me. Lorraine Brown helped me search for Hurston's lost play, *A Negro Lysistrata*. The staffs of many libraries were very helpful, but I cannot list them all here. Of special importance was the Library of Congress, the P. K. Yonge Library of Florida History at the University of Florida, and the Glenn G. Bartle Library at the State University of New York at Binghamton. Rochelle Moore and Ed Shepherd at Binghamton were generous with their time, finding materials and buying research sources for me.

Without a wonderful group of people in Florida, my work there would have been much more difficult. Jeanette Harris and her family provided me with a home on my numerous trips to Eatonville and Orlando. Rev. Jimmy Howard became a tour guide, taking me all over central Florida and introducing me to a number of local residents with stories to tell. Carol Mundy discussed her massive Florida collection with me. Ms. Louise Franklin, Larkin Franklin's daughter, and Mrs. Olga Mitchell, Joseph Clark's great-granddaughter, took me into their homes and their hearts. They also provided documents, photographs, and the benefit of their memories. Lois Hurston Gaston, Hurston's niece, graciously provided a key document. In Binghamton Dorothea Cornwell and her family, particularly her daughter, Rhonda Plunkitt Carbone, and her son-in-law, Michael Carbone, cared for me like my own family and were there to help when computers and printers failed and to drive me to Philadelphia to Temple University Press to deliver my manuscript. Their generosity was limitless.

My family was always so confident of my success. My mother did not live to see the completion of this book. She died in November 2002. My father, though grieving the loss of his lifelong partner, never lost interest in my work. My sister, Turnitta Rayburn, my brother, Jeffrey Patterson, my nieces and nephews, and my cousin provided love and encouragement. My gorgeous, wonderful grand-niece, Aria Faith Rayburn Peña, arrived in time to become the joy of my life. Damien Patterson, my nephew/son, lived with me during the years I worked to finish this book. He was killed on 8 August 2004 by the violence that continues to plague so many black lives. His spirit inhabits this book.

My students have always inspired me and many have also helped with my research. I am grateful to Rinah Fernandez, Jessica Flores, Alicia Dixon, Yumeris Morel, Sandra Fritz, Rafael Landron, Katrina Huffman, Natalie Bledman, Yanira Rodriquez, Shawanda Weems, Chris Gheeron, and graduate students Mio Matsumoto, Shannon King, Ivette Rivera-Giusti, Meredith Gadsby, Charles Peterson, Nicolas Veroli, and Peter Carlo. Risa Faussette, a brilliant student and now scholar, has enriched my intellectual endeavors beyond measure.

Very special thanks must go to Michael West, William Martin, and Tom Dublin, who graciously read several versions of some chapters. Jean Quataert read and edited early versions of the manuscript, yelling at me in a timely fashion when necessary. Kathryn Kish Sklar helped me to stay afloat in times of turbulence. Jeffrey Kerr-Ritchie also read and edited many chapters without complaint. Risa Faussette and Ricardo Laremont read the entire manuscript and made editorial suggestions.

There are two people for whom there are no words in any language sufficient to offer my thanks. Ari Ngaseo, my research assistant, is one of the most talented young men I have ever had the pleasure to work with. He stuck with me through this entire ordeal and challenged my ideas. My friend and my most loving critic, Karen Fields, deserves roses and champagne, bottles and bottles of it. For more than fifteen years she has supported and encouraged me when I didn't believe in myself. She spent many hours talking with me about my work, and her deep insights have sustained me over the years. A good deal of what is of value in this book I owe to her.

And most importantly, I thank God for his sustaining grace.

Prologue

ON A HOT AUGUST day in the 1920s, an unlikely couple motored through New England, stopping at an exclusive inn in Westchester County, New York. They were Fannie Hurst and Zora Neale Hurston, both writers, both female. One was an African American from the South whose rural southern heritage was imprinted in her color, language, and dress. The other was Jewish, and her heritage was hidden beneath her color, language, and dress. One was passing, the other could not. On many of their excursions together, they had discovered that race mattered in some places and not in others. They were welcomed into hotels and restaurants in Ontario, Canada.[1] At hotels in the United States, however, Hurston was often shunted off to the servants' quarters, if a place could be found for her at all. In a show of solidarity, Hurst once offered to refuse accommodation. But Zora Neale Hurston's response puzzled the white middle-class liberal, who detected no sense of indignation.[2] Unmoved by either the insult or Hurst's display of empathy, Hurston quipped, "If you are going to take that stand, it will be impossible for us to travel together. This is the way it is and I can take care of myself as I have all my life. I will find my own lodging and be around with the car in the morning."[3]

On this particular day in Westchester County, however, Hurston revealed a ripple in the apparent calm of her mental state. Fannie Hurst, dressed and behaving like a Fitzgerald heroine,[4] abruptly

1

requested that Hurston follow her as she pushed ahead at the entrance to the restaurant. Hurston, dressed in a "red head-scarf and a bizarre frock of many colors," trailed at her heels. Not giving the headwaiter time to discriminate, Hurst announced, "The Princess Zora and I wish a table." They were seated in a prime location. The meal that followed was filled with gaiety, and probably with a sense of triumph on Hurst's part. It was during the drive home that Hurston's "mental innards" surfaced. "Who would think that a good meal could be so bitter?" she mused.[5]

The responses of these two women—Hurst's surprise at Hurston's lack of indignation and Hurston's own reflection that "a good meal could be so bitter"—can stand as markers of the terrain that framed the consciousness of a southern black woman writer in the early twentieth century. This is a portrait of how an individual very much aware of the racial and gendered world she occupied made her way through that world with dignity, humor, and at times combativeness. Her response to her well-meaning white patron ("This is the way it is and I can take care of myself as I have all my life") stands as a classic response of fortitude in the midst of frustration. It stands, too, as a refusal to be a victim.

That is to say, Hurston took in the ugliness of her predicament as a black person yet remained fully open to the adventure of transgressing the color line and entering into a forbidden world of elegant service and excellent food. The one thing did not preclude the other: Both belonged to the American experience as she lived it. She took up her mission of documenting the lives of black southerners in a similar spirit. Certainly they were victims, and their predicament was indeed ugly, but she let no one persuade her to filter her understanding of their lives only through the lens of oppression and victimhood. Black southerners laid their tables in the presence of their enemies, in a manner of speaking. Zora Neale Hurston was on hand to record what they put there, how they spoke to one another around the table, and what they thought about the mysteries of life and the world they inhabited. Yet, while she trained her vision on the private homes and worlds that black southerners built, she never lost sight of the very public horror that haunted and hounded black lives. How Hurston's eyes watched both home and the horror, why she chose to focus on one without diminishing the other, and how she did so unbowed, unapologetic, and unashamed is the subject of the pages that follow.

Introduction

Rootedness—The History of Private Life

> I could blend the acceptance of the supernatural and a profound *rootedness* [emphasis added] in the real world at the same time with neither taking precedence over the other. It is indicative of the cosmology, the way in which Black people looked at the world. We are very practical people, very down-to-earth, even shrewd people. But within that practicality we also accepted what I suppose could be called superstition and magic, which is another way of knowing things. But to blend those two worlds together at the same time was enhancing, not limiting. And some of those things were "discredited knowledge" that Black people had; discredited only because Black people were discredited therefore what they *knew* was "discredited." And also because the press toward upward social mobility would mean to get as far away from that kind of knowledge as possible.
>
> —Toni Morrison, "Rootedness: The Ancestor as Foundation"[1]

ZORA NEALE HURSTON is a much-misunderstood historical figure. She faithfully chronicled black life—most notably the lives of working- and lower-class black women and men, especially in the rural South, but her very role as chronicler has been used to denounce her as a traitor to her race. Although her works stand among the richest documentary sources on black life, labor, and culture in the early twentieth-century South, most of the denunciation has emanated from the intellectual left, which has accused her of ignoring or minimizing the exploitation, oppression, and outright atrocities visited upon black people in the post-Reconstruction South.

In fact, Hurston's eyes were watching those atrocities, but her eyes were open to other aspects of the lives of southern black folk as well. Unlike her detractors, who preferred to view black people in relation to whites, Hurston sought first and foremost to study black people on their own terms. Although she recognized oppression as a daily fact of African American life, Hurston's literary and ethnographic work focused more on what black people were doing for themselves than on what their oppressors and tormentors were doing to them. Her contrarian gaze moved black people to the center of inquiry, establishing them as subjects, a place reserved for white people in the dominant race-relations paradigm in African American history and thought.

Hurston's intellectual and political posture is consistent with a venerable tradition in the African American experience. This tradition of black self-determination includes a kind of internal, territorial black nationalism and encompasses independent black communities such as Eatonville, Hurston's hometown and literary subject. If Hurston failed to pay as much attention to oppression as she might have, it was because she kept her focus on black self-determination. With an unflinching eye on her subjects, Hurston dissected the inner world of African American life with wit and provocative narrative. By all accounts, Zora Neale Hurston had a sharp eye, an acute ear, and a barbed tongue. Among her memorable barbs are, for example, "Niggerati," the term of disaffection she used when weary of the Harlem Renaissance elite, and "Negrotarians," her term for their condescending white elite patrons. As a novelist, Hurston created memorably articulate heroines, and as an ethnographer she recorded the delicious ins and outs of "telling lies" on southern porches.

Hurston's barbs invite careful scrutiny, for their meaning is anything but self-evident. Why is a proud black woman intellectual angry enough to puncture her peers with a term that was opprobrious even then, and downright taboo among progressive black people? And why does she imply that some white people behave as though black people are social projects? What do these terms imply about her detachment? My answer is that Zora Neale Hurston was an expert witness to her time. She imagined, as every great artist does; but she also made it her business to see, hear, and write as an ethnographer does—in detail, in depth, and by bringing to bear a deep understanding of human complexity. These qualities of Hurston's make her an invaluable witness to her era.

To understand what she meant, we must enter imaginatively into the world in which she lived, into a particular time in our country's past that formed the contours of Hurston's lived experience. This book examines what I think of as Zora Neale Hurston's "past present," centering on Hurston's folk: turpentine and sawmill workers in Florida's naval stores industries, workers in phosphate-mining industries, migrant workers in agricultural camps, and residents of an all-black town in Florida in the early twentieth century. I intend to demonstrate the value of Hurston's creative literary work as a source of historical knowledge about the period from the 1880s, when her parents married, to the 1940s, the most productive period of her life. To make this case I have used representative works from Hurston's canon: her well-known novel, *Their Eyes Were Watching God*, her unpublished short story, "Black Death," her play, *Polk County*, and her collection of vignettes, "The Eatonville Anthology"; I give these equal standing with her folklore study, *Mules and Men*, as well as selections from her journalism, letters, private papers, and her autobiography, *Dust Tracks on a Road*.

Hurston's portrait of black southerners, the culture and consciousness that distinguished their lives, and the peculiar forms of patronage that shaped southern as well as northern realities confront the larger historiography of the period. They challenge not only the cultural and political visions of her Harlem Renaissance contemporaries but also those of historians and literary critics in our own day. Thus we hear the judgments of writers such as

Richard Wright, Langston Hughes, Sterling Brown, and Stetson Kennedy echoed by such scholars as Hazel Carby. Few have appreciated Hurston's vision of southern black folk.

To move past these judgments, I argue that we must first understand the politics of the period in which Hurston and her contemporaries understood and misunderstood each other. Hurston's work, by placing in the foreground the everyday lives of residents of Eatonville, the Loughman sawmill/turpentine camps, and the phosphate-mining camp at Mulberry, cast a spotlight on the most sensitive issues in black culture—gender, sexuality, color, hoodoo, and violence. By revealing these aspects of black culture, she enables us to analyze them historically. Although these subjects were regarded as sensitive in the 1920s and 1930s, some of her contemporaries also dealt with them.[2]

Few writers other than Hurston, however, confronted black male sexism and violence toward women, whether among middle- or working-class people.[3] Hurston did, however. She also criticized black male leadership and acknowledged the violence that occurred in settled communities like Eatonville and in transient worlds like sawmill and turpentine camps. This was a bold position at a time when white violence against black people was destroying thousands in both the North and the South.

What is more, Hurston chose to represent the beauty of black culture using the very group of people that black intellectuals of the time considered the underbelly of black life.[4] She did so by not only celebrating the music and the poetry of their language but also by sanctioning the legitimacy of hoodoo and voodoo, an underground world of peasant cosmology that terrified and embarrassed the elite.

She entangled herself in the world of white patronage of the Harlem Renaissance and openly manipulated it to her advantage, but at the same time criticized this patronage for its ambition to be the custodian of black culture. If wealthy patrons sought the primitive and the childlike, Hurston accommodated them with her brightly colored clothing, off-color humor, and boisterous laughter. Her male contemporaries accepted white patronage but looked down their noses at Hurston for playing the primitive. I regard Hurston's manipulation of stereotypes as a far more honest stance in relation to the power of white patrons than her male counterparts' pretense of equality with their patrons.

Black southern life as recorded in Hurston's work was characterized by more than unrelenting work, violence, and imprisonment. While it was a place where bondage and racial domination persisted after the Civil War, the South, for her and her subjects, was also a place of cultural creativity, family, and religion, where everyday life was lived with integrity in the midst of struggle against racial oppression. It was, in short, a place called home. Southern black culture blended "the acceptance of the supernatural and a profound *rootedness* in the real world at the same time with neither taking precedence over the other," as Toni Morrison has described it.[5] Black people accepted what some would call superstition and magic as practical ways of knowing things. But theirs was "discredited knowledge," in Morrison's words, because black people themselves were discredited. Hurston rejected this dominant view of the South and instead understood southern culture as the material for creativity and survival. As Hurston put it in her unpublished short story, "Black Death," black people knew things that gave them power.

Hurston also recognized that color prejudice was a part of the fabric of black culture that had particular meaning for women. It takes a historically rigorous separation of our own present from Hurston's present to grasp the nature of the taboos she violated. Her contemporaries talked about color prejudice, for example, but this prejudice was an open secret in black life, one the black elite denied publicly even as they practiced color discrimination themselves. Nearly everyone discussed it as a source of both humor and pain. Hurston also acknowledged violence as a fact of life not only in Jim Crow society but also inside black communities. Many of her contemporaries turned a blind eye to violence within black communities for fear of undermining the struggle against racist violence. In Hurston's view, the Niggerati sloughed off this culture in their striving for upward social mobility.

For the "best-foot-forward Negroes," who sought social accept-ance, southern black folk knowledge was an impediment. Hurston, by contrast, validated this folk knowledge, its beauty and tragedy, its tensions, its contradictions, and its ethos of resist-ance. She recorded the humor, songs, poetry, sermons, stories, and social banter of her folk and their value as literature. For Hurston, folklore, "Sprites, fairies, Puck, Caliban, Twelfth Night celebrations, Mid-Summer's Night observances are just as much a part of English folk-lore and folk ways as hoodoo practices and Brer Rabbit are a part of Aframerican folk ways." Like Chaucer in an England conquered and denigrated by Normans, Hurston saw beauty in the language of ordinary people, despite the scorn in which their language was held. She saw rich cultural traditions that were the raw materials of great artistic creations.[6]

Hurston, if read carefully, gives us a nuanced and textured his-tory of the black experience not restricted to the area north of 125th Street in Harlem. She did not treat the northern metropo-lis as the quintessential cultural site of black expressive culture, but instead located this site in the South. She also criticized the promi-nent members of the Harlem Renaissance who had left the South and severed their ties to black folk. In their depictions, the folk became a free-floating signifier without a regional or cultural ref-erent. In the hands of Langston Hughes, for example, black folk were everywhere, but they lacked regional distinctiveness and were uncoupled from the political economy in which they were born and shaped. Hughes could therefore appropriate the lan-guage of the folk without confronting their identity as southern-ers. For Hurston, by contrast, location was a historical agent and producer of culture. In the South black culture emanated from the workers—debt peons, sharecroppers, and small-town dwellers. Hurston resituated the folk in the South, recognizing that their language, songs, folklore, etc., gave these people specific regional characteristics. At the same time, she illuminated the heterogene-ity of black people. In works like *Mules and Men*, Hurston depicted southern folk life as a cultural reference point for the construction of black interior life.

The chapters that follow maintain that Hurston understood the importance of people's lives and insisted that "the Negro farthest down" was a rich subject for literature. She was deeply critical of the black literati's inability to see the diversity of black people and allow them their individuality. Hurston's close-up view encompassed their names, family relations, friends and enemies; it acknowledged that they fished, gambled, quarreled, made love and discarded lovers. And it recognized that they found ways, within their southern sensibility, to resist the overt violence of Jim Crow as well as its psychic damage. In Hurston's view, each individual had a right to his or her particular identity and the ways in which that identity was shaped. Her published work and private papers suggest that she understood how living in a racist society forced groups to seek cohesion based on race, but she rejected the racist ideology that made that cohesion necessary.

She also knew that race did not govern every aspect of working people's lives in the South, in spite of what people with particular political agendas maintained. Hurston acknowledged that the South was the site of the violence and discrimination that filled northern newspapers. Indeed, her artistic and ethnographic works record the ways in which that violence was woven into the fabric of black life. But the South also encompassed homes and families, private lives that were defended even in the most wretched conditions. Hurston chose to emphasize the lives made by rural workers and members of the all-black town of Eatonville. Blackness for her was not a designation in the anthropological sense but a distinctive system of cultural particulars, of ways of thinking and acting, of commonplace expectations, humor, language, and style. In her determination to present black life in such terms, from the 1920s until her death in 1960 she expressed outrage at the liberals and radicals who focused only on racist violence. As a result, her public pronouncements and writing seemed more and more conservative. But a far more complicated political persona emerges from a close examination of the context in which she made these statements. If Hurston's insistence on rejecting the politics of victimhood sometimes led her to downplay the overt forms of violence in the South, especially in the 1950s, it is perhaps because some of her critics overemphasized them.

Hurston was an individualist, but she did not, as some have claimed, adhere to a philosophy of individualism that advocates egoistic isolation from community.[7] Hurston believed that she had a moral obligation to her community, and that obligation was fulfilled in her work as an artist and folklorist and in her everyday life.[8] At no time did Hurston see herself as disconnected from community, although there were times that she imposed exile upon herself.

This book, then, is an attempt to see Hurston and the world she depicted in their historical context. Chapter 1 examines the meanings of what I call "past presents" and the critical methodological issues at the heart of this study. It argues for combining the traditional methodology of historians with Hurston's ethnography and imaginative work in order to study African American culture. Chapter 2 compares and contrasts Hurston's portrait of the South with that of her contemporary, Richard Wright. Whereas Wright focuses so narrowly on the horror of Jim Crow in black southerners' lives that he omits everything else, Hurston presents their lives in a way that obscures Jim Crow, at least momentarily. The tension between these portrayals of the South establishes the framework for the next three chapters.

Chapter 3 explores the founding of Eatonville, Hurston's home and the site of much of her work. It links this community to the history of maroon societies and uses the concept of maroonage and territorial nationalism as a way of understanding all-black towns within the tradition of African American resistance. Hurston's angle of vision keeps these collective autonomous spaces in full view, but it never dismisses the ongoing struggle of black southern folk for autonomy and dignity. The population, institutions, economics, and politics of this community frame this chapter, which traces the many changes that took place in post-Reconstruction Florida. It also looks at the history of the naval stores industry, the social organization of capital and labor, the role played by the debt-peonage and convict-lease systems, and the nature of the work. The chapter ends with examples of the white terrorism that always threatened the relative safety of black towns. This violence was periodically visited upon individuals and whole communities for transgressing the norms of segregation or for exercising the rights of citizenship, and it had a profound effect on the climate in which everyday life was lived.

Chapter 4 explores the vibrant, complex culture of all-black towns through the lens of Hurston's work. Hurston depicts Eatonville as a community that operated outside the immediate reach of white control. She examines the ways in which gendered spaces were contested in this community, how race often took a back seat to class, and how color nevertheless remained a salient factor in daily life.

Chapter 5 discusses the everyday life of black workers who lived at a distance from the brutal world of turpentine, sawmill, and phosphate work yet were shaped by the violence of that world. Drawing on Hurston's folklore—as presented in *Mules and Men* and in her play, *Polk County*—this chapter sorts out the conflicting portraits of rural black southerners in Hurston's work, those presented to her public audience and those that remained hidden in unpublished documents. The chapter ends with some clues to Hurston's complicated politics, a subject explored more fully in the concluding chapter.

As Hurston tells her life, she had a white audience from the start and had to take that audience into account throughout her life, both in what she said and in how she said it. Chapter 6 examines that audience through Hurston's own stories about the human relationships that underlie the politics of "patronage." Hurston's depiction of South and North not only differed from that of her peers but also disturbed the selective nature of black artistic representations that developed during the Harlem Renaissance. The ideas discussed in this chapter expand on the portraits of the South discussed in Chapter 2.

IN SHORT, this book examines Hurston's work as a form of historical documentation. As part of the context for that work, it will be useful to turn briefly to a biographical sketch of Hurston's life.

Zora Neale Hurston was born on 7 January 1891 in Notasulga, Alabama, but she always claimed the all-black town of Eatonville, Florida, as her birthplace. She was the fifth of eight children. Hurston's father, John Hurston, was an Alabama sharecropper and a "yaller bastard... from over de creek," as Hurston's maternal grandmother described him.[9] Her mother, Lucy Ann Potts, was from the landowning Potts family, a class difference that influenced interfamily relations. Lucy Potts defied her family's wishes when she married John Hurston, who was considered unworthy of the proud, educated, comparatively well-off Potts family. John Hurston and Lucy Potts were typical of blacks who settled in Eatonville in search of a better life during the post-Reconstruction era.

John Hurston sought a place without the restrictions of Jim Crow, where a black man could have some say in how his life and community were run. He had high ambitions for his wife and eight children—a home, financial security, education, and protection from terror—elusive goals, more often than not, for a freedman. He found possibilities in Eatonville, where he could make a living as a carpenter and minister. In Eatonville, Lucy, a former schoolteacher, could be a mother and housewife and avoid "working out" in the homes of white people, one of the few black women in Eatonville able to do so.[10] Eatonville offered opportunities for political and economic freedom and therefore social and cultural comfort. John Hurston eventually served as mayor of Eatonville, from 1912 to 1916, as pastor of Macedonia Baptist Church, and as pastor of Zion Hope Baptist Church in nearby Sanford, Florida.[11] He was thus able to serve as a leader in his community while avoiding confrontations with the white power structure.

Zora was a precocious youngster who ran afoul of her father's conservative views on the proper behavior of both black people in general and young "ladies" in particular. His daughter's audacity and spirit needed to be contained, lest white folks get riled.

John Hurston's relations with his daughter show that his status as a minister and even as mayor of Eatonville did not erase the restrictions of Jim Crow, which he carried in his soul.

Zora's mother, by contrast, the symbol of strength in the family, encouraged her daughter to "jump at de sun" and encouraged the spirit of independence that later characterized her life.[12] Lucy felt that her daughter should be allowed freedom of imagination and behavior. In Hurston's account of her childhood, this freedom to think and wonder and move and explore was pivotal in the formation of her personality. In spite of the restrictions against which she would struggle in later life, she held on tenaciously to this psychic freedom, even when her physical freedom was held in check. This early experience placed the young Zora at the center of many family battles.

The death of Lucy Potts in 1904 was devastating for thirteen-year-old Zora.[13] She lost the maternal protection that had allowed her spirit and independence to flourish, and she was haunted by the death of her mother for many years. After Lucy's death, Zora's father struggled to hold the family together, but failed.

John Hurston sent his young daughter to a boarding school in Jacksonville, where her sister Sarah and brother John could look after her. Less than a year later, however, her father ran out of money for the tuition and at the same time married a woman Zora described as insensitive and self-serving. Thus Hurston was robbed of a home and became, in her own words, "a wanderer." Her wandering apparently lasted for several years, as she lived sporadically with her father, other family members, friends, and strangers. She tried to support herself as a maid but not too successfully. The humility expected of a maid was not her strong suit, nor was she available to the fancies of white men. Finally, in late 1915, Hurston joined a traveling Gilbert and Sullivan drama troupe and worked as a maid to an actress who eventually befriended her. She left the company in Baltimore eighteen months later to finish her education.[14]

Hurston entered Morgan Academy in Maryland in September 1917 and had fulfilled her high school requirements by June 1918, at the age of twenty-seven. In the fall of 1918 she attended Howard University Preparatory School. She entered Howard University in 1919 and received her Associate of Arts degree in 1920. She continued to take classes while working part-time at various jobs until 1924. She also met and fell in love with another struggling student, Herbert Sheen. Sheen wanted to be a doctor but instead became a musician, an occupation that led to long separations from his beloved Zora. Their relationship lasted for several years, with plans for marriage always postponed to sometime in the future.

Poverty stalked Hurston, and financial insecurity became a lifelong companion. Although she worked hard, she was rarely out of debt, and therefore her pace in school was slow. Despite her academic training and artistic brilliance, it was as a maid that she began and ended her working life. Domestic work was often her last resort, an experience she shared with many black and working women in both urban and rural areas, who made up a permanent service caste in nineteenth- and twentieth-century America.[15] Even after becoming a well-known writer, Hurston resorted to domestic service to support herself. Poverty was the familiar companion of many artists, of course. Langston Hughes, among many others, had many lean days. Most artists required the assistance of patrons. Literary success did not bring Hurston financial security, however.

In addition to working as a maid for prominent families, she was also a manicurist in a fashionable shop and a waitress at the exclusive Cosmos Club.[16] But Hurston's working-class existence did not exclude her from Washington's "Negro Society," and her experience in its circle undoubtedly left its mark on her life and work. She entered the black upper-class world of Washington society, where she forcefully asserted her southernness in an implicitly condescending northern milieu. Hurston's keen intelligence and stubbornness allowed her entrance into a world that she desired but also enabled her to move in and out of the working-class occupations that kept her afloat in hard times. This wandering across class and cultural lines meant that Hurston had continually to negotiate borders, which only refined her skills as a witness to the changes taking place in African American culture. As she migrated between rural and urban locales, between black and white society, Hurston learned how to unlock the doors that blocked her entrance to the world of artists and intellectuals.

She made connections with well-placed blacks and began what became a life of scholarship and letters, blending scholarly modes of expression with the southern folk vernacular that anchored her soul. Her efforts were encouraged and assisted by such luminaries as Alain Locke, poet and Rhodes Scholar, anthropologist Lorenzo Dow Turner of Howard University, and Georgia Douglas Johnson, a prominent black poet who entertained young artists at her home, known locally as Halfway House, with long evenings of poetry, music, and intellectual conversation. At Howard University the literary club Stylus admitted Hurston only after she had prevailed against stiff competition. Alain Locke and drama instructor Montgomery Gregory, the club's cosponsors, were intrigued by the dramatic presentation of folk life. Hurston's membership in Stylus undoubtedly facilitated the publication, in 1921, of her short story, "John Redding Goes to Sea," in Howard's literary magazine, also named *Stylus*.[17] Locke recommended Hurston's work to Charles S. Johnson, who in 1924 published her second short story, "Drenched in Light." Hurston learned quickly how to use these opportunities, impressing those she met with her wit and talent.

Buoyed by her experiences and with encouragement from Johnson, she left for New York in January 1925 with $1.25 in her pocket, though evidence suggests that she had visited New York as early as 1922 and had published both poetry and prose in Marcus Garvey's *Negro World*. In September she entered Barnard College, where she studied anthropology with the distinguished scholar Franz Boas.[18] Boas became her mentor and had a profound influence on her intellectual development. As with her writing, Hurston's education in anthropology was aided by a series of patrons who would come to play a significant role in her life, among them Annie Nathan Meyer, benefactor of Barnard College, and popular fiction writer Fannie Hurst, for whom Hurston worked as a secretary.

Hurston continued to write fiction while studying anthropology. In June 1925 her short story "Spunk" was published in *Opportunity*; another story, "Muttsy," was published in August 1926. In collaboration with Langston Hughes, Wallace Thurman, and others, Hurston edited the short-lived magazine *Fire!!* in which her short story "Sweat" appeared in November 1926. In 1930, again collaborating with Langston Hughes, she wrote a play entitled *Mule Bone*, a comedy about African American life that drew on Hurston's intimate knowledge of rural folk life. Never performed in her lifetime, *Mule Bone* highlighted Hurston's blending of scholarly and popular forms. With the aid of her most important patron, Charlotte Osgood Mason, Hurston wrote *Mules and Men*, a volume of anthropological folklore published in 1935. *Tell My Horse*, on Caribbean folklore, was published in 1938. Meanwhile, Hurston was turning her attention to the novel.

In 1934 she published her first novel, *Jonah's Gourd Vine*, loosely based on the lives of her parents, particularly her father. Her masterpiece, *Their Eyes Were Watching God*, was published in 1937, *Moses, Man of the Mountain* in 1939, and *Seraph on the Suwanee*, the least successful of her works, in 1948. Equally important in Hurston's canon is her autobiography, *Dust Tracks on a Road*. Published in 1942, this book situates Hurston within the turbulent cultural and political changes that shaped the period from the 1890s through 1940.

The way Hurston lived her life, the issues she addressed in her work, and especially her portrayal of the South and southern folk pushed to their limit the concerns over identity and representation that galvanized intellectual discourse in her day. This body of literature forms the basis for my examination of the interior worlds of turpentine, sawmill, and phosphate labor camps, and of the residents of rural southern black towns.

1

Reconstructing Past Presents

> Like the dead-seeming, cold rocks, I have memories
> within that came out of the material that went to make
> me. Time and place have had their say.
> —Zora Neale Hurston, *Dust Tracks on a Road*[1]

FOR ZORA NEALE HURSTON the presence of the past manifests itself even in the most ordinary things and the most ordinary lives. Layers of experience reside under their deceptively mute surfaces. For Hurston, everyday actions and interactions, while seemingly inconsequential, are actually set in motion by the complex interplay between the force of history and the creative efforts of those to whom Toni Morrison refers as "discredited" people. What may appear stone cold and devoid of vitality pulses with remembering. While "time and place have had their say" in the shaping of Hurston's memories, neither has the last word in her self-fashioning. Hurston recognizes the constraints imposed by Jim Crow conditions and their northern counterparts on her life and work, but she is never deadened by them. Instead she presents herself as an active agent, an "I" irreducible to any of her many components. How, then, can we recapture the lives that Hurston and her folk informants wrenched from the teeth of Jim Crow?

This book is about a "past present" in which Zora Neale Hurston's grandmother, Sarah Potts, said "nossuh!" to her daughter Lucy's intended marriage to John Hurston. Not "dat yaller bastard" from "over de creek."[2] That she regarded the match as unsuitable is clear enough to us from where we stand more than one hundred years later. But what did she mean by "yaller bastard?" And what did "de creek" have to do with a marriage? Census data can tell us how many "mulattoes" got counted in a particular area, but not why that status could render a marriage undesirable. A map of Macon County, Alabama, where the Pottses and the Hurstons lived, identifies the main creeks that have been flowing there since the glaciers melted, but not what makes living "over de creek" a disqualifier for the Hurston seniors. Sarah Potts's exclamation suggests a sense of class superiority, but Alabama statistics tell us that there was virtually no economic disparity among black people there. Through Hurston's testimony, we come to know what Sarah Potts's "Nossuh" meant. Hurston's testimony opens a window on what I think of as a "past present," raising questions about the nature of historical sources and what constitutes legitimate knowledge.

By past present, I mean spoken and written documents that embodied, for their producers, a real present, but that necessarily belongs to our own real past.[3] One part of that real present were the towns that blacks established as spaces where they could live out their lives at a distance from the raw, inhumane power of the Jim Crow regime. There they created their own ways of understanding the world around them that in turn formed the basis for social order, pleasure, work, spirituality, morals, art, mysteries, and everything else that makes for the distinctiveness of human life. Also in that past present are the sawmill, turpentine, and railroad camps, the mining towns, and the agricultural "mucks" where black people lived in the grip of racist exploitation of their labor. Yet, even at the lowest rung of the socioeconomic ladder, they lived and created human lives as well as a culture that cannot be defined by the oppression and degradation that characterized so much of their existence.

Without exploring that space for self-determination, we cannot adequately explain why "a yaller bastard" from "over de creek" was seen as a bad choice for a daughter of the landowning Potts in a black town. Nor can we fully comprehend how it came to pass that a high yellow, razor-wielding woman named Big Sweet dispensed law and order in a world where, historians have argued, law and order cowered in the shadow cast by powerful racist company overseers.

In short, it is easier to understand why some black people took part in the "Great Migration" than to understand how they lived in the South. If we fail to understand how they survived in the South, we will never know what cultural material they constructed and brought with them to the North. This failure would also limit our understanding of the South and the migrants' destinations in the North, because both regions were dramatically transformed in the years that followed the Civil War. Migration studies should, in essence, probe the micro-dynamics of human perspectives as well as the broad or macro-historical context that shaped people's decisions for staying or going.

An adequate description of a past present requires imagining a past moment as a present time—that is, as a time when the future is unknown. It has no place for anachronism. In Hurston's present, the period from 1900 to the 1940s, rural black folk are still very much embedded in southern black culture and its strategies of resistance, having stayed in the South through World War I and its aftermath. Even after the Great Migration that followed World War II, the South remained home to millions of black people.[4] Even those who resided elsewhere maintained southern family connections, as did their progeny. The failure to account for these realities is a failure to understand the past on its own terms, as well as a failure to recognize the past as something significantly more than the origins of the present.[5] Writing history as a past present, we attend to the contingencies and discontinuities that were an intrinsic part of the lives our forebears lived.

Writers have "designs upon their audiences," says Jane Tompkins; writers intend their readers to think, move, and act in particular ways.[6] The audience Hurston intended to move was the one she knew, who belonged to her historical moment and were members of her community. She could imagine what might move them, but not what might move us. People who are a "them" to us were a "you" to her. Though she traveled far, she never lost her connections with her home or region. She never became an outsider. Thus, I contend, historians may study Hurston's literature and the literature of other writers as artifacts of their time. Their work represents the broad contours of a historical moment filtered through an individual consciousness. Hurston's work takes us into the inner lives of sawmill and turpentine workers and residents of black towns, where we can observe men and women thinking about their condition and the world around them on their own terms.

Entering into their consciousness requires what Michael Woods calls "a heightened form of historical experience," which I take to mean finding history in "places where it ought not to have been lost," amid our favorite formalisms and decorums.[7] For example, age dictates that a certain tone be used when addressing an elder, while the names Skillet Blond and Blue Baby encode color consciousness and race.[8] Zora Neale Hurston's novels, folklore, autobiography, and personal correspondence are unique sources for bringing to light once lost histories. Together they provide us with discourses on race, color, ethnicity, gender, class, and sexuality as they were socially articulated within the African American communities of Zora Neale Hurston's time and place. These discourses constituted "a social language consisting of signs and symbols understood by Blacks,"[9] and they are embedded in Hurston's work. Her life offers other clues.

This book examines the broad features of African American social understandings by peering into the world of an African American novelist and anthropologist through her fiction and ethnographic fieldwork. The testimony of Hurston and other witnesses is often all the evidence we have of a world that has been erased by historical change but that was once immensely important and lives on in distant echoes. In her art and ethnography, we learn about such matters because she could not misrepresent them to us. As an ethnographer, Hurston recorded moments in time, and from those moments, as an artist, she constructed human dramas.

As a fiction writer, Hurston invented, and when she got around to writing her autobiography, she famously lied—about her age and love life, for example. For such reasons, she might be thought of as an unreliable chronicler. I regard such inventions as trivial matters for historians. The nicknames Skillet Blond, Blue Baby, and Big Sweet, with their overtones to class, color, and sexuality, whether or not they are inventions open a window onto the details of day-to-day life that are absent from official records or more reliable accounts. Stories heard on someone's porch, judgments made in ancient disputes, attitudes toward women called "vamps," assumptions about good behavior, acceptable solutions to social problems, decisions about when killing is justified together create the social world of Hurston's stories and represent the place and time in which she lived.

I regard Hurston as an expert witness. Hurston placed the ever-looming threat of white people at a distance in order to portray black communities from the inside and show that it was possible for black people to create a history of their own. Rather than focus solely on the power of the dominant class, Hurston peers into the bedrooms and waits in the shadows of front porches to capture the details of black life that are not constantly refracted through the lens of white oppression. We learn from her stories how black communities determined for themselves how color mattered, how property mattered, how class and status partly explained relations between black people, how social contracts were entered into and broken, how gender spaces were marked off, how men and women struggled for identity and dignity and how they managed their accounts with each other, how white folks mattered and didn't matter, how life unfolded. We learn about the imaginative worlds of black people in the twentieth century, about the folks who left few documents about that world and the intelligentsia who struggled to represent them.[10]

The Problem of Sources

Literature by its nature embodies the imaginative possibilities rooted in the time and place of its creation. Folk tales, sermons, written reports of neighborhood hullaballoos, and so on, by and large remain suspect sources for some historians. I contend that the choice of source material is more a matter of habit and training in methodology and epistemology than of carefully justified decisions. "Historians," Lawrence Levine has observed, "are prisoners... of their sources or what they perceive to be their sources."[11] They fail to take seriously the orally transmitted expressive cultures of the mass of African people "who, though quite articulate in their own lifetimes, have been *rendered* historically inarticulate."[12] Historians "imprison" themselves through their reliance on documents they deem "factual," such as census data and other government documents, private papers, public records such as newspapers, calculations derived from various kinds of statistics, and interviews. For traditional historical scholars, there is a sense that the historical record is comprised in these sources exclusively. Because the creation of imaginative literature and the collection of ethnographic material are not governed by rigidly prescribed rules, they are often dismissed as subjective, unreliable, and fictional in the sense of being untrue.

These criticisms lose their persuasive power if we look at them closely, for then we see that they are fraught with contradictions. Allegedly objective sources can contain elements of untruth without being discounted as sources, and admittedly subjective sources deserve at least the same consideration. The use of either kind of source therefore requires a critical methodology.[13]

Until the "new social history" transformed the discipline of history beginning in the 1970s, many historians dismissed the legitimacy of oral and folk sources in constructing historical narratives, and some still do. Such sources are devalued in favor of "great-man" history or "history from the top down." Gertrude Himmelfarb advocates the top-down, elitist approach to history when she complains that "kings, presidents, politicians, leaders, political theorists" are ignored in order to "understand any life... to explore the lowest depths of life, to probe the unconscious, unreflective, irrational aspects of life." C. Vann Woodward also laments the focus on "the family, the nursery, the bedroom, the deathbed... marriage, birth rates and sex roles... popular culture," at the expense of the "elites and the powerful."[14] He is right, of course, to insist that no plausible story about social life can be constructed as if the powerful did not exist. But this debate is really a struggle over the role of power and politics in history, and over what and who are appropriate subjects of historical inquiry.[15]

Historians who deplore the focus on ordinary people also tend to be suspicious of imaginative sources—autobiographies, ethnographic data, and literary creations—as sources of historical information. Such sources are acceptable only when coupled with "factual" materials—census data, government documents, letters, diaries—and even then imaginative sources serve more or less as supporting material that helps bolster an argument or enliven a narrative. Because imaginative sources consist largely in remembered or imagined worlds and stories, historians tend not to trust them without what they think of, often mechanically, as "corroborating" evidence. From this perspective, Sarah Potts's slur on John Hurston as a "yaller bastard" from "over de creek" would be judged worthless as a historical document.

Oral traditions were once viewed with similar suspicion.[16] Yet these traditions have been crucial to the writing of African history for several decades, after scholars finally dropped the argument that there was no African history to write or none worth writing about. My own training in African history taught me that it is possible to reconstruct the consciousness of a people who left scant written records but had a rich oral tradition. Jan Vansina defines oral traditions "as verbal messages which are reported statements from the past beyond the present generation."[17] These messages may be spoken, sung, or called out on musical instruments. According to Vansina, these messages must have been passed on by word of mouth for at least one generation in order to qualify as part of a "tradition,"[18] a criterion that folklore clearly meets.

Of course oral sources may require corroboration, for memory can be unreliable; and an ethnographer's role in the production of historical texts is inherently problematic, inviting the same criticisms of bias and subjectivity to which all other historical constructions are open. Nonetheless, when approached with care, oral sources can enable historians to explore past presents with fewer unwarranted assumptions than are customary.

Literary works, though they may contain few or no historically empirical data, are nevertheless historical artifacts. Before Schliemann excavated Troy, we knew rather a lot about it from *The Iliad*. Indeed, Schliemann found Troy partly with the help of that literary text.[19] Literary texts offer, at the very least, clues about the ideas abroad in a culture. They can tell us a great deal about the formation of racial and gender identities, political rights and struggles, privilege and oppression, and other features of everyday life that are not always recorded in more traditional historical sources.

Great literary works are great by virtue of going beyond "the limitations of their particular time and place" and speaking to us of universal truths. But they also provide "powerful examples of the way a culture thinks about itself, articulating and proposing solutions for the problems of a particular historical moment."[20] In short, literary artifacts reflect the social and psychological attitudes of a period.[21] These attitudes mediate social relations consciously and subconsciously, in both deliberate and habitual ways. They provide indications about "institutions and mores, formulated policies and unwritten codes, cultural traditions and tacit conventions."[22] Literary works dissect, examine, challenge, or affirm elements of social behavior. Statistics allow us to infer general conditions, but we need different information if we want to turn our attention inward.

The literary artist is permitted the freedom and the opportunity to probe what men and women mask, which is the internal circuits, the subconscious of their minds. Both the literary artist and the historian create mirrors of their worlds. If history is the raw material of literature, literature is an artifact of history. And as an artifact, it becomes a source, and a way of knowing history.

Autobiography

As a literary form, autobiography presents an especially thorny problem as a historical source. Historians have long approached autobiography with caution, since its claims cannot always be verified. As Elizabeth Fox-Genovese notes, "Memories fail. Authors deceive. Making a point sharply seems to require some tampering with facts."[23] Even so, autobiographies offer clues to the contours of the past. Of course they are not exhaustive or exclusive reservoirs of historical data, but they do contain essential information about the inner lives of their writers and those writers' subjects—in Hurston's case, of the black people of Eatonsville—that may be available nowhere else. Hurston's autobiography shows us instantly what is wrong with the conventional race-relations paradigm. Jim Crow decreed that black and white folk live in separate social, cultural, and economic spheres. But the conventional paradigm represents the black world simplistically (and tautologically) as "not white," and the white world as "not black," and on these grounds sees the two spheres as "related." In fact, these separate worlds require study before we can see how they are related.

In the case of Hurston's autobiography, race is a complex issue. In black autobiography in general, race becomes a trope that tends to blot out other group and individual identities and questions such as who is in the foreground? Who in the background? Who are the heroes and race leaders? Where are black families and communities? What are the demands of leadership and public life?

Hurston's politics of race, and her position on other social and cultural issues, have baffled some of her critics, but we can get to the bottom of some of them by delving deeply into her work.

Ethnography

For some historians, ethnography is perhaps the least suspect of all the sources used in this study. Many share Claude Levi-Strauss's view that "history and ethnography are concerned with societies other than the one in which we live," and for that reason have a "basic similarity and perspective," which consists in the remoteness (in time and space) of the investigator from the culture and value systems of the group under investigation.[24] Ethnographers have been charged with the same interpretive biases as historians: that their inherent subjectivity has made their work no more value-neutral than the work of any other social scientist or historian. But this criticism does not disqualify ethnography any more than it does any other discipline. Subjectivity and inherent interpretive bias cannot be remedied and must constantly be borne in mind, as we try to come as close as we can to that elusive quantity, historical truth.[25]

Like other anthropologists, Hurston studied populations marginal to the centers of power—those who were unable, until recently, to answer back. Unlike most anthropologists, however, Hurston was a native of the communities she studied. There is a longstanding debate within the discipline about which is more accurate or more valuable, studies done from within a culture by a member of that culture, or studies done from without, by a presumably detached, impartial observer. But, as we have just acknowledged, there is no such thing as strict impartiality. Moreover, I submit, understanding the inner lives of historical figures is difficult for either type of observer. There is a strong case to be made that only someone writing from within a given culture can truly understand it—particularly if that person is a gifted writer and observer like Zora Neale Hurston.

The subjects and the cultural world Hurston documented were largely hidden from full view; they had to hide themselves in order for them to survive. This was true even of the educated minority. Hurston disinterred the lives of these "insignificant others" at a time when the majority of her contemporaries were attempting either to refine and uplift these "others" or to hide them altogether.[26] She shared the same project as cultural historians like Emmanuel LeRoy Ladurie, Carlo Ginzburg, Robert Darnton, and Raphael Samuel, who have argued that the methods of the ethnographer "are more rigorous and revealing than they appear" in their own historical field.[27] In *Mules and Men*

Hurston is present, as all ethnographers are, as both observer and participant. Hurston's present is our past, and her work provides us tools for finding our own history in places where it ought not to have been lost.

In examining historians' debates over what constitutes proper historical sources, I have been trying to make the case that Hurston was an expert witness. But on what specifically was she an expert? Having lived in the North, she knew very well the world of the striving college graduate and the striving working-class black northern transplant. As a southerner, she knew the small town and the rural South and had lived her childhood and adulthood on back porches and at church revivals and chicken suppers. She knew the native language; she knew the adopted language. She knew the aspirations of people (like her own siblings) who had escaped the South; she knew their embarrassments. She knew their moments of dishonesty about their roots. She also knew that the two worlds were not the same, and that you could not accurately describe the one through the lens of the other. If you looked at the South through the lens of the North, the people looked too small, too far away, too blurred, too incoherent, and too "low down." If you look at the North through the lens of the South before southern blacks migrated there, you saw a mythical promised land, or nothing at all. If you looked at the North after the Great Migration, you saw a people transformed and sometimes distorted, the same and yet changed, a part of themselves extinguished. Hurston was an expert at crossing the border between North and South. She had enough knowledge of both regions and both cultures to provide a coherent picture of each. Her testimony has rescued both northern and southern blacks from the incomplete picture that showed them as merely the victims of racist prejudice and oppression. As James Baldwin pointed out in his critique of Richard Wright, to speak only of the horror of racism is to depict black people only through the eyes of their oppressors.[28]

Hurston was an expert witness to the "genius of the common people" and she illustrated this genius throughout her work. She examined the social structure neither in terms of the white elite who created it for their own benefit nor in terms of the black elite who sought a place within that structure. Her subject was the exploited center, and she probed the ways in which ordinary black people reconfigured the social structures that were designed to exploit them. In spite of his oppression, the "Negro farthest down" was able to invert the social structure through legal battles, flight, open rebellion, and a mentalité inaccessible to the elite.[29]

"Once we explore in greater detail those daily conflicts and the social and cultural spaces where ordinary people felt free to articulate their opposition, we can begin to ask the questions that will enable us to rewrite the political history of the Jim Crow South to incorporate such actions and actors," says Robin D. G. Kelley, one of several southern historians who have begun to probe the hidden history of black working-class people and establish its political significance.[30] Kelley maintains that "Black working people carved out social space free from the watchful eye of white authority or, in a few cases, the moralizing of the Black middle class."[31] That social space is, to be sure, difficult for us to enter. But we must do the best we can if we are to have a fuller portrait of black southern life. The tapestry of everyday life recorded in Hurston's work reveals that power does not impose "its will" without remainder. Rather, for many a black person, "without leaving the place where he has no choice but to live and which lays down its law for him, he establishes within it a degree of plurality and creativity."[32]

As Herbert Aptheker noted more than half a century ago, "an ever-present feature of antebellum Southern life was the existence of camps of runaway Negro slaves often called maroons," which "were seriously annoying, for they were sources of insubordination." These communities of flight "offered havens for fugitives, served as bases for marauding expeditions against nearby plantations and, at times, supplied the nucleus of leadership for planned uprisings."[33] For most historians, maroons were an important feature of the slave past. But the concept of "maroonage" became part of the worldview of black people and extended, I maintain, beyond the slave past. It found expression in the black towns that emerged in the antebellum period and those that developed after Emancipation. It was also expressed in the cultural creations that emerged from sites of resistance in the scattered sawmill and turpentine camps.

As a witness to her own time, Hurston provides us with a view of the inner worlds of African Americans. The following chapters examine what her work tells us about the consciousness of turpentine and sawmill workers and residents of small black towns in the South, and about her own relentless struggle as a southern black intellectual woman.

2

Portraits of the South

Zora Neale Hurston's Politics of Place

> I used to mull over the strange absence of real kindness
> in Negroes, how unstable was our tenderness, how lack-
> ing in genuine passion we were, how void of great hope,
> how timid our joy, how bare our traditions, how hollow
> our memories, how lacking we were in those intangible
> sentiments that bind man to man, how shallow was even
> our despair.
>
> —Richard Wright, *Black Boy:*
> *A Record of Childhood and Youth*, 37

> There were no discreet nuances of life on Joe Clarke's
> porch. There was open kindness, anger, hate, love, envy
> and its kinfolks, but all emotions were naked, and
> nakedly arrived at. You got what your strengths would
> bring you. This was not just true of Eatonville. This was
> the spirit of that whole new part of the state at the time,
> as it always is where men settle new lands.
>
> —Zora Neale Hurston,
> *Dust Tracks on a Road*, 68

FICTION, as Eudora Welty reminds us in her cele-
brated work *Place in Fiction*, requires the creation of a sense of
place that renders a drama real enough to gain the reader's complicity.[1] Welty's observation could be applied to the works of
Zora Neale Hurston and her critics, both contemporary and
present-day, were it not for one major complication—the role

that politics played in the production, circulation, and consumption of African American fiction during the Harlem Renaissance and the role it plays today.

When we look at the politics of Hurston's writing we see the problem in Welty's graceful argument: How much reality will do, and for whom? Which reality should be used to entice the reader? How should this reality be conveyed? When politics matters deeply, gaining the reader's complicity involves more than the writer's art. Hurston's many rounds with her critics bring into full view what we may call "a politics of place" that accounts, at least in part, for the different portraits black writers and others have painted of the South and its history. Understanding this politics can offer us clues to what it took for Hurston to gain—or, as was often the case, to lose—her readers' complicity.

At first sight, the politics with which Hurston and her critics had to contend seems simple enough. For many black writers in Hurston's time, the prevailing sense of the South was framed by the horrors of racism and the flight from those horrors. For them, representing the South outside that frame seemed at best beside the point and at worst possibly harmful to the struggle against racism. For other black writers, and especially for Hurston, that framing of the South and its people impoverished the depiction of both. It meant portraying black southerners without life, culture, or opportunity, and therefore without complexity. Hurston's sense of place is so vivid and so full of human complication that, paradoxically, it has prevented many readers from entering into her work, precisely because so much rides on how the South is depicted.

Among Hurston's readers, Richard Wright is perhaps the most influential. In his now well-known essay "Between Laughter and Tears," Wright accused Hurston of having no interest in serious fiction. He claimed that *Their Eyes Were Watching God* had no "basic idea or theme that lends itself to significant interpretation," and that its prose was "cloaked in that facile sensuality that has dogged Negro expression since the days of Phillis Wheatley." For Wright, Hurston may have managed to capture "psychological movements of the Negro folk-mind in their pure simplicity, but that's as far as it goes."

> Miss Hurston voluntarily continues in her novel the tradition which was forced upon the Negro in the theater, that is, the minstrel technique that makes the 'white folks' laugh. Her characters eat and laugh and cry and work and kill; they swing like a pendulum eternally in that safe and narrow orbit which America likes to see the Negro live: between laughter and tears.[2]

But what Wright disparaged as a narrow orbit "between laughter and tears" marks off a territory that present-day historians can profitably explore.

A first approximation of Wright's and Hurston's contrasting portraits of the South can be seen in the epigraphs that open this chapter. Wright and Hurston seem to agree at least on the "bareness" of black feeling, its "nakedness" and lack of "nuance." But while Wright's observations are haunted by a sense of despair, a sense that black life has somehow been stripped of emotional depth, Hurston's observations are brightly colored. For her, "discreet nuances" were not to be expected from relaxed conversation on a back porch. If black people's emotions were naked and nakedly arrived at, this was part of the frontier spirit in which those people found themselves at that time. Hurston thus historicizes black feeling. Wright's black southerner, by contrast, lacks the feelings—perhaps, Wright suggests, even the capacity for feelings—that fundamentally define humanity itself. This, in Wright's view, was one of the tragic legacies of the racist oppression and apartheid that characterized the American South.

Dreams and Disappointments

It was and remains an accepted belief that the South oppressed black people in a way different from the North. Both systems of oppression were violent, economically discriminatory, and segregated. Both regions challenged blacks to find safe spaces in which to live, where the impact of racism might be softened. But people believed then and believe today that the North allowed black people breathing room in a way that the South did not. The belief that the North was a "promised land" somehow even survived the experiences of violence and discrimination that took place in the North just as they did in the South. The myth that the South provided few or no educational opportunities for black people, that police and courts oppressed them more harshly than in the North, that economic success was rarely if ever possible, that segregation was more rigid, persists in the minds of many Americans, white and black, even today. Although other writers—Jean Toomer and Sterling Brown, for example—painted a more complex picture of the South, one in which black people could forge a personal and cultural identity even against terrible odds, the myth of a monolithic South remains.[3] Black migrants to the North soon learned that they would not find there the promised land of their dreams, but they made allowances for their new home while harboring conflicting visions of the South, a place that was both home and dangerous.

Hurston and Wright both knew that racial discrimination was just as debilitating in the North as in the South. But Hurston rejected the notion that black people were defined by the conditions of their existence in either place, while Wright saw the South as a place where violence defined every aspect of black life.

Wright, like many intellectuals of the 1920s and '30s, viewed black southerners with ambivalence. Even if black culture could be mined creatively, one sees in the work of black intellectuals like Wright doubts about the equality of the "Negro farthest down" with the educated and cosmopolitan elite. Many black writers and intellectuals privately harbored the belief that "the Negroes farthest down" brought violence on themselves by being immoral and uncivilized. The moral and well-behaved poor were candidates for moral and social uplift, for educational opportunities and protection from economic exploitation. The immoral and uncivilized poor were to be condemned or ignored; they were a source of shame to be hidden from view, if possible.[4] Even as they fought bitterly against white racism, black artists and intellectuals blamed the black masses for not doing more to "civilize" themselves.

This deep sense of doubt and shame about blackness could not be completely eradicated by tributes to the greatness of the African past or the creativity of black folk. Toomer wrote a lyrical masterpiece based on what he saw and heard in the cane fields of Georgia, where he taught school for three months, but as an adult he fled so far from folk spiritually that he became a follower of a Russian holy man.[5] Marcus Garvey's celebration of dark skin and of Africa did not prevent his newspapers from advertising skin-lighteners. Countee Cullen could write wonderful poetry about drum beats, but one of his poem asks, "What is Africa to me? / Copper sun or scarlet sea."[6]

The ambivalence of black intellectuals is understandable if we acknowledge the impact of racism on oppressed people, an acknowledgment that most black scholars and intellectuals have been unwilling to make.[7] As Arnold Rampersad has observed, "the individual psychological impact on black artists and writers of the staggering weight of racism aimed at them during this period" is a neglected subject. Rampersad describes "the racism that bred—and breeds—what we call low self-esteem and even self-hatred" and that has led to "the resulting divisions within the 'black' community along color lines as well as class lines." It is not hard to understand how such low self-esteem could drive one to deny or try to escape one's race. It leads, in Rampersad's words, to "issues not only of literal racial 'passing' and flight, but also of metaphorical versions of passing and flight; and the ways, admittedly impossible to map, in which the black mind reconstituted and reconstitutes itself in the face of the repeated woundings inflicted by racism."[8]

Hurston and her fellow African American writers worked in an intellectual and political climate in which people of African heritage were still regarded as naturally inferior. Such views were advanced in the nineteenth century by such revered figures as Thomas Jefferson in his *Notes on the State of Virginia*, which argued that racial difference was fixed in nature. The ideas of Immanuel Kant, Johann Gottfried von Herder, George Leopold Cuvier, and Georg Wilhelm Friedrich Hegel all shaped race consciousness among America's educated elite. By 1856 Count Joseph Arthur de Gobineau's *Moral and Intellectual Diversity of Races*, announcing that blacks had an absolutely fixed and unchangeable set of undesirable traits, had been published in the United States. At the beginning of the twentieth century, theories linking race with intellectual ability, behavior, and morality proliferated. Works such as Frederick L. Hoffman's *Race Traits and Tendencies of the American Negro* (1896), William Patrick Calhoun's *The Caucasian and the Negro in the United States* (1902), Charles W. Carroll's "The Negro a Beast" or "In the Image of God" (1900), and Robert Wilson Shufeldt's *The Negro: A Menace to American Civilization* (1907) were widely discussed and generally accepted by white readers. Theodore Roosevelt, for instance, stated authoritatively that "a perfectly stupid race can never rise to a very high plain; the negro, for instance has been kept down as much by lack of intellectual development as by anything else."[9] Social Darwinists suggested that native whites would not be displaced by the "inferior" European immigrants, colored migrants from the colonized world, and black migrants pouring into urban neighborhoods (though they constituted a threat to public health, morals, and safety). At the extreme, white supremacist ideologies supported brutal acts of violence and vicious pogroms to keep nonwhite people in their place.

The eugenics movement, which originated in Europe, offered a scientific foundation "for legislation and policies born of racist and nativist sentiments."[10] In popular culture, Thomas Dixon's *The Clansman: An Historical Romance of the Ku Klux Klan* (1905) and D. W. Griffith's film, *The Birth of a Nation*, and such pseudo-scientific scholarship as Madison Grant's *The Passing of the Great Race* fueled a racially charged intellectual and social environment.

Black elites and their white supporters advocated racial "uplift" to counter racist representations of and attacks against black people. This ideology at once celebrated black culture and regarded it as "low." By the 1920s, racial violence was reaching new levels of viciousness, with pogroms against black communities in places like Tulsa, Oklahoma, and Rosewood, Florida. Hundreds of lynchings propelled throngs of migrants northward. Some black intellectuals believed that they should not publicly express their anger at such atrocities, because only reasoned dialogue would persuade white power elites to intervene.

In this context black writers navigated a thicket of constraints, some of them self-imposed. The creative possibilities open to black writers and artists were limited by rules set forth under such headings as "Instructions for Contributors," "Criteria of Negro Art," and "Blueprint for Negro Writing." Such limiting regulations irritated Zora Neale Hurston, who condemned them as the work of "best-foot-forward Negroes." Hurston and other writers who refused to be bound by such prescriptions answered an earlier call. Like nineteenth-century writers Frances E. W. Harper, Thomas Hamilton, and W. S. Scarborough, they responded to the call for African Americans to tell their own story, to speak for themselves and establish themselves as leaders of their own liberation.

In 1859 Thomas Hamilton had published an introductory "Apology" in the first issue of his new journal, the *Anglo-African Magazine*. "[B]lack people," he wrote, "in order to assert and maintain their rank as men among men, must speak for themselves," for "no outside tongue, however gifted with eloquence, can tell their story." Their chief concern should be "what was then, and has remained, the preoccupation of Afro-American male writers: the great and terrible subject of white racism."[11] Frances Ellen Watkins Harper rejected this narrow focus and declared in a letter to the editor, "If our talents are to be recognized we must write less of issues that are particular and more of feelings that are general. We are blessed with hearts and brains that compass more than ourselves in our present plight... We must look to the future which, God willing, will be better than the present or the past, and delve into the heart of the world."[12]

Hamilton and Harper established the parameters of a debate regarding the proper content of African American literature that lasted well into the twentieth century; the dispute between Richard Wright and Zora Neale Hurston echoes their disagreement. W. S. Scarborough sided with Harper and called on the black novelist to "portray the Negro's loves and hates, his hopes and fears, his ambitions, his whole life, in such a way that the world will weep and laugh over the pages, finding the touch that makes all nature kin." Scarborough challenged writers to forget "completely that hero and heroine are God's bronze images, but [know] only that they are men and women with joys and sorrows that belong alike to the whole human family. Such is the novelist that the race desires. Who is he that will do it? Who is he that can do it?"[13] Most Renaissance writers followed Hamilton in addressing the terrible subject of racism, but Zora Neale Hurston followed Harper.

The question of what black writers should write, and how, was openly debated in the mid-1920s. In 1926 Langston Hughes's now familiar declaration testified to the determination of black artists to claim their freedom of expression: "We younger Negro artists who create now intend to express our individual dark-skinned selves without fear or shame. If white people are pleased we are glad. If they are not, it doesn't matter. We know we are beautiful. And ugly too. If colored people are pleased we are glad. If they are not, their displeasure doesn't matter either. We build our temples for tomorrow, strong as we know how, and we stand on top of the mountain, free within ourselves."[14]

In the same year that Hughes made his declaration, W.E.B. DuBois prescribed several "criteria of Negro art," arguing that "all Art is propaganda and ever must be, despite the wailing of the purists. I stand in utter shamelessness and say that whatever art I have for writing has been used always for propaganda for gaining the right of black folk to love and enjoy. I do not care a damn for any art that is not used for propaganda. But I do care when propaganda is confined to one side while the other is stripped and silent."[15] DuBois's idea of propaganda excluded the focus on the inner lives of black folk that would eventually distinguish Hurston's work. At the time that DuBois published his essay, Hurston was one of the young Turks who assembled around the magazine *Fire!!* — a publication supported by Carl Van Vechten and dedicated to literary insurgency. Van Vechten's novel, *Nigger Heaven*, had enraged DuBois, and Bruce Nugent's "Smoke, Lilies and Jade," which has been described as a "paean to pederasty and androgyny," further inflamed him. DuBois's position was rather prudish, though he directed most of his barbs at white writers and publishers.[16]

Like DuBois, George Schuyler believed in art as propaganda, but he disagreed that there was such a thing as a black subject. In a 1926 article entitled "The Negro-Art Hokum," Schuyler sneered that "the Afraamerican is merely a lampblacked Anglo-Saxon." "If the European immigrant after two or three generations of exposure to our schools, politics, advertising, moral crusades, and restaurants becomes indistinguishable from the mass of Americans of the older stock... how much truer must it be of the sons of Ham who have been subjected to what the uplifters call Americanism for the last three hundred years."[17] In 1929 Schuyler went further, designing a rigid set of rules for writers that were prominently displayed in the Negro press of the day as an "illustrated feature section." His "Instructions for Contributors" addressed style, tone, morality, and audience. Schuyler insisted, for example, that every manuscript submitted "must be written in each-sentence-a-paragraph style. Stories must be full of human interest. Short, simple words. No attempt to parade erudition to the bewilderment of the reader. No colloquialisms such as 'nigger,' 'darkey,' 'coon,' etc. Plenty of dialogue, and language that is realistic." No stories that were "depressing, saddening, or gloomy" would be accepted, nor would anything "that casts the least reflection on contemporary moral or sex standards." Writers were instructed to "[k]eep away from the erotic! Contributions must be clean and wholesome." The heroine was to be always "beautiful and desirable, sincere and virtuous"—and "of the brown-skin type." The hero "should be of the he-man type, but not stiff, stereotyped, or vulgar." Finally, overt references to racial matters were to be strictly avoided: "All matter should deal exclusively with Negro life. Nothing will be permitted that is likely to engender ill feelings between blacks and whites. The color problem is bad enough without adding any fuel to the fire."[18]

Expected continuously to prove their merit, black intellectuals like Schuyler censored themselves and attempted to censor others, believing that restraint was needed to secure white support. According to Schuyler, black writers who expressed outrage in response to racial oppression were regarded as unduly emotional and unreasonable, perhaps even naturally violent and lacking in self-control.

W.E.B. DuBois, a writer who commanded a range of narrative voices, disagreed, and drew on a time-honored tradition of confrontational discourse that had its roots in black abolitionist tracts. DuBois, the editor of *The Crisis*, the media arm of the NAACP, was well known for his use of rational, scholarly arguments to condemn racist violence, economic discrimination, and the social marginalization of African Americans. But when decades of violence culminated in vicious attacks on black people in 1919, DuBois summoned the voice of outrage to indict the white race for its bigotry and hatred. Unlike the quiet power of *The Souls of Black Folk* (1903), his *Darkwater: Voices from within the Veil* (1921) raged against white supremacy. In one chapter, "The Souls of White Folk," DuBois recounted personal observations of racial hatred and charged that they were not isolated. "We have seen, you and I, city after city drunk and furious with ungovernable lust of blood; mad with murder, destroying, killing, and cursing; torturing human victims because somebody accused of crime happened to be of the same color as the mob's innocent victims and because that color was not white!"

> We have seen,—Merciful God! in these wild days and in the name of Civilization, Justice, and Motherhood,—what have we not seen, right here in America, of orgy, cruelty, barbarism, and murder done to men and women of Negro descent.
>
> Up through the foam of green and weltering waters wells this great mass of hatred, in wilder, fiercer violence, until I look down and know that today to the millions of my people no misfortune could happen,—of death and pestilence, failure and defeat—that would not make the hearts of millions of their fellows beat with fierce, vindictive joy! Do you doubt it? Ask your own soul what it would say if the next census were to report that half of black America was dead and the other half dying.[19]

A reviewer in the *Outlook* condemned the book as "a creation of passion rather than intellect";[20] another reviewer deemed it "a remarkable example of the elemental race-hatred which [DuBois] himself so fiercely denounces."[21]

Questions of appropriate tone and subject matter still preoccupied black writers as Nazism swept across Europe.

Hurston and Wright

When Richard Wright contributed to the ongoing debate about the tone black writing should take with his "Blueprint for Negro Writing" (1937), he challenged writers to address "the color problem" in a wider historical and philosophical context.

> [I]n order to do justice to his subject matter, in order to depict Negro life in all of its manifold and intricate relationships, a deep, informed, and complex consciousness is necessary; a consciousness which draws its strength upon the fluid lore of a great people, and moulds this lore with the concepts that move and direct the forces of history today. Every short story, novel, poem, and play should carry within its lines, implied or explicit, a sense of the oppression of the Negro people, the danger of war, of fascism, of the threatened destruction of culture and civilization; and, too, the faith and necessity to build a new world.[22]

Raised in Mississippi, Richard Wright bore the imprint of disruption and discrimination. Like Hurston, he was a wanderer. As recorded in his autobiography, *Black Boy*, Wright's memories included a father who deserted his family, a mother broken by the hardship of caring for two children on a domestic's wages, and an existence haunted by hunger, fear, and white violence directed at him and his family. For Wright the South meant little more than pain and isolation. The northern ghetto, where southern migrants went seeking freedom, was similarly bleak. In his novel *Native Son*, racism and isolation suffocate Bigger Thomas in the North no less than in the South.

In Bigger Thomas, Wright develops a character with the courage to rebel against the dehumanization of Jim Crow society.

In Wright's eyes, only Bigger can challenge this totalitarian system, though he is destroyed by it in the end nevertheless. But as James Baldwin and other critics point out, Bigger Thomas exists apart from human kin. In Baldwin's view, "Bigger has no discernible relationship to himself, to his own life, to his own people, nor to any other people—in this respect, perhaps, he is most American—and his force comes, not from his significance as a social (or anti-social) unit but from his significance as the incarnation of a myth." The southern conditions that produced Bigger are no different from conditions in the North, and Bigger is isolated in both places.[23]

This, of course, was exactly Wright's point. Such an individual is possible because he has no connection to community or to self. Baldwin defines community as "the relationship that Negroes bear to one another, that depth of involvement and unspoken recognition of shared experience which creates a way of life."[24] In such communities African Americans developed psychic defenses against degenerating into "monsters." Bigger Thomas, lacking community, has no such defenses.

For Wright, neither North nor South offered many alternatives to African Americans. They were so hemmed in by repression and violence that human development was permanently arrested. As he said of *Native Son,*

> the Bigger Thomases were the only Negroes I know of who consistently violated the Jim Crow laws of the South and got away with it, at least for a sweet brief spell. Eventually, the whites who restricted their lives made them pay a terrible price. They were shot, hanged, maimed, lynched, and generally hounded until they were either dead or their spirits broken.[25]

Wright's espousal of politically didactic literature presents a strong contrast to Hurston's desire to undermine stereotypes and depict a broad spectrum of characters and their social relations. Hurston documented black communities as places inhabited by complicated individuals, where humor and conflict as well as violence and discrimination are facts of life. But these communities are also graced with unique cultural beauty. Hurston's article "What

White Publishers Won't Print" complained that "Everybody is already resigned to the 'exceptional' Negro, and willing to be entertained by the 'quaint,'" but "the average, struggling, non-morbid Negro is the best-kept secret in America."[26] The depiction of average black people whose everyday lives were permeated by Jim Crow but not defined by it was one facet of her political struggle to destroy racism.

In Hurston's view, the conception of black people as fundamentally different from whites inspired fear and made racist violence acceptable. For her, portraying the inner world of black life was "the thing needed to do away with the feeling of difference which inspires fear, and which ever expresses itself in dislike." Art had a function beyond presenting racial attitudes, as well. "Literature and other arts," she wrote, "are supposed to hold up the mirror to nature. With only the fractional 'exceptional' and the 'quaint' portrayed, a true picture of Negro life in America cannot be. A great principle of national art has been violated." Acknowledging the role that stereotypes play in the national consciousness, Hurston argued that a true picture of black people and their lives "will destroy many illusions and romantic traditions which America probably likes to have around."[27] For Hurston, this was as much a political as an artistic stand. In *Their Eyes Were Watching God*, Janie's search for self and love, Tea Cake's complicated conception of manhood, and Jody Starks's desire for material wealth and power speak to Hurston's political aims as surely as Bigger Thomas's destruction by racism and reactionary politics speaks to Wright's.

Even so, Hurston's South remained personal. It was about family and friends, acceptable and unacceptable characters, love and hate, values and norms, social rewards and social punishments, spiritual strength and material practicality. Finally, it was about making sense of a world dominated by Jim Crow while trying to live a normal life. Conversely, Richard Wright depicted South and North abstractly; they were grounded in the general fact of racist discrimination rather than in the relationships that anchor human society.

Baldwin's critique of *Native Son* raises some important issues regarding questions of community and the ways in which black people survived. Wright's novel was an attempt to challenge "the abstraction and romanticization of the proletariat that had infected Western Communist ideology" by presenting a more authentic example of the impact of racism on black culture. Herein lies the tension between Wright and Hurston. Bigger Thomas is a tool for Wright's engagement with the Communist Party and communist ideology. Hurston's depiction of black folk emerged out of a very different kind of political commitment that freed her to portray a whole culture from the inside out.

In 1941 Wright published a poignant folk history of black people entitled *Twelve Million Black Voices*, a history that moved from South to North. "Each day," he wrote in the opening pages, "when you see us black folk upon the dusty land of the farms or upon the hard pavement of the city streets, you usually take us for granted and think you know us, but our history is far stranger than you suspect, and we are not what we seem."[28] In a strikingly similar passage in *Mules and Men*, Hurston writes, "And the Negro, in spite of his open-faced laughter, his seeming acquiescence, is particularly evasive. You see we are a polite people and we do not say to our questioner, 'Get out of here!' We smile and tell him or her something that satisfies the white person because, knowing so little about us, he doesn't know what he is missing."[29]

Wright seemed to understand that the South was far more complicated than his portrait suggested, but it was Hurston who was willing to peel away the layers and expose the core of southern life. Though Wright's point, that the dehumanization wrought by racism produces Bigger Thomases, is valid, Hurston's point is that monsters are the aberration; most black people managed to retain their humanity even in the face of unrelenting hardships.[30]

Wright's portrait of the South, however compelling, put the horrors of Jim Crow so prominently in the foreground that black southerners' lives are always seen in relationship to it, leaving everything else unimagined. Hurston's portrait, by contrast, so diminished the role of white racism that at times her contemporaries branded her a conservative in denial of reality.

Their differences aside, both Wright and Hurston objected to the Communist Party's understanding of "the proletariat." Communist ideology was as guilty of idealizing black working people as white racism was of demeaning them. There was no place in the romantic communist vision for either Bigger Thomas or Hurston's turpentine workers. It was this failure of the left that so disturbed Hurston. Consequently, she rejected Wright's depiction of black people through the distorted perspective of white liberals and leftists. Wright, for his part, faulted Hurston for creating a facile picture of "happy darkies."

Wright's and Hurston's projects were different but not necessarily antagonistic. Too sharp a dichotomy has been drawn between them, first by Wright himself and then by critics, both at the time and since. Both Hurston and Wright rejected the romantic fantasies of white people who idealized the primitive. And Hurston was no more enamored of the North than Wright was. But Wright came to his art through leftist politics and sought to infuse his art with political purpose, in the hope that his stories would force white society to acknowledge the destructive and tragic effects of racism. His collection of short stories, *Uncle Tom's Children*, which languished for a long time before finding support, was finally published in March 1938 and, to his surprise, was a critical and popular success. "The South that Mr. Wright renders so vividly is recognizable and true and it has not often been within the covers of a book," announced Sterling Brown.[31] Some southerners even liked the book. Hurston was less impressed, and she wrote scathingly in the *Saturday Review*, "This is a book about hatreds... Not one act of understanding and sympathy comes to pass in the entire work... All the characters in this book are elemental and brutish."[32]

In a letter to William Stanley Hoole, Hurston sketched the kind of novel *she* wanted to write. It was "to be a novel about a woman who was from childhood hungry for life and the earth, but because she had beautiful hair, was always being skotched upon a flag-pole by the men who loved her and forced her to sit there. At forty she got her chance at mud. Mud, lush and fecund with a buck Negro called Teacake... [who] took her down into the Ever-glades where people worked and sweated and loved and died vio-lently, where no such thing as flag-poles for women existed."[33] It was to be, in other words, a novel about living and dying, loving and hating, gender and class, working and playing—in short, about the fullness of life lived in the South.

When *Their Eyes Were Watching God* was published in 1937, Wright, as we have seen, condemned it as a throwback to the days of Negro minstrelsy. Sterling Allen Brown was also critical of Hurston's novel. Although he had been impressed with some of Hurston's earlier work, he received the publication of her anthro-pological work, *Mules and Men* (1935), without enthusiasm.[34] Though he found the folklore she presented interesting, he was disturbed by what he considered an incomplete portrait of black life: *Mules and Men* recorded no misery, no exploitation, and no violence. Brown dismissed Hurston's assertion that her informants had not presented this side of their existence. He also objected to Hurston's portrayal of "socially unconscious characters living carefree and easy-going lives." This was not the South that Brown knew.[35]

The notion that blacks could escape the violence of Jim Crow, even partially or provisionally, was as unthinkable for Brown as it was for Richard Wright. Brown was not from the South, which helps to explain his response. Even so, unlike Wright or Alain Locke, he found some good in *Their Eyes Were Watching God*, pub-lished just a year later. He recognized subtle aspects of the work that other reviewers missed, and wrote, "Living in an all-colored town, these people escape the worst pressures of class and caste. There is little harshness, there is enough money and work to go around. The author does not dwell upon the 'people ugly from ignorance and broken from being poor' who swam upon the 'muck' for short-time jobs. But there is bitterness, sometimes oblique, in the enforced folk manner, and sometimes forthright."[36]

But despite finding positive elements in *Their Eyes Were Watch-ing God*, Brown finally sided with Wright, who wrote a scathing review of the novel. Charles Scruggs agreed, saying, "if minstrelsy means placing blacks in a context where whites find them non-threatening, then [Wright] is making a shrewd observation."[37] Brown, however, like other critical contemporaries, failed to see that if black life in the South was depicted entirely in terms of Jim Crow and white racism, then black people were reduced to helpless victims with no agency of their own. Like other black artists and intellectuals, Brown was disturbed by the violence, sex, and immoral behavior the characters in *Their Eyes* engaged in. He may have praised the creativity of black folk in his own work, but the messy realities of real life were too big a threat to his precarious sense of self, of having made it, if just barely, in the larger white world. He remained trapped within the "uplift ideology" of his time.

The Problem of Anachronism

The foregoing discussion of the politics of black writing in Hurston's time offers several lessons for the writing of history and the reconstruction of the past present in which Hurston wrote. Reconstructing the past requires that the writer move away from his or her vantage point. Only then can a writer capture a "then" and a "them" that are remote in time. The failure to change one's perspective results in anachronism, which distorts both the "then" and the "them" that historians aim to capture.

The literary critic Hazel Carby, for example, reads the folk in Hurston's works as though they lived in a time that is not theirs, that is, as "a folk who are outside history."[38] Carby sets up Hurston's work as the polar opposite of Wright's by arguing that Hurston's version of black cultural forms is outside "the culture and history of contestation" that inform Wright's work. Fair enough, but only if we can agree that Wright's work contains all we need of "culture," "history," and "contestation." Carby also sets Hurston in opposition to Langston Hughes: "Langston Hughes shaped his discursive category of the folk in direct response to the social conditions of transformation, including the newly forming urban working class and socially dispossessed, whereas Hurston constructed a discourse of nostalgia for a rural community."[39]

But is it "nostalgic" to present or study one aspect of southern culture and to set one's fiction within it? Social transformation may always be taking place, but its pace is uneven. More important, though many thousands of black southerners moved north, most did not. And even those who moved north did not entirely abandon the South as home for several generations. Indeed, migration was both a cyclical and circular process for many, not merely a one-way avenue of permanent escape. Many moved back and forth between the North and the South; others moved north but maintained their ties to the South through culture and family.[40]

Hurston's work was grounded in the lived experiences and conditions of ordinary black folk in the South. Her work, though generally avoiding the circumscription of black life, offers a remarkably rich view of the interior lives and labors of poor black rural southerners. Although she did not define it in a confrontational way, her fiction and ethnography reveal the slave-like status to which the South's post-Reconstruction regimes had reduced the rural black masses. It is a tribute to the resiliency of these people that they refused to be broken spiritually in spite of the tremendous obstacles they faced. Hurston's genius lay in her ability to chronicle unobtrusively this story of the triumph of the human spirit over adversity. It is to her chronicles that we now turn.

3

A Place between Home and Horror

> Hurston, who claimed to have been born in 1901, but whose records show her birth year as a decade earlier, most certainly lived through the race riots and other atrocities of her time. However, she does not mention even one unpleasant racial incident in *Dust Tracks on a Road*. The southern air around her most assuredly crackled with the flames of the Ku Klux Klan raiders but Ms. Hurston does not allude to any ugly incident.
>
> —Maya Angelou[1]

IN THE OPENING PAGES of her autobiography, *Dust Tracks on a Road*, Zora Neale Hurston writes, "I was born in a Negro town. I do not mean by that the black back-side of an average town. Eatonville, Florida, is, and was at the time of my birth, a pure Negro town—charter, mayor, council, town marshal and all. It was not the first Negro community in America, but it was the first to be incorporated, the first attempt at organized self-government on the part of Negroes in America."[2] Hurston's Eatonville was a place where families lived, worked, played, fought, prayed, and loved. It was a corner of the world constructed upon an intricate web of complex relationships, a part of the New South but one with an inner cultural logic of its own. This world comes to life in the pages of Hurston's books, which are filled with effervescent language, humor, and great depth of feeling. The race riots, lynchings, and desperation that partly characterized this time and place are documented in her richly detailed journalism, but her fiction has another focus.

As I argued in the previous chapter, the racial oppression of Jim Crow was an atrocious fact of life for virtually every black person in the postwar South, but it did not completely define everyday life in Eatonville. After the failure of Reconstruction, African American migrants created towns of their own whose *raison d'etre* was to keep Jim Crow at a distance. There they built homes and established networks of family and community relations, and lived their lives with as little racial discrimination and violence as possible. Hurston conveyed what she meant by "home" in a poem published in 1922 in the *Negro World*, the newspaper published by Marcus Garvey's Universal Negro Improvement Association:

Home

> I know a place that is full of light
> That is full of dreams and visions bright
> Where pleasing fancy loves to roam
> And picture me once more at home.
>
> There nothing comes to mar my days
> And dim for me the sun's loved rays
> To shake my faith in things divine
> And bare the cruelty of mankind.
>
> Ah, that I to that spot might flee
> That peace and love may dwell with me
> To brush away the somber shrouds
> And show the lining of the clouds.[3]

The poem was penned early in her career, at the beginning of her "wanderings" in the North; its sentiments were meant to evoke Hurston's hometown of Eatonville, described twenty years later in her autobiography as "the city of five lakes, three croquet courts, three hundred skins, three hundred good swimmers, plenty guavas, two schools, and no jail house."[4] Both descriptions are nostalgic and describe a place far removed from the harsh realities of Jim Crow. Eatonville was a place to which Hurston could always return, at least in her thoughts and memories. Her literary works offer a portrait of all-black towns in the late nineteenth-century South, capturing the spirit that animated them.

More than sixty all-black towns emerged at the end of the Civil War, where African Americans could have a semblance of autonomy between the teeth and within the cavities of Jim Crow. Driven by the need to protect themselves from racial violence and to mitigate the abuses of economic exploitation, residents of some of these towns incorporated themselves as independent legal units. Others remained unincorporated but emerged as independent cooperative communities. Even in the black sections of segregated white towns (which Hurston referred to as the black backsides of all-white towns), African Americans managed to create a sense of community cemented by biological and fictive kinship ties, racial solidarity, and institutions for social, spiritual, and economic development. Throughout her career, much of Hurston's literary and ethnographic work was drawn from Eatonville. In this she presented an alternative southern experience that made good the promises and possibilities of freedom that Reconstruction failed to deliver.

Hurston also traveled extensively through those "black backsides of average towns" in central Florida, from the agricultural migrant camps in the Everglades to the turpentine, sawmill, and railroad camps and the phosphate mining towns, as well as the black enclaves of the cities and ports on Florida's Atlantic coast.[5] In these places her identity took shape as she grew into womanhood. Hurston returned to these towns to conduct research after "wandering" in the North, and here, among those who stayed behind in the South, she found subjects for both her social science and her literary work. Hurston immersed herself in the rich history and culture of Florida and that history infused her work. She studied the history of imperialism in Florida as well as the history of maroonage and the wars and rebellions waged by runaway slaves and native peoples. She was well aware of the transformation of Florida as the country's leading citrus producer, and of the streams of migrant labor that supported that industry.[6]

Hurston also explored the expansion of the naval stores industry and its system of debt peonage—which kept workers in forced labor for payment of debt—a key component of the economic landscape of Florida in the late nineteenth and early twentieth centuries. Turpentine and agricultural workers were a familiar presence in the region. Hurston describes turpentine workers as part of the human environment on a boat trip from Jacksonville:

> A group of turpentine hands with queer haircuts, in blue overalls with red handkerchiefs around their necks, who huddled around a tall, black man with a guitar round his neck. They ate out of shoe-boxes and sang between drinks out of a common bottle. A stocking-foot woman was with them with a dirk in her garter. Her new shoes were in a basket beside her. She dipped snuff and kept missing the spittoon. The glitter of brass and the red carpet made her nervous.[7]

Mucksteppers, a derogatory term for those who worked on the "muck" (the fields where agricultural products were grown), and turpentiners lived both in settled black communities and in migratory camps.[8] Their relationships and outlook informed the ethos of black southern folk life to which Hurston devoted so much of her writing.

The violence that framed Jim Crow society, both the racist violence meted out by whites and the violence within black communities, especially the migratory camps, was never far from view.[9] Hurston sought inspiration for her fiction in the black towns and the inner lives of their inhabitants. Her stories render the connectedness of these communities and their standards of behavior. They depict individual transgressions and the social basis for conflict. Hurston's fiction brings to life the culture and society of Eatonville and its surrounding migrant camps, and provides glimpses into the life and passions concealed from the outer world. Black people used forbearance and fortitude to camouflage the rage and contempt that smoldered beneath the surface of social relations in a segregated society. They reserved their time and emotions, as much as possible, for those that mattered—family, friends, and neighbors.

Despite the frequent incidents of violence and humiliation and the restrictions on education, social mobility, and economic opportunity, African Americans in central Florida built independent black towns with effective institutions and a vibrant social structure. In the black sections of some predominantly white towns, they also established institutions and networks of cooperation that thrived in spite of racial segregation. Much of the black South remained depressed and underdeveloped, yet in many of Florida's small towns and urban areas black people managed to achieve a respectable degree of autonomy and institutional independence. Even in the most depressed areas—those based on debt peonage and migratory labor—a particular culture and system of values ordered black life. In order to appreciate this achievement, let us turn briefly to the outside world of racial hierarchies, which will provide a useful contrast to the private worlds of African Americans that are the subject of the next two chapters.

Post-Emancipation Florida

In *Dust Tracks on a Road*, Hurston captured images of labor and industry that were at once a distinct feature of a modernizing era and a throwback to a premodern era.

> All of these places have plenty of men and women who are fugitives from justice. The management asks no questions. They need help and they can't be bothered looking for a bug under a chip… The wheels of industry must move, and if these men don't do the work, who is going to do it?…
>
> Polk County. Black men laughing and singing. They go down in the phosphate mines and bring up the wet dust of the bones of pre-historic monsters, to make rich land in far places, so that people can eat.
>
> Polk County. Black men from tree to tree among the lordly pines, a swift, slanting stroke to bleed the trees for gum. Paint, explosives, marine stores flavors, perfumes, tone for a violin bow, and many other things which black men who bleed trees never heard about.[10]

The end of the Civil War brought social chaos and economic instability to central Florida as throughout the South. The system of plantation agriculture that had dominated the region for generations was badly crippled by political upheaval, economic change, and social confusion. The beginnings of a free-labor system and declining cotton prices hit planters hard as they tried in vain to return to prewar production levels. Cotton was no longer king, and planters had to find new sources of revenue and a cheap, manageable labor pool. Northern and central Florida were both underpopulated and underdeveloped, and planters soon saw an opportunity to rebuild their fortunes in the lush green forests, with their virgin stands of pine and cypress. All they needed was labor, and for that they turned first to immigrants, then to local whites, and finally to imported black labor.[11]

The planters' efforts to regain their economic strength were aided by the development of the railroad. Railroads had come to Florida in the late 1870s and 1880s and linked the region's numerous undeveloped waterways. Improved systems of transportation were a key factor in economic revitalization throughout the country, and Florida was no exception. Towns and villages sprang up along the rail lines and waterways, and immigrants were recruited by talented entrepreneurs seeking to take advantage of Florida's industrial possibilities and untapped natural resources. In a relatively short time, railroads, sawmills, phosphate mines, cotton mills, and naval stores factories dotted the landscape. Florida had began a steady march toward modernization.[12] This economic expansion brought people and goods to Florida and created a demand for labor that could not be satisfied by immigrants alone.[13] Black and white laborers migrated into Florida in record numbers, drawn by a vibrant economy and the promise of economic opportunity. Many workers were also recruited from Alabama, Georgia, and the Carolinas by agents of businessmen eager to create a manageable pool of labor.

In Florida as elsewhere in the South, an "oppressive body of law" established segregation and political disfranchisement of black people as a constituent element of the New South.[14] High levels of labor mobility brought social upheaval and economic insecurity. In this context, Florida became as violent as any state in the South. Debt peonage, convict leasing, lynching, and whitecapping (a term that referred to white vigilante gangs who invaded black communities in masks) were commonplace, and in undercapitalized industries like turpentine and lumber they were a common means of obtaining and maintaining a labor force.[15] Thus Florida, along with the rest of the South, entered the modern industrial era.[16]

In the late nineteenth century, northern industrialists, European businessmen, and local developers bought vast acreages of virgin long-leaf pine and cypress for the rapidly developing naval stores and timber industry; more than 20 million acres of lush forest waited to be developed.[17] But the movement toward economic stability was erratic owing to high fixed costs and labor shortages. While extractive industries such as phosphate mining and timber took advantage of new labor-saving machinery, the naval stores industry continued to use primitive methods. A key factor in its failure to modernize was its lack of access to adequate capital. Though all of these industries exploited their workers, the turpentine industry was the worst and failed to modernize at all; naval stores production held on tenaciously to these antiquated practices well into the twentieth century.[18]

Turpentine and resin extracted from pine trees were used in making paint, varnish, soap, sealing wax, oil, paper sizing, pharmaceuticals, and lubricating compounds. From 1890 to 1900, Jacksonville was the center of the state's turpentine industry; after the turn of the century, the industry spread across northern and central Florida. By 1900 Georgia, with 19,199 workers, and Florida, with 15,073, employed more than 70 percent of turpentine workers in the nation and continued to lead the country until the decline of the industry after World War II.[19]

Turpentining was a year-round process in Florida, labor intensive and migratory in nature. Equipment was primitive, consisting of only rudimentary forms of extraction. Modern equipment and techniques of production were difficult to achieve in an industry that was chronically short of capital to reinvest in development.

During the winter months, trees were located by a "woods-rider" and the bark was stripped by a "wood-puller." Grooves were made in the wood fourteen inches wide and seven inches deep near the base of the tree, and clay pots were hung under each groove to collect the sap.[20] After stripping the wood, the wood-puller had to move up the trunk of the tree to keep the resin flowing, often as high as eight feet. Once a month a "dipper" came to collect the sap, which was then poured into barrels on the back of a wagon and taken for distillation. Sap and water were poured into the "cap" over the kettle above the mill's firebox and the firebox was lit. The sap and water flowed through the "worm," a metal tube ringing the still, and came out the bottom. The turpentine and water separated at the end of the process, each going into a different barrel.[21] The pure turpentine was sent to market. The water left from the process was called "low wine" and, according to Stetson Kennedy, some workers actually drank this liquid.[22] Any detritus left over from the process was used as gunpowder.

Trees were severely damaged by this process of boxing, leaving the forest vulnerable to heavy winds and devastating fires. The amount and quality of the resin began to decline after two years, so that after three to five years the manufacturers moved on to find fresh trees. This was a wasteful and destructive practice and did not inspire economic confidence in investors.[23]

Turpentine operations were located deep in the woods, which provided cover for manufacturers, who controlled and disciplined their workforce with methods similar to those of slavery. Though living conditions varied, most workers were housed in shacks owned by the company. A sawmill was built nearby to cut wood for barrels, and a commissary provided goods to workers at a very high cost, which conveniently kept them in debt. The work week lasted from Monday until Saturday at noon, and the workday from 6:00 A.M. until dark. A jook joint in each camp provided liquor, gambling, and "promiscuous love." Children rarely attended school and women attended to domestic duties. Some camps were worse than others. While collecting folklore and taking photographs in west Florida, near Cross City, Hurston and Stetson Kennedy found some of the most wretched conditions. Kennedy reported that Hurston felt "that in all of her research in all the industries employing Negroes, the intelligence quotient of these West Florida Negro families was 'rock bottom.'" Oddly, according to Kennedy, in this particular camp "there is very little drinking among the Negros especially," though its families, like those in all the camps, were in perpetual debt.[24]

Financing for the turpentine industry drew on an antiquated system of factorage houses that began in the antebellum period.[25] By the late nineteenth century these houses were located in the port facilities of several southern cities, among them Mobile, Alabama, Savannah and Brunswick, Georgia, and Jacksonville and Pensacola, Florida. Factorage houses depended on indebtedness, lending money for leases and other goods and holding a mortgage on the camp. By 1900 they controlled 90 percent of the trade in turpentine. Commercial southern bankers were reluctant to provide financing to an industry with a narrow profit margin and very little collateral. Turpentine manufacturers tended to buy leases that were intangible assets and a poor credit risk for long-term loans. Turpentine was also vulnerable to loss resulting from fire; and the migratory nature of the business suggested instability. Manufacturers, always desperate for cash, could not turn to commercial bankers and had no choice but to rely on the factorage houses that provided the capital for leases. The houses loaned the money for tools and supplies as well, and their agents directed the transportation and marketing of turpentine and resin to dealers in major ports. They also provided financing for the material needs of a turpentine farm: food, clothing, household goods, and anything else needed to sustain production. All of this was provided on credit.[26] As Michael David Tegeder has noted, "After receiving their 2.5 percent commission at the end of a harvest, factors balanced their accounts from the past year; with deductions for leases and labor costs, credit advances, inspection fees, product insurance, and accrued interest, manufacturers rarely cleared their debts."[27] Constant debt therefore plagued manufacturers, and they responded by cutting costs and seeking the cheapest possible labor.

By the early twentieth century, competition from big timber interests exacerbated the situation. Operators had to cut costs even more radically in an industry that already required a steady supply of cheap labor. The turpentine industry had failed to invest in labor-saving technology, which would have reduced labor costs. As a result, it was trapped in antiquated methods of production. In order to survive under these conditions the industry had to rely on a system of debt peonage and violence not terribly different from slavery.[28]

Phosphate mining and railroad companies followed a different path. Using advances in technology, these industries were not dependent on factorage houses for capital, and their willingness to modernize made them a better financial investment for banks. But their need for labor, particularly in the underpopulated regions of Florida, was as great as that of the turpentine industry. According to Jacqueline Jones, "Pioneer Florida phosphate companies had relied on indigenous white labor, but these 'crackers,' accustomed to an 'indolent life,' were, in the words of one observer, 'most independent in their views, and as most them own a homestead and cattle of their own, they liked a holiday after a week's work.'"[29] The seasonal nature of the work also affected labor supply. Work decreased in the brutal heat of summer, but during the winter months workers spent up to eighteen hours a day in the mines.

For a more dependable and tractable workforce, phosphate employers recruited blacks from nearby states. Black family men became the dominant group of laborers in the work camps by 1919, and they and their families became increasingly dependent on the companies for their livelihoods. By 1930 Florida was producing four-fifths of the phosphate in the United States, yet mechanization had actually decreased the number of workers. Of the 450,000 workers in the state, only 2,200 were employed in the phosphate industry by the 1920s. Whites held all the supervisory jobs while blacks toiled in the pits. For twenty cents an hour, twelve hours a day, six days a week, workers dynamited barrel-size chunks of rock out of earth as they stood knee deep in water and mud. The work was dangerous and explosions frequently killed or crippled workers. Miners lived in ramshackle company housing with poor sanitary facilities and were dependent on the company store for provisions, as they were paid in scrip that could be redeemed only at the commissary. Armed guards patrolled the camps to ensure that workers did not run away.[30] Like their counterparts in the turpentine and sawmill businesses, phosphate mining companies regularly manipulated the debt peonage system to guarantee a stable labor supply.[31] By the 1920s an increasing number of single white men worked alongside black workers, and they experienced some of the same discrimination. But companies went to great lengths to distinguish between black and white workers. Housing for black workers lacked bath facilities and blacks were required to pay for their own insurance. In Bartow, Florida, a school was provided for whites within one mile of their homes. Black children had to walk six miles to attend segregated classes.[32]

After World War I, black and white workers joined the International Union of Mine, Mill and Smelter Workers and went on strike in May 1919. The strike occurred at the Mulberry Mines, one of the most important mining towns in phosphate country and one of the towns where Hurston collected folklore. Workers demanded better housing, higher wages, and freedom from the company store. The company brought in black strikebreakers from Georgia and several people were killed in the ensuing violence. The union collapsed after this failed strike and was not revived until the 1930s, but this early challenge to the company's control of labor was an important difference between the phosphate industry and the sawmill and turpentine camps.[33]

Railroad companies also recruited heavily from black labor pools. Henry Flagler, a wealthy railroad tycoon, had built the Florida East Coast Railway and sought to extend that line into Key West. Recruiters solicited labor from as far away as New York

City. Railroad workers were lured into debt like the workers in other industries, and they likewise found conditions in railroad camps harsh and marred by violence. With the full force of the law at his disposal, Flagler ruthlessly maintained his workers in these conditions despite challenges from the courts. One of Flagler's agents, David E. Harley, and three others were arrested in 1908 for violating peonage laws and tried by the government for forcing several thousand men to work on Flagler's railroad. But the U.S. Circuit Court judge ordered the jury to find the defendants not guilty on the grounds that the government had failed to prove evil intent.[34] Like phosphate mining companies, railroad companies acquired modern technology and labor-saving devices, but they also controlled their workers in the same brutal manner as other industries.[35]

Across the South, the efforts of freedmen to exert some control over their social, economic, and political circumstances were thwarted by post-Reconstruction policies. After the national government withdrew its support for freedmen in 1877, African Americans rapidly lost the few gains they had made during Reconstruction. By the late 1880s, before the blind eyes of the federal government, Jim Crow legislation rapidly spread throughout the South, sanctioning racial segregation and discrimination. While labor patterns were diverse and complex in many areas, the basic employment arrangements that emerged reduced the freedman to a condition that many scholars have argued was little different from slavery.

In addition to debt peonage, convict leasing emerged throughout the South in the 1870s under Republican leadership. Formerly enslaved, blacks became part of these new labor patterns.[36] The prison population was predominately black, generally young men in their teens and early twenties who were typically arrested in urban areas on minor charges such as gambling, vagrancy, and petty theft. Once in custody they found themselves leased to industries like turpentine or railroad companies in desperate need of labor. Whites picked up in similar circumstances went to prison; blacks were sent to work camps.[37]

Convict leasing was a major source of labor for the lumber industry, which gave company owners even more control over prisoners' lives.[38] Most studies of convict leasing have demonstrated the system's corruption, brutality, profitability, and racism. "The convict lease system," observes C. Vann Woodward, "did greater violence to the moral authority of the Redeemers than did anything else. For it was upon the tradition of paternalism that the Redeemer regimes claimed authority to settle the race problem and 'deal with the Negro.'"[39] As Mary Curtin argues in her fine study of the penal system in Alabama, this system was part of the underpinning of Jim Crow and capitalism in the New South.[40]

Convicts were leased out to private businesses and went to the highest bidder every two years. The official reason for convict leasing was to keep prison costs down, but the system invited abuse and corruption, and collusion between local officials and business firms was widespread.[41] Vagrancy laws in this period were used to force many former slaves and some poor whites into prisons, and as the prison population grew, so did the labor pool.

The debt peonage system was nearly as harsh and brutal as the penal system, shaped and perpetuated as it was by the racial caste structure of the South. Debt peonage began with tenant farmers, both black and white, but soon spread to include other workers, particularly in the lumbering and naval stores industries.[42] Immigrant workers such as Jews were part of the forest crews, many of them tricked into signing on with promises of good pay and housing when they arrived on the East Coast from Europe. They soon found themselves in debt and under the watchful eye of gun-toting bosses. Debt peonage thrived thanks to the collusion of state and corporate interests and the federal government's lack of concern. The abuses of the system did not receive serious notice until the case of Martin Tabert drew the attention of the national media.

The state of Florida had prohibited the leasing of convicts to private companies in 1919, but counties routinely ignored the law and continued the practice with little interference. Martin Tabert, a young white South Dakota farm boy, found himself in a camp owned by the Putnam Lumber Company in Putnam County. He ran afoul of a prison guard named Walter Higginbotham and was beaten to death. Perhaps because he was white, his death made it onto the front pages of the nation's leading newspapers and touched off an investigation that was to be a turning point in the saga of debt peonage. Higginbotham was convicted of Tabert's murder, but his conviction was overturned by the Florida Supreme Court. While awaiting retrial, Higginbotham was accused of murdering another worker, Lewis "Peanut" Barker, who was found beaten and shot to death at another Putnam Lumber camp in Dixie County, where Higginbotham had resumed his duties. Higginbotham never served a day for either murder, nor did other officials suspected of involvement in Barker's murder.[43]

Outright murders of this kind were rare, but lesser abuses were common. Even after laws prohibited the use of convict labor and outlawed peonage following the Tabert case, the practice of debt peonage went unchecked, and brutality in turpentine and sawmill camps continued. Investigations into these abuses by Gainesville district attorney Frederick C. Cubberly revealed a sadistic pattern of fraud, beatings, rapes, and other violence. The details of Cubberly's investigations filled the newspapers in Florida and throughout the country, and more crimes and violations made it to court, but the pattern of violence and abuse continued nevertheless.[44]

As Barbara Fields has argued, "The work of instilling discipline into people no longer subject to slavery but not yet susceptible to compulsion mediated solely through the market took many forms. Overt physical violence was by no means the least of these... Debt peonage, an expedient that confirmed the departure of slavery even while trying to recreate it, persisted into the twentieth century, limiting freedom of movement."[45] Debt peonage and the convict-lease system were the most brutal and violent forms of labor to take shape in the South after slavery was ended, but other forms also left much to be desired. Sharecropping and the credit system—both contingent on monoculture of the cash staple—limited freedmen's independent access to the means of subsistence, as did tightened hunting regulations and laws putting a stop to open-range grazing of livestock.

The labor conditions that characterized the post-Emancipation South were part of an evolving process in the development of modern industrial society. While the racial violence built into southern labor relations was not all that different from the violence of slavery, the economic oppression that came with it was part of capitalist modernization.

The expanding naval stores, railroad, and phosphate mining industries were not the only major enterprises to alter the economic landscape of Florida. Florida's climate was ideal for certain agricultural products, especially citrus fruits. Once drainage operations had turned wet marshes into arable fields and orchards and copper sulfate was added to the soil, Florida's citrus industry became a central factor in the state's economic development.[46]

The local labor supply was insufficient to meet the growing need for workers, and migrants began to pour into Florida to take advantage of the economic boom in agriculture. They came first from the Northeast, a source of seasonal labor for some time. Immigrant farmers from Southern and Central Europe migrated along the Atlantic coast and became a part of the seasonal migration stream. Black migrants soon joined the trek from Maryland, the Carolinas, and Georgia. By the turn of the century, black workers had begun to dominate on the Atlantic Coast stream.[47] The improvement in soil composition meant bumper crops, and large agricultural towns grew up, particularly in the Everglades. The areas around Belle Glade and Pahokee teemed with workers during the harvest season. In the 1920s, as Americans demanded more fruits and vegetables in their diet, the migrant worker stream expanded further. Hurston documented this process in *Their Eyes Were Watching God*.

> Day by day now, the hordes of workers poured in. Some came limping in with their shoes and sore feet from walking. It's hard trying to follow your shoe instead of your shoe following you. They came in wagons from way up in Georgia and they came in truck loads from east, west, north and south. Permanent transients

with no attachments and tired looking men with their families and dogs in flivvers. All night, all day, hurrying in to pick beans. Skillets, beds, patched up spare inner tubes all hanging and dangling from the ancient cars on the outside and hopeful humanity, herded and hovered on the inside, chugging on to the muck. People ugly from ignorance and broken from being poor.[48]

Hurston understood the harshness of labor conditions intimately. She also knew well the vibrant worlds that black workers managed to create in spite of work conditions, and the black towns that mitigated the harsh realities of migrant work in the new South.

Black Towns: The Outlines of a History

The formation of all-black communities was one of many responses to slavery and the terrifying world of Jim Crow. In autonomous or semi-autonomous enclaves, black southerners sought ways to turn segregation to their advantage and build a "nation within a nation." Black towns had their own banks, schools, post offices, newspapers, general stores, churches, fraternal orders, and law enforcement and other municipal offices. Residents of towns like Mound Bayou, Mississippi, Boley, Oklahoma, Goldsboro, Florida, and Eatonville, Florida, managed to live in relative harmony in a segregated world. Many black communities on the edge of white towns were equally successful. In black communities in Tulsa, Oklahoma, the Georgetown section of Sanford, Florida, Ocoee, Florida, and the village of Rosewood, Florida, people prospered and felt secure. The racial tensions inherent in the larger society could still be felt, but they were muted by the sense of solidarity and relative safety, which encompassed the poor as well as the better-off members of these communities. Although vicious pogroms could be visited on these people without warning, self-imposed segregation was one answer to oppression and a way to prove to the world what black people could do on their own. Their independence, however, often invited the very violence they hoped to avoid.

There has been considerable debate over what constitutes a black town.[49] Sundiata Keita Cha-Jua has argued that the criteria must include incorporation, purpose of founding, and political control. In his view a black town's "origins involved a distinct 'racial' or proto-nationalist purpose in which nearly 90 percent of the population is Black and the reins of government are controlled by Blacks."[50] This definition has limitations because it bases the legitimacy of territorial nationalism on recognition by the state.[51] It also ignores maroon communities, which often had considerable political control, were proto-nationalist in purpose, and certainly existed outside the legal confines of the state.[52] A slightly modified definition allows for the inclusion of communities that lacked formal recognition but were located at a distance from the scrutiny of the state and white society and were effectively run by a black power structure. Under this definition, all-black communities may have been more widespread than has previously been acknowledged.[53]

At the end of the nineteenth century more than sixty documented black towns had been formed in the South, though even before that time autonomous black communities were not uncommon. Sundiata Keita Cha-Jua's study of Brooklyn, Illinois, in the antebellum period demonstrates the vitality of an all-black organized community in the North.[54] But even before Eatonville, there were all-black towns in the South. Kenneth Hamilton, for example, identified Kendleton and Broad House, Texas, as having been founded on 8 June 1869.[55]

In 1910 Hiram Tong described the founding of Mound Bayou, Mississippi, as "a definite, deliberate race movement."[56] Benjamin Green and Isaiah Montgomery, both ex-slaves, purchased 840 acres from the Yazoo-Mississippi Valley Railroad in Bolivar County in 1887, the same year Eatonville was incorporated.[57] Like the founders of Eatonville, these freedmen envisioned a colony that would be self-governing and self-supporting. Montgomery and Green sold smallholdings to farmers, and the success of the village scheme was such that within three years they were able to pay for the original purchase and add 4,000 acres.[58] Tong's observations

on the biological traits of the population of Mound Bayou suggest their color and class origins. "The Mound Bayou Negroes,"
he says, "are not a hybridization of the African and the Caucasian
stocks in America. They are essentially a new efflorescence of
the African stock."[59] The sheriff of Bolivar County appointed "a
colored deputy sheriff," which was the extent of white interven-
tion in the business of the town; all the other town leaders were
black. The adult males elected their mayor, constable, village
marshal, and three aldermen. The actual governance of the town,
however, was based on consensus; all decisions were decided in
town meetings. And although the right to vote in elections was
limited to males, Tong reports that women were fully represented in town meetings.[60]

Booker T. Washington wrote several articles on Mound Bayou
and on Boley, Oklahoma, another black town. "It is striking evidence of the progress made in thirty years," Washington wrote
for the *Outlook* in 1908, "that the present northward and westward movement of the Negro people has brought into these new
lands, not helpless and ignorant hordes of black people, but land-
seekers and home-builders, men who have come prepared to build
up the country." Attributing this success not to their white masters or employers but to their African forebears, Washington
proudly reported that "In the thirty years since the Kansas Exodus the Southern Negroes have learned to build schools, to establish banks and conduct newspapers. They have recovered something of the knack for trade that their foreparents in Africa were
famous for. They have learned through their churches and their
secret orders the art of corporate and united action."[61]

Similar magazine articles praised the industriousness and ingenuity of the founders of these towns. An article in the *Colored
American Magazine* in 1909 described Mound Bayou's founders as
"highly patriotic, unselfish and aggressive men of the race, who are
making history for the race that shall be permanent... The men
who conduct the municipal business and financial affairs of Mound
Bayou are of rugged character, sterling worth, and are well and
favorably known for their honesty of purpose."[62] The editors of

this magazine wrote within the prevailing framework of uplift ideology. For them, good moral character led to business success, which in turn testified to black skill and ingenuity. The businesses that flourished in Mound Bayou, among them a lumber company, a cotton merchant's shop, a cotton gin, and a general merchandise store, offered physical proof of the moral character and business sense of the town's leaders. A newspaper called the *Demonstrator*, a Grand Lodge fraternal organization, the Mound Bayou Land and Investment Company, the Mound Bayou Normal and Industrial Institute, which was supported by the American Missionary Association, and Methodist and Baptist churches all testified to the onward march of racial progress.[63] The article contained the names of distinguished business owners, ministers, and educators, complete with their college affiliations. An article in the same magazine two years later congratulated the founders of Boley, Oklahoma, for their ingenuity and commitment to racial progress.[64]

Black Communities in Central Florida and Eatonville

Eatonville was formed between the teeth of Jim Crow. It was an extension of the legacy of maroonage, those runaway-slave communities that dotted the physical and political landscape of colonial and antebellum Florida. In the seventeenth and eighteenth centuries, African-born slaves in the English colony of South Carolina knew of the Spanish edict promising religious sanctuary to runaway slaves. They were aware too of the competition between England and Spain for control of the territory between South Carolina and Florida. With the aid of Indian allies, fugitive slaves made their way south into Spanish territory, the first group, a party of eight men, two women, and a nursing child, arriving in 1686. By 1738 there were more than 100 African fugitives in St. Augustine, and in that year they established a fort and community just north of the Spanish town. The fort was called Gracia Real de Santa Teresa de Mose. Thus the first black town in Florida was organized by runaway slaves, and it became the first legally sanctioned free black town in the territorial United States and a precursor to Eatonville.[65] Fort Mose, as it was known, was only the beginning. Runaway slaves and Africans seeking freedom from American, Spanish, and Indian slaveholders also developed all-black communities in east and west Florida. Though many of these settlements were destroyed in the War of 1812, they nevertheless offer proof of how African Americans fought valiantly for their freedom.

As noted above, many investors moved into the central Florida region with the aim of profiting from the economic opportunities of the New South. One such investor was Henry Shelton Sanford, the father of the citrus industry in Florida and the founder of the city of Sanford. Born in Connecticut to a life of privilege, Sanford had visited Florida in 1860. He returned there after the Civil War and made several bad investments. In 1870 Sanford purchased 12,535 acres of raw land along Lake Monroe and spent the next twenty years importing varieties of citrus fruit and experimenting with it in a grove he developed in the region called Belair.[66] In this wild, undeveloped, and underpopulated frontier region—at the time a mere 200,000 people were scattered over 60,000 square miles—the potential for profit was great, but Sanford was a poor manager and he lost millions. Nevertheless, he helped to develop the area, and his need for labor also added to its population. He first tried working with local whites, whom he detested. He then turned to white immigrant labor, which also proved unsuccessful.[67] Finally he brought sixty black workers from Madison to clear groves and plant citrus. In a letter to his son in 1890, Sanford commented on the reaction of local whites to his patronage of black workers: "They were driven off and some slain with shot guns; and to that very act, the Georgetown suburb of Sanford owes its existence for when I was strong enough to defy the shotgun policy of men, I offered and secured a home and protection there to peaceful, laborious worthy colored people—they have fulfilled my expectation."[68]

The lots Sanford sold his black workers were turned into homes, schools, churches, and businesses that the residents called Georgetown, an area later incorporated into Sanford. Other workers developed a town near the railroad yards that they incorporated as Goldsboro in 1891, five years after the founding of Eatonville. The laborers in these towns laid the track for the railroads that crisscrossed the region, moving both people and goods. Others manned steamboats that connected Sanford to Jacksonville. The cars for the South Florida Railroad were built in shops near Goldsboro. In short, Georgetown and Goldsboro were the basis for the region's emergence as the commercial and railroad hub in the late nineteenth century, according to local historians Altermese Smith Bentley and Brenda Elliott. They also attribute Sanford's coveted position as the county seat to the toil of the black laborers Sanford hired to work his citrus groves.[69]

Residents of Georgetown worked in barbershops, boarding houses, laundries, lunchrooms, and various shops. Schools such as Crooms Academy, a private school for blacks, were modeled on Tuskegee. Churches were built on land donated by Sanford. Zora Neale Hurston's father served as pastor of one such church, Zion Hope Baptist, for twenty years, and the Hurston family owned and continues to own a house in Sanford.[70] By 1910 Goldsboro and Georgetown were thriving communities. Most residents worked as laborers, the majority in the citrus industry and celery fields, and many owned their own homes.[71]

The familial and community networks in Georgetown and Goldsboro made it possible for some to find success within their segregated world, but that success did not protect them from white racism. In 1911, for example, the state legislature revoked Goldsboro's charter so that the white town of Sanford could expand westward—a "theft" that Zora Neale Hurston wrote about three decades later. When Goldsboro leaders William Clark and the town council would not voluntarily relinquish their charter, state senator Forest Lake, of Orange County, devised a solution. Hurston wrote:

> He induced the legislature to rule that since that body had the right to grant a charter, they also had the right to take one back.

They voted to take back the charters of both Sanford and Golds-borough [as the name was spelled at the time]. Then Sanford speedily reorganized itself and included the Goldsborough tract in their next application for a charter, which was speedily granted. Thus ended the existence of the second incorporated Negro town in Florida.[72]

The officials in Sanford promised that Goldsboro's indebtedness of $10,375.90 would be paid; the good citizens of this formerly all-black town had nothing to worry about. The promise was broken. With characteristic understatement, Hurston recorded the pathos of another betrayal of black Americans: "William Clark is an old man who cherishes a mass of jumbled yellow papers all about the debt that he and some others hope to collect someday. But busy Sanford selling millions of dollars' worth of celery every season has forgotten all about those papers years ago."[73]

The Founding of Eatonville

Eatonville was incorporated as an all-black town by a group of African Americans who held on to the dreams of the post–Civil War generation.[74] Led by Joseph E. Clark, who figures prominently in Hurston's literary work, blacks from Maitland, Florida, purchased land and established Eatonville in 1887.

Clark was born into slavery in 1859, the third child of William and Angelina Clark, slaves on the plantation of N. N. Clark in Covington, Georgia. His father worked as a drayman on the plantation, hauling goods to other parts of the state, which gave him a measure of freedom not available to most slaves. When slavery ended, William Clark, like so many former slaves in the turbulent days after the war, moved his family "north" to Tennessee, where he heard that the Union army was in control and that ex-slaves could find opportunities for work and a good education for their children. Clark and his family headed to Chattanooga with the hope and promise of a new life.[75]

In 1869, after the passage of the Fifteenth Amendment, William Clark, still working as a drayman, proudly exercised his right to vote. Joseph, now ten, worked as a drayman with his father. By all accounts, the family was adjusting to life after slavery. William Clark taught his children frugality, while in school they learned reading, writing, and arithmetic. According to the 1870 census, William Clark's net worth was $400, a considerable sum for a former slave.[76]

The political climate in Tennessee and throughout the South began to darken as former confederates moved to disfranchise blacks who supported Republican political candidates. In 1866 the Ku Klux Klan was founded in Pulaski, only 150 miles from Chattanooga, and in 1868 a riot in Pulaski killed two black people and wounded five others. In 1870 William Clark decided to move his family back to Georgia, where they settled in Atlanta and did well, in spite of the death of Joseph's sister, Mary, at age thirteen, and the death of his mother shortly thereafter.[77] The Clarks were active members of the community and helped to build Morris Brown College, sponsored by the African Methodist Episcopal Church.

Joseph was ambitious. In the 1870s he married Julia Hightower, and by the time they moved to Maitland, Florida, around 1880, they had three daughters, Mattie, Mande, and Marnie. Like many freed slaves, the Clarks understood freedom as an opportunity to lead their lives free from discrimination, own their own land, develop their own institutions, and provide for their families.[78] According to the *Eatonville Speaker*, Joseph Clark and his friend Allen Ricketts had tried to establish a town for freedmen in other parts of Florida between 1875 and 1877, when Clark was still in his teens. But, according to the newspaper, "so great was the prejudice then existing against the Negro that no one would sell the land for such a purpose."[79]

For ex-slaves, land ownership was a crucial element of freedom. Though they failed to achieve their "forty acres and a mule," land ownership remained a cornerstone of economic independence.[80] As historian Jimmie Franklin has argued, "To many blacks, land in the rural South represented a terrible economic entrapment, a natural resource for sustaining economic subservience.

Yet work on the land and its products played a significant part in an individual's view of personal worth and identity. Land, then, had a close association to the idea of place, even among those persons who failed to own it."[81] It was this relationship to land that inspired Clark and others to pin their hopes on acquiring it. This relationship also partially explains why many exploited workers remained in the South in spite of the hardships there, as well as why many left the land and migrated north. The dual relationship to land, characterized by resentment and pride, imprisonment and liberation, is often missed by literary scholars. Land was a symbol of social, political, and economic autonomy, the aspirations of freed people at the end of the century.[82]

As freed slaves quickly lost ground after the failure of Reconstruction, Clark and his supporters, Allen Ricketts, Tony Taylor, and others, struggled to maintain control over their lives by continuing to try and acquire land. Their initial attempts failed as whites in the surrounding area refused to sell, but finally circumstances and philanthropy opened a way.

By 1883 small groups of African Americans had drifted into the area that was to become Eatonville from further north, joining residents of the black section of Fort Maitland, a town named for the colonel who had commanded the old fort there, which had been used against the local Indians. In 1883 Maitland had not yet been incorporated, but in the post-Reconstruction period blacks had migrated to the area to work its rich citrus groves as pickers and caretakers.[83] These laborers also helped to build the magnificent homes of the wealthy whites who settled on the shores of Lake Maitland. As Hurston recalled in her autobiography,

Negroes were found to do the clearing. There was the continuous roar of the crashing of ancient giants of the lush woods, of axes, saws and hammers. And there on the shores of Lake Maitland rose stately houses, surrounded by beautiful grounds. Others flocked in from upper New York State, Minnesota and Michigan, and Maitland became a center of wealth and fashion. In less than ten years, the Plant System, later absorbed into the Atlantic Coast Line Railroad, had been persuaded to extend a line south through Maitland, and the private coaches of millionaires and other dignitaries from North and South became a common sight on the siding. Even a president of the United States visited his friends at Maitland.

These wealthy northerners, with their "glittering carriages behind blooded horses and occupied by well-dressed folk, presented a curious spectacle in the swampy forests so dense that they are dark at high noon." The dense, swampy forests were frightening; they swarmed with "deadly diamond-back rattlesnakes, and huge, decades-old bull alligators bellowed their challenge from the uninhabited shore of the lakes. It was necessary to carry a lantern when one walked out at night, to avoid stumbling over these immense reptiles in the streets of Maitland."

Black laborers constructed their "hastily built shacks around St. John's Hole, a lake as round as a dollar, and less than a half-mile wide" in the shadow of the white estates on Lake Maitland. They found employment and developed good relations with their white employers.

> The Negro women could be seen every day but Sunday squatting around St. John's Hole on their haunches, primitive style, washing clothes and fishing, while their men went forth and made their support cutting new ground, building, and planting orange groves. Things were moving so swiftly that there was plenty to do, with good pay. Other Negroes in Georgia and West Florida heard of the boom in South Florida and they came. No more back-bending over rows of cotton; no more fear of the fury of the Reconstruction. Good pay, sympathetic white folks and cheap land, soft to the touch of the plow. Relatives and friends were sent for.[84]

By the early 1880s, black people outnumbered whites in Maitland. The town was finally incorporated in 1884. Several historical accounts written by the Florida researchers for the Federal Writers' Project of the WPA suggest that political tensions emerged immediately between the black and white residents of the town.[85]

According to Hurston, the white founders of Maitland had supported emancipation, and when it came time for local elections there was no attempt to exclude blacks from the franchise. As Hurston recalled, "the Eatons, Lawrences, Vanderpools, Hurds,

Halls, and the Hills, Yateses and Galloways, and all the rest including Bishop Whipple, head of the Minnesota diocese, never for a moment considered excluding the Negroes from participation."[86] Whites nominated one candidate for mayor and blacks, under the leadership of Joe Clark, put up Tony Taylor. Tony Taylor won and Joe Clark was elected town marshal. This was a surprise, but according to Hurston both men took office without incident and served for a year. They were then ousted for reasons that remain unclear. Frank Otey, Maitland's historian and the former principal of Hungerford Academy, suggests some sort of political rift. A member of the Federal Writer's Project, writing on Eatonville in the 1930s, described the situation as follows: "Men walked boldly about the streets with revolvers strapped to their sides; saloons dotted the town. The whites were afraid of the Negro situation."[87] While the writer does not elaborate on "the Negro situation," and while it is difficult to sort out fact and legend, it appeared that for a brief moment Maitland would become a unique experiment in political harmony in the post-Reconstruction South. But rising political tensions increased black residents' desire for a separate town. In Hurston's words, "a yeast was working. Joe Clarke had asked himself, why not a Negro town? Few of the Negroes were interested. It was too vaulting for their comprehension. A pure Negro town! If nothing but their own kind was in it, who was going to run it? With no white folks to command them, how would they know what to do? Joe Clarke had plenty of confidence in himself to do the job, but few others could conceive of it."[88]

Some residents suggested that Clark had never given up on the idea and that his assistance in establishing Maitland and testing the political waters was his way of "working the white folks." Whatever his motives, he did gain the attention of two northern white philanthropists. In 1875 a Mr. Lewis Lawrence from Utica, New York, had moved to Maitland and established a large citrus grove.[89] Joe Clark went to work for Lewis and was well liked by the majority of his fellow blacks. He also had a gift for exerting his leadership without arousing white offense.[90] Captain Josiah Eaton, an

English sea captain who ran a large manor known as Boyington Estate, appointed Clark foreman of the citrus groves.[91]

In 1883 Joe Clark purchased a twenty-seven-acre tract of land on a mortgage from Mr. Lawrence.[92] The town was named Eatonville in honor of Josiah Eaton, who also at one time or another employed almost all of the residents in Eatonville in his citrus groves.[93] In addition to Clark, its settlers included Matthew Brazwell, Tony Taylor, David Yelder, Fred Lewis, Walter Thomas, Tom Pender, C. H. Boger, John Watson, Tim Everett, Ishmael Williams, and Syke Jones. On 18 August 1887 twenty-seven registered voters met in the public hall of Eatonville and voted unanimously to incorporate as a town, and by the turn of the century Eatonville had become a well-organized black community.[94]

In this all-black enclave, residents developed a political and social system that existed to some extent as a "safe cocoon" free of the usual tensions between the races. In the town's first elections, held 18 August 1887, C. H. Boger was elected mayor,[95] J. R. Johnson clerk, W. T. Thomas marshal, J. B. Brazell tax assessor, J. N. Watson tax collector, and L. D. Brazell treasurer. All were elected unanimously by twenty-seven votes. The new leaders established a post office, and Joe Clark was appointed postmaster. Court was held in the local church, and a newspaper was established and lasted for a few years.

Eatonville quickly grew into a cozy and contained village. By 1900, 297 households were recorded in the census.[96] Most men were employed as day or farm laborers in the surrounding citrus groves. Women worked as domestics and washwomen, probably for the whites who lived in neighboring Winter Park and Maitland. By 1920 the town had grown to more than 900 households,[97] and during the 1920s and 1930s several residents acquired their own citrus groves. Men like Sam Weston had come to the area looking for work and become orange pickers. After years of hard work and sacrifice, Weston was able to purchase 100 acres of land and plant his own grove on land west of Eatonville and Forest City roads. He undoubtedly was able to employ citizens of Eatonville.[98] Larkin Franklin, a Mohawk Indian who married a black woman, also moved to Eatonville in the 1920s and became a squatter on ten acres of land on Lake Sybelia, just outside Eatonville.[99] He found work in the citrus groves and worked his way up to the position of caretaker, finally acquiring his own grove; his descendents still own this land.

James T. Steele was another black resident who established his own citrus grove and provided employment for many in the town. Steele and his wife came to Eatonville in 1917 from Mississippi with nothing but the clothes on their backs. Steele became an expert on citrus fruit and managed several large estates for wealthy northerners who had winter homes in the area. He bought his own citrus grove and with the income from these enterprises acquired several homes and other businesses. His holdings made him the wealthiest member of the community. Steele was able to employ members of the community as fruit pickers and eventually positioned himself as a benefactor in Eatonville.

Residents developed the institutions that cemented a loose collection of households into a community. They built churches, schools, and businesses. Joe Clark opened one of the first businesses in Eatonville, a general store, and sold land to new residents for a nominal fee. In an essay on Eatonville, written for a WPA guidebook on Florida, Hurston described the landscape that Clark helped to create:

> Maitland is Maitland until it gets to Hurst's corner, and then it is Eatonville. Right in front of Willie Sewell's yellow painted house the hard road quits being the hard road for a generous mile and becomes the heart of Eatonville. Or from a stranger's point of view, you could say that the road just bursts through on its way from Highway #17 to #441 scattering Eatonville right and left.

After leaving the Sewell home one encountered open space until arriving at the Green Lantern on the corner.

> That corner has always been the main corner because that is where Joe Clarke, the founder and first mayor of Eatonville, built his store when he started the town nearly sixty years ago, so that people have gotten used to gathering there and talking. Only Joe

Clarke sold groceries and general merchandise while Lee Glenn
sells drinks of all kinds and whatever goes with transient rooms.[100]

Joe Clark's store figures prominently in Hurston's novels and
folklore. It was on the porch of this store that Hurston observed
the social structure and public culture of Eatonville. There men
and women negotiated for social space, sparred with each other,
told tall tales, and entertained themselves with ribaldry and
jokes. While literary scholars have focused on the gender and
social relations Hurston described in Eatonville, it is evident from
these exchanges that community residents were also concerned
with the politics of color, internal codes of justice and retribution, and preserving their sense of humor in the face of spo-
radic racial violence.

Religion has always been a central part of African American
community life. Eatonville residents decided that they needed
a church of their own and in fact built one, the African
Methodist Church, in 1881–82, before the town was incorporated. Church members eventually named the church after
Lewis Lawrence, who had donated the land on which it was
built, and it became the St. Lawrence African Methodist Episcopal Church. An Odd Fellows Hall, the St. Lawrence Lodge,
was also named in his honor. As the town grew and the number of worshippers increased, a second, larger church was built
on the same site.[101]

Citizens who felt the need for a Baptist church established the
Macedonia Baptist church in 1882, and the small group met in
the same structure as the Methodists on alternating Sundays. In
1889 the Baptists bought a building on Eaton Street and by 1895
the small church was led by Reverend John Richardson. They
soon outgrew this building and built a new church at the corner
of Calhoun and Eatonville roads. In 1902 John Hurston became
its second pastor and the third mayor of Eatonville. This congregation grew at such a rapid pace that a new church was needed
by 1909.[102]

After the establishment of churches, businesses, and lodges,
a school was the next logical project. The Robert Hungerford

Normal and Industrial School was the first of its kind in the South. It was an all-black private boarding and day school for students from grades four through twelve. Founded in 1897 by Russell C. and Mary Calhoun of Tuskegee Institute, its aim was to educate black children in both trades and academic subjects.[103] Dr. Robert Hungerford became the school's benefactor and assisted the Calhouns with funding from white patrons. The school was named in memory of the young white physician who was "a permanent inspiration in the lives of so many Negroes."[104] After Hungerford's death, his father, Edward C. Hungerford, became a patron of the school and donated forty acres of land to be used in the teaching of agriculture. The Hungerford family solicited more assistance from relatives, who responded by donating more land. Other benefactors made cash contributions. Early records indicate that Booker T. Washington gave $400 to erect the school's first large building, which was named in Washington's honor.[105] Later, George B. Cleutt, a manufacturer from Troy, New York, gave $8,000 for the construction of its second large building.[106]

By 1935 the school had expanded to 340 acres and developed a reputation for its excellent academic program, which was based on the curricula of Tuskegee Institute and Hampton Institute. Students were required both to study academic subjects and to acquire a vocational skill. When Russell Calhoun died in 1909, Mary took over and ran the school for ten years. After her departure, the school fell into less capable hands. By the mid-1940s it was in decline, and in the early 1950s it was taken over by the state and became a public vocational institution.

During its forty years of health, however, the school was the educational mainstay of the community. Eatonville parents were eager to send their children to Hungerford, confident that it would prepare them for a world in which economic opportunities were limited. The 1900 census listed children in almost every household, including the Hurston children, as "at school." The opportunity for these children to attend a private boarding school was made possible by the continued patronage of sympathetic whites and those blacks financially secure enough to donate to the school. Students also came from all over the state, since there were few high schools for black children. Yet not everyone in Eatonville received an education. Frank Otey leaves the impression that education was universal even in the 1920s and 1930s, but Hurston's neighbors were often uneducated.

Eatonville continued to grow, and with its growth came the inevitable changes. Hurston had boasted that there was no jailhouse in Eatonville during her formative years; Joe Clark, likewise, had reportedly contended that his town did not need a jail. Those who didn't behave themselves were simply run out.[107] But crime eventually came to Eatonville. During John Hurston's tenure as mayor, 1912–16, the first jailhouse was built, a makeshift structure that was destroyed by the first prisoner, Doc Biddy, who tore down one side and escaped. During the administration of Hurston's successor, the town purchased cement blocks for the building of a more substantial structure, but the same Doc Biddy stole the blocks. The partially completed jail was used for some years to hold the lawbreakers who frequented the jook joints, beer and wine parlors, and other social establishments that respectable residents viewed as "undesirable havens of vice."[108]

Apart from drinking establishments, Eatonville was a quiet place suitable for raising families. Law and order were maintained and the town leaders lauded discipline, education, and religious values. According to Otey, "In its first three score years, the town produced one doctor, one dentist, two pharmacists, two nurses, two well known preachers, two high school principals, ten school teachers, and one author."[109] Black men in Eatonville could elect their own leaders, run unhindered for public office, and help make the laws that governed the town. And if Elsa Barkley Brown's argument for Richmond and other areas of the South—that women participated in the vote by making it a family affair— holds true for Eatonville, then women also had a say in the democratic process.[110]

Yet Eatonvillers did not live in a cocoon. Despite their strong institutions and vibrant public culture, black Floridians were not insulated from the larger realities of the Jim Crow South. Most residents were not professionals, wealthy landowners, or business-men. They were day laborers in the citrus groves and domestics. Only a small percentage worked for black owners like Steele and Weston; the rest had to commute to white Maitland for work. Contacts outside the town were sufficient to remind residents that life continued to be difficult for the majority of black people in the New South. And beyond Eatonville's borders, black life in the rural areas of Florida was as harsh as in other parts of the South, a subject that undoubtedly occupied the private and public con-versations of Eatonville residents. The residents of Eatonville whom Hurston wrote about were well aware of the discrimina-tion and violence of agricultural migrant camps in the mucks and turpentine and sawmill camps.

Still, Eatonvillers lived as freely as they could, which was undoubtedly more freely than most southern blacks. They built their own homes, married, raised families, and worked hard to educate their children. They loved and fought and laughed and prayed. Most whites had no sense of the vigorous life that existed in such communities. As they drove by on the road from Orlando they saw workers moving in and out of their "shacks," or they heard the music from the local jook and imagined the depravity inside. As W.E.B. DuBois said, these "car-window sociologists" never ventured to the inside of these worlds; instead they con-structed a knowledge based on bits and pieces of reality under-stood through the distorted lens of race. Even now, few imagine life as it was really lived in that time and place. What white passersby saw as homely shacks were the homes from which future generations of upwardly mobile, landowning, educated black people emerged, among them the civil rights activists who changed the face of American society, both North and South, a few short decades later.

Criticisms of Hurston's portrayal of southern black life as ide-alized are both inaccurate and unfair. Hurston's depiction of the rural South actually reminds us of the desperate conditions in which black men and women had to live and labor, and over which, in no small measure, they managed to triumph. Her narrative begins with the desperation but it does not end there, for she offers a more intimate view of her characters than that. Neither ugly nor broken, they are actually as whole and as beautiful as we can dare imagine.

The Rough Side of Southern Life

Much has been written about the systematic racial oppression suffered by black communities throughout the South. The effort to reduce free blacks to a condition as close to slavery as possible began before the ink had dried on the Emancipation Proclamation. Indeed, the more successful black people were in creating autonomous communities, the more vulnerable they often were. Nell Painter's study of black migration to Kansas in the 1870s and 1880s demonstrated the degree to which the wave of lynchings was driven by white resentment of the political gains that blacks achieved.[111] The targets of many of those lynchings were black men elected to political office after passage of the Fifteenth Amendment; others were black community leaders. In Memphis in early 1892, for example, three successful merchants and owners of the People's Grocery Company—Thomas Moss, Calvin McDowell, and Henry Stewart, were arrested after a game of marbles escalated into a fight. Spirited away by a white mob, they were lynched on the outskirts of town. No one witnessed the deed, but the lynching was reported in the next day's paper. Ida B. Wells was a friend of the three unfortunate businessmen, and she began a crusade against the violence that took their lives in the *Memphis Free Speech*, the newspaper she owned. In May, after months of investigation, Wells challenged the spurious charge of rape on which the mob had lynched the men.

> Eight Negroes lynched since last issue of the Free Speech. Three were charged with killing white men and five with raping white women. Nobody in this section believes the old thread-bare lie that Negro men assault white women. If southern white men are not careful they will overreach themselves and a conclusion will

be reached which will be very damaging to the moral reputation of their women.[112]

Wells barely escaped her own lynching as a result of her brazen outspokenness. Her newspaper was destroyed, and she went on to work for the *New York Age*.

By the end of the decade, violence against blacks had reached new levels of barbarity. The lynching of Sam Hose in Georgia signaled the beginning of a pattern of violence as a "deadly amusement," entertainment so gruesome it remains difficult for modern minds to comprehend.[113]

On 23 April 1899, near Newman, Georgia, a lynching took place that brought out 2,000 people on a warm Sunday afternoon. Some had arrived on a special excursion train. The crowd included some of the region's most prominent citizens, many of whom participated eagerly in the day's activities. The body to be lynched and mutilated that day belonged to Sam Hose, a literate, articulate, ambitious farm laborer in rural Georgia. Hose wanted to pursue his education, but an invalid mother and retarded brother required his support, so in 1898 he accepted a job with a planter named Alfred Cranford in Coweta County, outside Atlanta. In April 1899 he requested permission to visit his mother and asked for an advance in pay for the trip. For reasons unknown, Cranford not only refused but insulted him, prompting a heated exchange between the two men. The next day, as Hose chopped wood, the planter resumed the argument, drew his pistol, and threatened to kill Hose. Hose defended himself, flinging his ax and planting it in Cranford's head, killing him instantly. Although he had acted in self-defense, Hose knew that if he were caught he would be lynched, so he did the only thing he could and fled the scene.

The stories that circulated over the next two days portrayed Hose as a deranged monster who had murdered his employer without provocation. The murder scene was embellished in the retelling, such that, as "the brains were oozing out of her husband's head," Mrs. Cranford was ravaged by the monster. Mrs. Cranford's mother, who had not witnessed the killing, provided a positive identification of Hose. Her word was enough for the crowd that gathered on 23 April to witness Hose's torture and execution.

Sam Hose was stripped of his clothing and chained to a tree. His executioners cut off his ears, fingers, and genitals and skinned his face. He was doused with oil, and kerosene-soaked wood was stacked around him. Many in the crowd plunged knives into his flesh, while others watched "with unfeigning satisfaction" as the torch was applied and "the flames rose, distorting his features, causing his eyes to bulge out of their sockets, and rupturing his veins." As he burned alive, Hose managed to loosen his ropes. The executioners put out the flames, retied him, covered his body in more oil, and set him on fire again. "As his blood sizzled," Hose whispered, "Oh, my God! Oh, Jesus." After his charred remains had cooled, participants cut out his heart and liver and cut them into pieces. His bones were crushed into small particles. "The crowd fought over these souvenirs" and some made fine profits on the sales: "small pieces of bone went for twenty-five cents, while a piece of liver, 'crisply cooked,' sold for ten." The *New York Times* reported that shortly after the lynching one of the participants left for the state capitol with a gift for the governor, a slice of Sam Hose's heart.

The next day all that remained of the previous day's events was a pile of smoldering ashes, a blackened stake, and a placard on a nearby tree that read, "We Must Protect Our Women." Further "celebrations" resulted in a reign of terror that included the torching of a black church and the torture and lynching of a popular black preacher, Lige Strickland, who was thought to be involved in the Cranford murder. Also lynched was Albert Sewell, for threatening revenge and for talking too much.

Investigations carried out by a white detective who interviewed Mrs. Cranford, and a separate investigation by Ida B. Wells, revealed that Hose had come to the house to pick up his wages and the two men had quarreled. When Cranford went for his revolver, Hose in self-defense had picked up and hurled the ax, which killed Cranford instantly. Hose then fled the scene. He never entered the house, Mrs. Cranford confessed, nor did he assault her. The results of the investigations were of no interest to the press or the public. Between 1890 and World War I, nearly 3,000 black southerners suffered the same fate as Hose, "with only slight variations in the rituals performed and in the hymns that were sung."[114]

In 1923, Rosewood, Florida, located in Levy County, experienced the worst pogrom in the history of the state. A white woman alleged that a black man had beaten her, an explanation she offered for the bruises on her face. As the story circulated, the beating became a rape, and whites in the nearby town of Sumner formed a posse to capture the culprit. They moved toward Rosewood, a small black community of about thirty homes. To the baying of hounds and the sound of voices yelling, "kill him," "kill the nigger!" Rosewood was attacked and most of its inhabitants massacred; the town's homes and its churches, Masonic lodge, and school were leveled. Only a few children and adults, with the help of white engineers on the railroad, escaped death.[115]

Atrocities such as this occurred on a regular basis in the post-Emancipation South, and Florida was no exception. Perhaps no incident depicts the depravity of Jim Crow more vividly than the Ocoee Riot of 1920, on which Zora Neale Hurston reported.

> This happened on election day, November 2, 1920. Though the catastrophe took place in Ocoee, and it is always spoken of as the Ocoee Riot, witnesses both white and Negro state that it was not the regular population of Ocoee which participated in the affair. It is said that the majority of whites of the community deplored it at the time and have refused to accept full responsibility for it since.[116]

So began Hurston's account of the Ocoee Riot, which culminated in the lynching of July Perry and the destruction of another African American community. The following details are drawn from Hurston's account and from a report by Walter White, a member of the NAACP and its future director.

The trouble began in the citrus town of Winter Garden. The Harding presidential campaign had been a lively one and black

Republicans were turning out to vote in record numbers. The elections of 1920 were of great significance. Women now had the right to vote and black women availed themselves of this historic opportunity for the first time, giving some areas a potential black majority. On 16 September the *Jacksonville Metropolis* ran a headline that blared, "Democracy in Duval County Endangered by Very Large Registration of Negro Women."[117] The accompanying article claimed that white women had not registered in the same numbers as black women and asked, "Are the white men and women of Duval County going to permit 'negro washerwomen and cooks' to wield the balance of political power?" In Orange County, where Ocoee was located, allegations were made that black votes cost white jobs. Blacks in Ocoee swarmed to the polls, while whites from Winter Garden went to Ocoee to stop what they perceived to be a black takeover.

After much pushing and shoving and many angry exchanges, many black voters left the polls, but some persisted. Among these was Mose Norman, who was struck and driven off for attempting to vote. He consulted a local judge named Cheney who urged him to return and collect the names of those denied their rights and the names of the white culprits who had violated the law. Norman was driven off again and several blacks were beaten in his place. The mob decided to seek Norman out and give him a good beating for his "officiousness and for being a smart-aleck." Norman "was unpopular with the whites because he was too prosperous; he owned an orange grove for which he had refused offers of $10,000 several times. The prevailing sentiment was that Norman was too prosperous 'for a nigger.'"[118] Someone saw him visiting the home of July Perry, a prosperous farmer and labor contractor, and the mob decided to go to Perry's home and drag Norman out. According to Hurston, the "Black Dispatch" (the local grapevine) had published reports of these events, and most of the Negroes had left town or hidden out in the orange groves. "July Perry armed himself and prepared to defend himself and his home. His friends all took to the woods and groves and left him to his courage. Even his sons hid out with the rest. Only his wife and daughter remained in the house with him," according to White. By late evening two of the town's three black churches had been burned and the whole community was under siege. At least one man, a carpenter named Langmaid, had been castrated. Mose Norman himself had disappeared. Hurston reported that as night fell, "no Negro except July Perry had maintained his former address. So night dusted down on Ocoee, with the mobs seeking blood and ashes and July Perry standing his lone watch over his rights to life and property."

> The night color gave courage to many men who had been diffident during the day hours. Fire was set to whole rows of Negro houses and the wretches who had thought to hide by crawling under these buildings were shot or shot at as they fled from the flames. In that way Maggie Genlack and her daughter were killed and their bodies left and partially burned by the flames that consumed their former home. The daughter was far advanced in pregnancy and so felt unequal to flight since there was no conveyance that she could get. Her mother would not leave her alone as all the others vanished out of the quarters. They took counsel together and the old woman and her pregnant daughter crept under the house to escape the notice of the mob. Roosevelt Barton died of fire and gunshot wounds when the barn of July Perry was put to flames. He had thought that that would be a good hiding place, but when the fury of the crowd swept over the Perry place, the barn was fired and when Roosevelt tried to rush out he was driven back by a bullet to die in the fire. But this only happened after a pitched battle had been fought at Perry's house, with July Perry against the mob.

This scene was fictionalized in Beverly Coyle's novel *In Troubled Waters* (1993). Coyle's grandfather, a cattleman from Seminole County, had been a member of the KKK. During a visit in 1990, he began telling Coyle a story about a night in 1920 when he was awakened by friends to go to Ocoee, where "[s]ome of the boys had gone on a tear." There he saw a house where eight blacks had been hiding. "The people inside had tried to run from the flames but had been entangled and burned alive in a chicken-wire fence at the rear of the burning structure."[119] Coyle did not know whether to believe her grandfather, but the vividness of his account disturbed her.

Perry waited with his high-powered rifle. He wondered about the white people with whom he had worked and known so long who were coming now with strangers from Winter Garden to destroy him, his family, and his property. The mob outside assaulted his front door and Perry defended his property with all his might. "He was effective," says Hurston, so effective that the mob thought Perry was not alone. In Hurston's telling, the mob continued the assault on the front of the house while several sought entrance from the rear. Sam Salisbury kicked in the door and in his surprise he began shooting at the "gaping mouth of the door."[120] In shock, Perry's daughter ran out the door and caught a bullet from her father's gun. The next shot struck Sam Salisbury in the arm. Elmer McDonald and a man named Overberry were fatally wounded. The mob retreated to seek reinforcements.

July Perry had also been struck with bullets. His wife persuaded him to leave and they scurried into the cane patch, leaving behind their wounded daughter. The mob returned with fresh recruits and found his wounded daughter the only occupant in the house. They ignored her and proceeded to hunt Perry down. At dawn they found him and took him to jail in Orlando. But the mob was not finished. As Hurston wrote, "It was after sun-up when the mob stormed the jail and dragged him out and tied him to the back of a car and killed him and left his body swinging to a telephone post beside the highway… That was the end of what happened in Ocoee on election day, 1920."[121]

But that was not the end of the story. July Perry's death certificate recorded the cause of his death as "By being hung." Sometime later, no one knows when, someone wrote across the official death certificate, "not by violence caused by racial disturbance." Several weeks after the riot, a black midwife in another small town slipped a letter into a citrus crate and mailed it to a friend in New Jersey.[122] She said she hoped her friend would like the navel oranges and the smaller fruits in the crates, which were kumquats. She suggested boiling the strange fruits to draw out their sourness. Then came a whispered urgency. "We were speaking of lynches and other ill happening to colored people in the south," she wrote.

There had never been any near enough for me to see it, but at last one of the most wickedest happenings of a lifetime happened here. On the north side of town, all the homes and some of the people were burned, one man was shot and killed and carried to the county seat and hung up as lynched. The people on the south side of town are being threatened that they must sell out and leave or they will be shot and burned as the others have been. I don't know the first step to take.

The author of the letter, Mrs. J. H. Hamiter, was speaking of Ocoee. According to an article in the *Orlando Sentinel*, her letter supports other evidence that the riot may have been spontaneous, but the aftermath was deliberate. Blacks in Ocoee were forced by threat of violence to sell or abandon their property and leave town.[123] The letter continued, "It seems to have been a pre-arranged affair to kill and drive the colored people from their homes as they were getting more prosperous than the white folks." Before Election Day, 495 black people lived in Ocoee. After the riot, no one lived there.

Historian Pam Bordelon has commented that "Hurston knew that in vividly documenting the atrocities at Ocoee and the needless suffering of helpless victims, she was informing the wider world of the violence perpetrated against blacks."[124] When Hurston wrote about horror, she described it just as thoroughly and with as much attention to detail as she did when writing about home. Racist violence, however, was not the subject of her literary and ethnographic work. This kind of horror found its way into the stories she told, but the subject of her work was the life that was lived every day. I turn now to that story.

4

Sex and Color in
Eatonville, Florida

> In the world of [Hurston's] novels, history lies in persistence in the memory, in lost hidden places that wait to be found and to be known for what they are. Such history is barely accessible, the shell of it is only frailly held together, it will be loseable again. But the continuity is there.
>
> —Eudora Welty, "The House of Willa Cather"[1]

IN THE WORKS of Zora Neale Hurston, as in those of Willa Cather, history lies not in official proclamations or authorized texts but "in lost hidden places that wait to be found." "Barely accessible" to our own understandings, "frailly held together" by the shell of their own cultural logic, these places are sustained by the persistent memories of their inhabitants. Our task as careful readers is to enter these places with an open mind and a willingness to let go of our most cherished presuppositions. Only then can we attend to the memories that resound through these places and know them "for what they are." This strategy is of great importance for those of us concerned with retrieving histories and recovering lives that have been consigned to the margins of our individual and national consciousness. In her brilliant essay on the politics of memory, Karen Fields argues that while memories can sometimes fail as representations of unvarnished truth, they can also succeed as the basis for "social order" and, in the case of

African American memories, as a resource for the writing of alternative histories.[2] By taking seriously the memories recorded in Hurston's works and the "lost hidden places" from which those memories emerged, we can re-create the history of resistance that led to the formation and endurance of all-black towns. We can also learn of the "social order" that bound their inhabitants together and the cultural life that nurtured them in the face of Jim Crow.

Hurston's willingness to draw on real events and real people to fuel her imagination increases the value of her fiction as a historical source. We shall see her direct use of real life again and again in this chapter and the next. I do not read her fiction as fact but show how the real world that she draws on is close at hand and available to the historian. I want to complicate the historian's task by testing novels in the same way that we test all historical documents—i.e., by considering them in light of other sources to develop an accurate (if incomplete) picture of the past.

When Hurston returned to Eatonville in 1927 to collect folklore, she had been away from home for several years. But Eatonville was home for Hurston no matter how long her absence. She claimed it as her birthplace even though census records identify her birthplace as Notasulga, Alabama.[3] Evidence suggests that all but three of her siblings were also born in Alabama, but they too claimed to have been born in Eatonville.[4] Returning home meant returning to memories of place that shaped her encounters with friends and family. Those memories and the folklore she collected became the raw material for her literary creations.

In 1925 Hurston submitted four pieces to the first *Opportunity* magazine contest. Her short story "Spunk" and her play *Color Struck* won prizes; the play *Spears* and short story "Black Death" received honorable mention. These were her first works to portray life in Eatonville and to record the names and characteristics of its inhabitants. They also introduce the topics that concerned Hurston's work for more than two decades after her arrival in New York: such everyday matters as marital relations, sexual improprieties, love and desire, freedom and the search for self, social status, religious and spiritual issues, and violence. In "Spunk," for example, the title character, a sawmill worker, commits adultery with Joe Kanty's wife and then kills Joe in a fight. Hunted by a black bobcat, Spunk believes Joe has returned to seek revenge. When he is pushed into a circular saw by an unseen hand, Spunk believes Joe's spirit pushed him, and the men on the store porch concur.

Color Struck introduces Hurston's life-long interest in questions of color bias. Believing that her dark skin disqualifies her for love, the central character is incapable of accepting the love of a man who is unconcerned about a matter as trivial as color. Despite his declaration of love, the woman is convinced that his heart belongs to a lighter-skinned woman. Her self-hatred and anguish is so deep that she destroys the love she so desperately yearns for.

That Hurston allowed her readers to peer into this world was more significant than it might seem now. Segregation limited and structured the encounters of blacks and whites. Black people were integral parts of the households of the white gentry and middle classes, working in the shadows of their porches, parlors, kitchens, and even bedrooms. All but the poorest of whites brought black people into their private worlds. In Rosewood, Florida, Sarah Carrier knew that Fanny Taylor's lover was white because she had served in the Taylor home as a washerwoman. White people, by contrast, rarely found their way into black people's homes or towns, which were genuinely hidden from view, except when matters of law and economics required breaching segregated boundaries. The few whites who were aware of African American spiritual beliefs or cultural practices viewed them as proof of backwardness.

Most black writers of Hurston's era dared not tread on this terrain. These private matters were avoided in published work and not discussed even in letters. Hurston depicts feelings, attitudes, prejudices, and desires that were probably edited out of other writing. The "Negroes farthest down" rarely wrote autobiographies, and when they did they were not always forthcoming on these matters.

As historian Earl Lewis put it, "At home... many black residents lived in an almost all-black world, one shaped but not totally defined by limited interactions with whites. In such a world notions about power changed. In churches, on windowsills, street corners or other places of congregation, African Americans sermonized, joked, sang, and for moments at a time altered power relations."[5] In such settings Eatonvillers talked freely about private and public matters. Hurston's stories and ethnography provide a privileged view of this aspect of home for African Americans in which "concepts like minority, difference, and other meant something other than what we have come to accept. When read from inside the black community outward place helped resituate the colored 'other.'"[6]

The private life that interests me is the one that exists in the face-to-face exchanges of black southern communities. These exchanges do not always disclose personal information, because such information belongs to the realm of what is collectively known and, as such, goes unsaid. Rather, what is disclosed in these exchanges is the knowledge people have about each other's ways and customs, the shared worldviews of people who live and work together in close quarters over a long period of time. To map the interior world of black southern folk we do not need to know who struck whose wife, but we can extract from back-porch stories the rules and norms that governed a community.

Hurston's basic recipe for creating her stories included various combinations of imagination, folklore, and memory. To these ingredients she added the sparkling language of the "Negro farthest down." She also added her own keen sense of history and sophisticated cultural understanding, as well as a political awareness that allowed her to sketch the outlines of a Jim Crow framework in such a subtle way that her stories seem to be far removed from political matters. Hurston's award-winning story "Black Death" is a good place to begin. Robert Hemenway, her biographer, is uncertain about the source of the story's plot, believing it "either a direct redaction of an Eatonville folktale, or a work of fiction Hurston permitted to masquerade as authentic folklore."[7]

The basic story outline also appeared in her article "Hoodoo in America," which was published in the *Journal of American Folklore* in 1931, six years after she wrote "Black Death." Whatever its origins, its opening paragraph anticipates Toni Morrison's definition of rootedness:

> We Negroes in Eatonville know a number of things that the hustling, bustling white man never dreams of. He is a materialist with little care for overtones.
>
> For instance, if a white person were halted on the streets of Orlando and told that Old Man Morgan, the excessively black Negro hoodoo man can kill any person indicated and paid for, without ever leaving his house or even seeing his victim, he'd laugh in your face and walk away, wondering how long the Negro will continue to wallow in ignorance and superstition. But no black person in a radius of twenty miles will smile, not much. They *know*.[8]

The subject of the story is sexual conflict and the cultural knowledge of how to protect oneself against pain and destruction at the hands of an intruder. Recall Morrison's observation that African American culture blends "the acceptance of the supernatural and a profound *rootedness* in the real world at the same time with neither taking precedence over the other."[9] Black people accepted what some would call superstition and magic, which for them were practical ways of knowing things. Because their way of looking at the world was not accepted by whites or even by some elite blacks, these beliefs were viewed at best as backward and superstitious, at worst as ignorant and evil. A faithful portrait of the black experience must include the worldviews of black people from another time and place that many continued to value in the early twentieth century.

"Black Death" tells the story of Docia Boger, a pretty, naïve young maid who works at a resort hotel, and Beau Diddley,[10] a suave and charming northerner working in the same hotel. Docia is smitten and Beau easily seduces the country girl. She becomes pregnant, and he not only cruelly denies his responsibility but maligns her good name, telling the other waiters "how that piece of the earth's refuse had tried to inveigle, to force him into a marriage... It couldn't have happened with the *right* kind of a girl, and he thought too much of himself to marry any other than the country's best." By the next day all Eatonville knows of the pregnancy, and to her heartbreak over Beau's betrayal is added the malicious gossip of the townspeople.

Docia is devastated and turns to her mother for protection. Mrs. Boger is distressed by the loss of the family's honor but even more she is deeply wounded by her daughter's grief and shame.

> Drip, drip, drip, went her daughter's tears on the old woman's heart, each drop calcifying a little the fibers till at the end of four days the petrifying process was complete. Where once had been warm, pulsing flesh was now cold heavy stone that pulled down pressing out normal life and bowing the head of her. The woman died, and in that heavy cold stone a tiger, a female tiger—was born. (5)

Mrs. Boger wants vengeance, but even more she wants the justice typically denied black women, and she will do whatever is necessary to get it. This means transgressing the boundaries of Christian belief and reaching back to an older tradition.

She consults Old Man Morgan, the village hoodoo priest, for assistance in ridding the community of Beau Diddley and avenging her daughter. Morgan "lives in a two-room hut down by Lake Blue Sink, the bottomless... His eyes are reddish and the large gold hoop ear-rings jangling on either side of his shrunken black face make the children shrink in terror whenever they meet him on the street or in the woods where he goes to dig roots for his medicines." As she nears his cabin, Mrs. Boger is filled with fear: "As she approached Blue Sink she all but turned back. It was a dark night but the lake shimmered and glowed like phosphorous near the shore... She remembered that folks said Blue Sink the bottomless was Morgan's graveyard and all Africa awoke in her blood." But she does not turn back, even as "a cold prickly feeling stole over her and stood her hair on end. Her feet grew heavy and her tongue dry and stiff." In this moment she returns to the ways of her ancestors: "three hundred years of America passed like the mist of morning. Africa reached out its dark hand and claimed its own. Drums, tom, tom, tom, beat in her ears. Strange demons seized her. Witch doctors danced before her, laid hands upon her alternatively freezing and burning her flesh, until she found herself within the house of Morgan" (6).[11]

The witchdoctor offers Mrs. Boger her choice of weapons— "By water, a sharp edge, or a bullet?" he asks. She chooses the bullet, and Morgan tells her to shoot into a mirror in which Beau's apparition appears, which will kill Beau without implicating her in the crime. Beau's face appears in the mirror, filled with all the contempt he has heaped on her daughter, but his scorn turns to fear as Mrs. Boger fires. Dropping the gun, she throws the money at the priest and flees in fear, putting as much distance as possible between herself and the hoodoo place.

Since the days of slavery, black women have resorted to violence to protect themselves and their own. Female slaves who had the courage to confront their masters and mistresses earned the admiration of their communities.[12] It was not unusual for women and men to consult their African beliefs to find both solace and justice in a world that provided them neither. "Black Death" affirms both a black woman's right to pursue justice and the local cultural knowledge that African Americans could draw upon to protect themselves in a hostile world. It affirms community cohesiveness in the face of betrayal.

Vigilante justice was often the only means by which black women could defend their honor in an era when they were assumed to be unchaste and to need no protection from the judicial system. Not only is legal justice in court unavailable to Mrs. Boger, but the courts themselves are neither impartial nor nonviolent institutions. We know that Docia Boger is most unlikely to win justice in any white courtroom in the early twentieth-century South. Mrs. Boger's recourse to the art of hoodoo makes perfect sense in this context.

"Black Death" is therefore also about codes of honor. The honor of a young woman and her family has been violated by an outsider, and the family's honor must be vindicated. Black people pursued this satisfaction through methods unsanctioned by the white world that denied them justice. "The coroner's verdict was death from natural causes—heart failure. But they were mystified by what looked like a powder burn directly over his heart. But the Negroes knew instantly when they saw that mark, but everyone agreed that he got justice. Mrs. Boger and Docia moved to Jacksonville where Docia married well" (6).

Though "Black Death" does not provide details about the Boger family, there was such a family in Eatonville. According to census data, C. H. Boger, the first mayor of Eatonville, had a daughter named Docia. I am not suggesting that the story draws upon "factual" information about a leading family in the community but that Hurston's knowledge of the community included all social strata. Because of her social position, Docia's transgression was embarrassing, but she was not forced to leave. The community may have passed judgment on Docia, but they would not have banished her. As Toni Morrison has noted, in these small communities there was "eccentricity and freedom, less conformity in individual habits—but close conformity in terms of the survival of the village, of the tribe. Before sociological microscopes were placed on us, people did anything and nobody was run out of town."[13] But there were rules, and when they were violated the community passed judgment and sometimes meted out punishment. Many in Eatonville objected to Hurston's use of their identities, but it is not clear whether her violation was to reveal secrets or to use their names.[14] The result was that Hurston, too, was judged and talked about.

"Black Death" is also significant in the way it draws on the supernatural beliefs that were part of black American culture, a mixture of Christian and hoodoo beliefs and practices. In recounting the death of a rival hoodoo doctor whom Morgan allegedly disposed of, Hurston wrote, "The white coroner from Orlando said she met her death by falling into the water during an epileptic fit. But the villagers *knew*. White folks are very stupid about some things. They can think mightily but cannot *feel*." If the white audience saw this as exoticism it did not matter.

What white people thought mattered more to the black elite than to the residents of Eatonville and the black working poor. Hurston kept her eyes on the folk. Yet the tensions surrounding these issues were also present in Eatonville, for all-black rural towns had their elites just like all towns everywhere. Questions of upward mobility, respectability, tensions between various Christian denominations, and competing religious practices like hoodoo were part of the cultural fabric.

In openly acknowledging folk religion, Hurston was not spreading the virus of primitivism, so much in vogue in Harlem and the preoccupation of her patrons, particularly of Charlotte Osgood Mason. Rather, she depicted a belief system that was alive and well *within* black communities and that coexisted with traditional Christian religious beliefs in nearly every country in the Americas with a large slave population. The endurance of older beliefs such as those embodied in hoodoo is an uncomfortable subject for many African Americans, but Hurston did not shy away from documenting their persistence in the culture of Eatonville.

"The Eatonville Anthology," published in 1926 in the *Messenger*, was, in Hemenway's words, "the literary equivalent of Hurston's memorable performances at parties" as well as a rich historical source.[15] The short stories and vignettes contained in it were humorous excursions into folks' "business" in the town and portrayed the texture of life in all its complexity and contradictions. Hurston's stories draw upon the lives of ordinary people and their conventional activities as well as ones that the leading citizens would have preferred to conceal. Hurston's characters are probably composites of several real-life Eatonvillers and are therefore, strictly speaking, fictional.

Consider Mrs. Tony Roberts, the main character in the story "The Pleading Woman." She is the town beggar, even though her husband "gives her all he can rake and scrape, which is considerably more than most wives get for housekeeping, but she goes from door to door begging for things."[16] She starts her begging at Joe Clarke's store: "'Mist' Clarke,' she sing-songs in a high keening voice, 'gimme lil' piece uh meat tuh boil a pot uh greens wid. Lawd knows me an mah chillen is SO hongry! Hits uh SHAME! Tony don't fee-ee-eee-ed me!'" Clarke, like everyone else, knows that Mrs. Roberts is well provided for. Her constant begging is an irritant, particularly since she is critical when she does not get the amount she wants. "Thass right Mist' Clarke. De Lawd loveth de cheerful giver. Gimme jes' a lil' piece 'bout dis big (indicating the width of her hand) an de Lawd'll bless yuh" (813). Instructing Clarke on how to cut the meat but failing to get the size she desires, she leaves commenting "on the meanness of some people who give a piece of salt meat only two fingers wide when they plainly asked for a hand-wide piece." She repeats this exchange with several other members of the community until she has collected her rations for the day. Each day the scenario is repeated.

Hurston's story humorously depicts the beggar that every small rural community seems to have. Regardless of their own economic position, these beggars generally resent those they perceive as being better off. Mrs. Roberts calculates both what she needs and how much her benefactor can afford to give:

> Mrs. Pierson picks a bunch of greens for her, but she springs away from them as if they were poison. "Lawd a mussy, Mis' Pierson, you ain't gonna gimme dat lil' eye-full uh greens fuh me an' mah chillen, is you? Don't be so graspin': Gawd won't bless yuh. Gimme uh han'full mo'. Lawd, some folks is got everything, an' theys jes' as gripin' an stingy!" (813–14)

In this way, class distinctions are embedded in everyday exchanges, often having less to do with what people have or how they are socially located than with how they feel about themselves in relation to others.

Residents in Eatonville interviewed by Anna Lillios in 1989–90 about Hurston's work suggested that elder members of the community were disturbed by the stories she told and by her use of real people's names. Clara Williams, for example, who as a child heard adults talk about Hurston, stated that "She'd written some things about Eatonville and when she came back, they said they were going to fix her.[17] [Laughs.] They didn't like some of the things she said or the way she said them."[18]

Others denied subtly that the portrait Hurston painted was real. Mrs. Hoyt Davis, who became acquainted with Hurston as an adult even though they were close in age, insisted that everyone in Eatonville had plenty to eat. "I don't know of one person being hungry at that time in Eatonville. Everybody out here planted gardens and they grew chickens. They could eat chickens whenever they wanted and they fished. So I never heard of anybody asking for food."[19] Notice the terms in which Mrs. Hoyt took issue with Hurston. She reiterated the image of Eatonville as an oasis of black self-sufficiency in a desert of hunger and poverty. Hurston takes us past that general self-conception to the reality that some people have more and some less; some make demands on their neighbors and enforce those demands through gossip. Class differences in the community were evident in how people dressed, how they decorated their houses, whether they had phones, and so on.

Historian John Bracey has provided an interesting tidbit about community response. His paternal grandparents, Scipio and Katie Bracey, lived at 809 Locust in Sanford. When Hurston was writing *Jonah's Gourd Vine*, she rented a house at 806 Locust, after sensing that she was not at that time welcome in Eatonville. It seems that Hurston made known her intention to write a novel about a philandering minister modeled on her father. This project did not sit kindly with community members, given their reverence for ministers and respect for Rev. Hurston. The church and its pastors were sacred to black folks, and certainly a daughter ought not to betray either father or pastor. It is not that the community wanted to banish Zora, merely to chastise her for daring to speak out about her father. Thinking it best to leave town for a little while, she settled in Sanford. Helen Harris Bracey, Professor Bracey's mother, was Hurston's friend and the source of his knowledge of Hurston's time in Sanford. He recalls that she was much loved in spite of her irritating ways. She spent many hours at the Bracey home, living there for a short while after she ran out of money and was evicted from her house. She would sit on the porch and wait for the trucks to deliver farm workers from the fields, and as they walked pass the Bracey home she would ask if she could measure their heads. They graciously allowed the measurements. Helen Bracey would then explain that she was doing very important work. Though puzzled by Hurston's strange request, residents seemed proud to have made her acquaintance. In short, the townspeople may have been displeased with some of her behavior, but they accepted her.[20] In the words of Annie Davis, "She was just Zora. She never looked over none of her people because she had more education… She was always Zora… When she spoke to any of her people she always spoke nice… Some liked her. Some loved her. Some didn't… She wasn't doing nothing but telling the truth."[21]

Hurston's stories tell us a great deal about the enforcement of community norms. Convention required that respectable people marry before having children, as this piece from "The Eatonville Anthology" shows:

> Becky Moore has eleven children of assorted colors and sizes. She has never been married, but that is not her fault. She has never stopped any of the fathers of her children from proposing, so if she has no father for her children it's not her fault. The men round about are entirely to blame. The other mothers of the town are afraid that it is catching. They won't let their children play with hers. (814)

Respectability was a condition of social acceptance that cut across class lines in this small town as elsewhere. Sexual transgressions were particularly frowned upon. Black women who expressed their sexual appetites, whether in conversation or behavior, brought shame not only on themselves but on the community. Men and women were expected to conduct their private business quietly, though men were judged less harshly than women for their indiscretions.[22] But there were few secrets in a small community. In "Characteristics of Negro Expression," Hurston wrote, "It is said that Negroes keep nothing secret, that they have no reserve." Privacy was valued but difficult to achieve. "There is no privacy in an African village. Loves, fights, possessions are, to misquote Woodrow Wilson, 'open disagreements openly arrived at.' The community is given the benefit of a good fight as well as a good wedding. An audience is a necessary part of the drama" (839–40). Once a person's business was in the street, the community felt free to sit in judgment, particularly on matters of sexual propriety.

Hurston specifically addressed the battle of the sexes in two stories. "The Head of the Nail" told the story of Daisy Taylor, the town vamp, and how she met her downfall:

> Not that she was pretty. But sirens were all but non-existent in the town. Perhaps she was forced to it by circumstances. She was quite dark, with little brushy patches of hair squatting over her head. These were held down by shingle-nails often. No one knows whether she did this for artistic effect or for lack of hair pins, but there they were shining in the little patches of hair when she got all dressed for the afternoon and came up to Clarke's store to see if there was any mail for her. (820)

Checking the mail was Daisy's cover for her real objective, the men who hung out on Joe Clarke's porch. "There were only two single men in town. Lum Boger, who was engaged to the assistant schoolteacher, and Hiram Lester, who had been off to school at Tuskegee and wouldn't look at a person like Daisy. In addition to other drawbacks, she was pigeon-toed and her petticoat was always showing. There was nothing else to do except flirt with married men" (820).

Wife after wife complained about Daisy's advances on their husbands, but her affair with Albert Crooms became a more serious matter. "Mrs. Laura Crooms was a meek little woman who took all of her troubles crying and talked a great deal of leaving things in the hands of God." Nevertheless, Daisy's brazen behavior finally forced a confrontation. "The town was collected at the porch-post office as is customary on Saturday nights. The town had its bath and with its week's pay in pocket fares forth to be merry. The men tell stories and they treat the ladies to soda-water, peanuts and peppermint candy." Daisy tries to participate but the assembled group ignores her. "Ah don't keer if you don't treat me," she finally bursts out. "What's a dirty lil nickel?... The ever loving Mister Crooms will gimme anything atall Ah wants" (821). Daisy is warned that Laura is approaching, but instead of backing off discreetly she issues a challenge: "If she ain't a heavy hipted Mama enough to keep him, she don't need to come crying to me." She begins needling Mrs. Crooms, who is all for withdrawing and leaving the matter in the hands of the Lord until the others give her enough encouragement to act. When Daisy comes out of the store, Mrs. Crooms takes up an ax handle and knocks her in the head. A second blow sends her into the town ditch. No one comes to Daisy's aid except Elijah Moseley. When Joe Clarke asks how badly she's hurt, Moseley replies, "I don't know... I was just looking to see if Laura had been lucky enough to hit one of those nails on the head and drive it in" (822). By week's end, Daisy has moved to Orlando, where her talents as a vamp are more appreciated.

Morality and color are intertwined in this story. Daisy is "quite dark" and her hair is so kinky that nails are needed to hold it in place. The not-so-veiled message here is that dark-skinned women are not only unattractive but immoral as well, a widely held belief among black people that embarrassed the elite. Daisy appears in another of Hurston's works, *Mule Bone*, this time as an attractive dark-skinned vamp.

Hurston addressed the politics of color in "Characteristics of Negro Expression" as well, suggesting there another side of the question.

> Negro shows before being tampered with did not specialise in octoroon chorus girls. The girl who could hoist a Jook song from her belly and lam it against the front door of the theatre was the lead, even if she were as black as the hinges of hell. The question was "Can she jook?" She must have a good belly wobble, and her hips must, to quote a popular song, "Shake like jelly all over and be so broad, Lawd, Lawd, and be so broad." So that the bleached chorus is the result of a white demand and not the Negro's.

The insidious practice of grading people's desirability according to darkness, then, both generally and in particular as sexual partners, is a white convention that has been assimilated and internalized by black people. But Hurston makes clear that black folk are not of one mind about this, and that such pernicious conventions do not always prevail. "The woman in the Jook may be nappy headed and black, but if she is a good lover she gets there just the same." Black attitudes about skin pigmentation are also influenced by class and region. "Of course," says Hurston, "a black woman is never the wife of the upper class Negro in the North. This state of affairs does not obtain in the South, however. I have noted numerous cases where the wife was considerably darker than the husband. People of substance, too." In general, however, color prejudice is as prevalent among the poorer classes as among the richer. "This scornful attitude towards black women receives mouth sanction by the mud-sills. Even on the works and in the Jooks the black man sings disparaging of black women. They say that she is evil. That she sleeps with her fists doubled up and ready for action. All over they are making a little drama of waking up a yaller wife and a black one" (843).[23]

We see marital infidelity judged by Eatonville's court of opinion in "Pants and Cal'line," a story Hurston wrote about her own family and published in the *Messenger*. The protagonist of the story is Cal'line Potts (based on Hurston's aunt, Caroline Potts), whose husband, Mitchell (Caroline's husband and Hurston's uncle, John Mitchell Potts), had a roving eye. "Once he took up with Delphine—called Mis' Pheeny by the town. She lived on the outskirts on the edge of the piney woods. The town winked and talked. People don't make secrets of such things in villages. Cal'line went about her business with her thin black lips pursed tight as ever, and her shiny black eyes unchanged." One evening Cal'line follows her husband to a rendezvous with his paramour, ax in hand. They pass the porch where the town is assembled, he smiling sheepishly, she silent and unsmiling. So ends the version presented in "The Eatonville Anthology." Hurston offered a longer version of this story in her autobiography:

> About an hour later they saw a figure darting behind trees who appeared to be in his underpants. The figure jumped over Clarke's

strawberry patch and headed toward the Potts house. Then Cal'-line emerged with ax over her shoulder, her husband's pants draping the ax. All she said was "Good evening, gentlemen" and kept walking. When the town saw Cal'line's husband they wanted to know how she got into Mis Pheeny's house. "Dat ax was her key." "Oh, dat old stubborn woman I married, you can't teach her nothing. I can teach her no city ways at all."[24]

This story probably was based on fact, for Hurston's autobiography elaborated on her uncle's infidelities and her aunt's retribution. In the expanded version that appears in *Dust Tracks*, another rival received a lesson in proper behavior from Cal'line. This bodacious vamp not only slept with Cal'line's husband, she announced in the "Black Dispatch" (the local grapevine) that she wore only a petticoat and no underpants under her dress. Cal'line decided to find out and knocked the woman off the steep church steps. She landed on her head, her bottom in the air, proving that she was as good as her word. Cal'line aimed her spit at the woman's bare bottom and then tried to wipe it off with her foot. The woman thought it best to change her address and left town, never to be seen or heard from again.

Not all Eatonville women handled their disputes with Cal'line's determination, but many did. While men were often critical of such women, there was at the same time a healthy respect for a woman who had the gumption to take an ax to an errant husband. Hurston's uncle liked to boast that women needed to be handled with a fist if necessary and berated Hurston's father for refusing to hit Lucy Hurston. These stories, both the factual and the ostensibly fictional, attest to the hollowness of his boast.

Like her novel *Their Eyes Were Watching God*, another of Hurston's short stories, this one about Joe Clarke's wife, depicts violence within a marriage.[25]

Mrs. Clarke is Joe Clarke's wife. She is a soft-looking, middle-aged woman, whose bust and stomach are always holding a get-together.

She waits on the store sometimes and cries every time he yells at her which he does every time she makes a mistake, which is quite often. She calls her husband "Jody." They say he used to beat her in the store when he was a young man, but he is not so impatient now. He can wait until he goes home.

She shouts in Church every Sunday and shakes the hand of fellowship with everybody in the Church with her eyes closed, but somehow always misses her husband. (817)[26]

Mrs. Clarke is an abused wife who finds solace only in her religion. The church offers her the opportunity to comment publicly on her husband's conduct, even as it continues to allow the abuse. Another story suggests that the community will intervene to some extent in such cases:

Mrs. McDuffy goes to Church every Sunday and always shouts and tells her "determination." Her husband always sits in the back row and beats her as soon as they get home. He says there's no sense in her shouting, as big a devil as she is. She just does it to slur him. Elijah Moseley asked her why she didn't stop shouting, seeing she always got a beating about it. She says she can't "squinch the sperrit." Then Elijah asked Mr. McDuffy to stop beating her, seeing that she was going to shout anyway. He answered that she just did it for spite and that his fist was just as hard as her head. He could last just as long as she. So the village let the matter rest. (818)

Community norms did not necessarily sanction domestic abuse, but neither did they sanction too much interference when husband and wife were equal participants. Most men went only so far in challenging other men. Even so, abusive relationships were generally held in contempt, certainly by Hurston but also, she suggests, by the community. By contrast, women who tolerated no abuse or other transgressions from their menfolk earned the community's respect, even if they had to resort to violence to keep their men in line. A man who used violence against his wife received a mixed reaction. Dragging private business into public view was frowned upon, but it did not necessarily earn the man universal disapproval. Among some men, such behavior was even admired, as John Mitchell's boast suggests.

Hurston depicts the community's norms of acceptable conduct and its modes of enforcing them in flesh-and-blood detail. Her stories are safe containers within which to explore sensitive issues like domestic abuse and sexual norms and to bring into focus the private, interior life of a rural black town.

Public entertainment is another lens through which to view that interior life. Hurston opens her "Double-Shuffle" with an observation about Eatonville's idea of correct demeanor and the way it was changing in the 1920s.

> Back in the good old days before the World War, things were very simple in Eatonville. People didn't fox trot. When the town wanted to put on its Sunday clothes and wash behind the ears, it put on a "breakdown." The daring younger set would two-step and waltz, but the good church members and the elders stuck to the grand march. By rural canons dancing is wicked, but one is not held to have danced until the feet have been crossed. Feet don't get crossed when one grand marches.

The older generation and the pious could still kick up their heels, however, in a way that white people never could.

> Among white people the march is as mild as if Volstead had passed it on. But it still has kick in Eatonville. Everybody happy, shining eyes, gleaming teeth. Feet dragged 'shhlap, shhlap!' to beat out time. No orchestra needed. Round and round! Back again, parse-me-la! Shlap! Shlap! Strut! Strut! Seaboard! Shlap! Shlap! Tiddy bumm! Mr. Clarke in the lead with Mrs. Moseley... Lizzimore about to break his guitar. Accordion doing contortions. People fall back against the walls, and let the soloist have it, shouting as they clap, old double shuffle songs. (818–19)

Church deacons, respectable ladies, and town officials abandon themselves to the music. "Sweating bodies, laughing mouths, grotesque faces, feet drumming fiercely. Deacons clapping as hard as the rest" (819). The lyrics of the songs echo the humor and the prejudices that Hurston's stories convey:

> Great big nigger, black as tar
> Try to git tuh hebben on ur 'lectric car.
> Some love cabbage, some love kale
> but I love a gal wid a short skirt tail.
>
> Long tall angel—steppin down
> Long white robe an' starry crown.

'Ah would not marry uh black gal (bumm bumm!)
tell yuh de reasons why
Every time she comb her hair
She make de goo-goo eye.

Would not marry a yaller gal (bumm bumm!)
Tell yuh de reason why
Her neck so long an' stringy
Ahm 'fraid she'd never die.

Would not marry uh preacher
Tell yuh de reason why
Every time he comes tuh town
He makes de chicken fly. (819)

The themes of these songs recur in Hurston's ethnography and fiction. She documents issues of color and class, gender tension, female virtue, domestic violence, and religion, but always as embedded in ordinary activities. The gender issues that have become the subject of feminist scholars in the past thirty or forty years are depicted as natural, age-old facts of everyday life in Hurston's work. Present-day feminists tend to see women as victims of male abuse and oppression, while Hurston shows them as powerful individuals quite capable of defending themselves. The current emphasis on "patriarchal hegemony" often suggests that black men's identities were simply copied from white society. But Hurston does not reduce identity to such a caricature; in her skillful hands identity, whether class, racial, or individual, is the product of a complex combination of cultural elements. Hurston's stories convey a nuanced understanding of gender relations seen in context, not abstracted and forced into the mold of some theoretical model.

Mules and Men and *Their Eyes Were Watching God* expand upon the material presented in "The Eatonville Anthology." The Eatonville section of *Mules and Men* explores community concerns over religion, gender, love, color, age, and work. Joe Clark's porch registered the pulse of the town. There men told stories that expressed their concerns, humor and anger often alternating as flip sides of the same coin. Women were not traditionally the storytellers in this setting, but they interrupted freely, affirming or contesting what was told. Women negotiated for respect, defended their position as wives, mothers, and sexual partners, and defined their identity within traditional borders as well as outside those borders.[27]

In one of Hurston's collected folktales, tensions between a couple named Gene and Gold are expressed in the language of gender and color during a "lying session." After Ellis Jones tells a tall tale about a preacher, a favorite subject on the porch, Gold chides him for lying and uses the opportunity to criticize men in general:

> "Dat's all you men is good for—settin' 'round and lyin'. Some of you done quit lyin' and gone to flyin'."

Gene Brazzel feels compelled to defend his brethren:

> "Get off of us mens now. We is some good. Plenty good too if you git de right one. De trouble is you women ain't good for nothin' exceptin' readin' Sears and Roebuck's bible and hollerin' 'bout, 'gimme dis and gimme dat' as soon as we draw our pay."

As Cheryl Wall has noted, such exchanges could be fierce, resting as they did on gender tensions that lay just beneath the surface.[28] Other women join in, both to defend Gold and to diffuse the anger that has begun to surface. Shug, a member of the gathering, challenges Gene:

> "Well, we don't get it by astin' you mens for it. If we work for it we kin git it. You mens don't draw no pay. You don't do nothin' but stand around and draw lightin'."

Gene takes offense:

> "Ah don't say Ah'm detrimental... but if Gold and Shug don't stop crackin' us, Ah'm gointer get 'em to go."

Gold stands her ground:

> "Man, if you want me any, some or none, do whut you gointer do and stop cryin'."

Gold has challenged Gene's manhood publicly, and he responds in anger:

> "You ain't seen me cryin'. See me cryin', it's sign of a funeral. If Ah even look cross somebody gointer bleed."

Gold retorts:

> "Aw, shut up, Gene, you ain't no big hen's biddy if you do lay gobbler eggs. You tryin' to talk like big wood when you ain't nothin' but brush."

Finally Gene attempts to smooth the waters:

> "We ain't mad wid one 'nother... We jus' jokin'."

What begins as a good-natured exchange turns to questions about manhood. Unemployment haunted the men who worked in the citrus industry. Almost all of the women worked steadily as domestics, and their comparative economic independence certainly contributed to men's insecurities and shaped the pattern of relations between the sexes. But more than that, black women had cultural permission to be outspoken, even when men resented this show of independence. Since the days of slavery and continuing through the twentieth century, tradition sanctioned women's confrontational behavior. Exchanges like the one between Gene and Gold demonstrate the relative gender equality within the black community that was denied them in the outside world. Certainly not all women challenged male authority as Gold and Shug did, but such confrontations were not uncommon.

Although the disagreement on the porch was temporarily laid to rest, it surfaced again a little later, when Gold wanted to tell a story "about a man as black as Gene." Gene responded:

> "Ah ain't a bit blacker than you."

Gold strikes back:

> "Oh, yes you is, Gene. Youse a whole heap blacker than Ah is."

"Aw, go head on, Gold. Youse blacker than me. You jus' look my color cause youse fat. If you wasn't no fatter than me you'd be so black till lightnin' bugs would follow you at twelve o'clock in de day, thinkin' its midnight."

"Dat's a lie, youse blacker than Ah ever dared to be. Youse lam' black. Youse so black till they have to throw a sheet over yo' head so de sun kin rise every mornin'. Ah know yo' ma cried when she seen *you*."

"Well, anyhow, Gold, youse blacker than me. If Ah was as fat as you, Ah'd be a yaller man."

"Youse a liar. Youse as yaller as you ever gointer git. When a person is poor he look bright and de fatter you git de darker you look."

"Is dat yo' excuse for being so black, Gold?"[29]

Calling someone black was a deliberate insult. Comments about size, especially directed at a woman, compounded the injury. Lighter skin color not only signified beauty but also often marked one as of a higher class (though, as we have seen, not always). The ambivalence blacks felt about color had its roots in centuries of racism and miscegenation, and it found its way into the social relations between men and women and the social structure as a whole.

Back on the porch, one of the bystanders to Gold and Gene's dispute again intervened to defuse the situation. Gold used the opportunity to tell a tale of how African Americans became black. In her telling, God set aside one day to assign physical characteristics. When he was assigning skin color, blacks were the last in line. God waited "three and one half hours and no niggers." He sent the angels to fetch the "niggers" and the angels found them asleep under the tree of life. They were awakened and told that God wanted them, at which "They all jumped up and run on up to de th'one and they was so skeered they might miss sumpin' they begin to push and shove one 'nother, bumpin' against all de angels and turnin' over foot stools. They even had de th'one all pushed one-sided. So God hollered 'Git back! Git back!' And they misunderstood Him and thought He said, "Git black," and they been black ever since" (32–33). This tale injected humor into a situation that was growing increasingly ugly.

Color was an issue within the community just as it was outside the community, but with wholly different results. Within the community, color prejudice sometimes resulted in more integration. Many sought to "whiten up" the family through marriage, an investment in the future. Lighter-skinned children potentially had more opportunity, at least within the black fold. Unlike the color prejudice of Jim Crow, which was always economically, politically, and emotionally destructive, color prejudice within the community, while often damaging psychologically, could sometimes be overcome.

Color permeated the consciousness of African Americans. It was referenced in names like Skillet Blond (an exceptionally black person), Good Black, and Black Baby.[30] It was a source of pride and shame, status and beauty. This feature of black culture, though seldom acknowledged openly by scholars, shaped attitudes and social relations. It defined who was in and who was out in particular social circles. Color, therefore, was about power. It was a determining factor in who achieved success, position, and recognition. African Americans, unlike Africans in the Caribbean and Latin America, were far more reluctant to admit their color consciousness openly. It was considered politically incorrect to be "color struck," though it was more common in the early twentieth century than it is today to openly admit such prejudices. At the very least, those who attempted to move up the social ladder wanted to distance themselves from dark-skinned people, who were often perceived as poor, even while those who represented themselves to the larger white community as leaders sought to present unity among African American people. Cultural material like folklore, blues music, novels, and poetry confronted color matters more directly than did polite exchanges among the elite. The elite, however, maintained color barriers quietly within their own circles while publicly ignoring the subject. In her willingness to discuss color openly, Hurston must have seemed to the elite as rude in her way as Marcus Garvey was in his willingness to celebrate dark skin and African appearance.

Zora Neale Hurston beating the hountar, or mama drum.
Credit: Library of Congress, Prints and Photographs Division, NYWT&S Collection, LC-USZ62-108549.

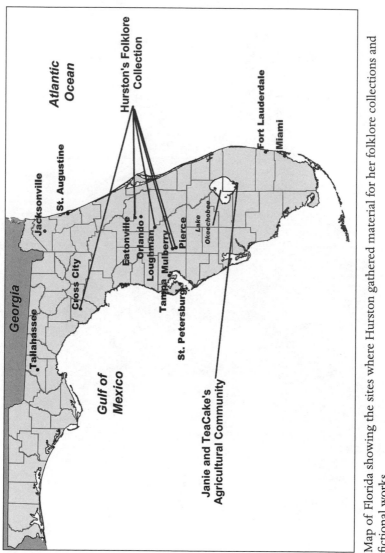

Map of Florida showing the sites where Hurston gathered material for her folklore collections and fictional works.

Credit: Courtesy of ESRI, Binghamton University, GIS Core Facility.

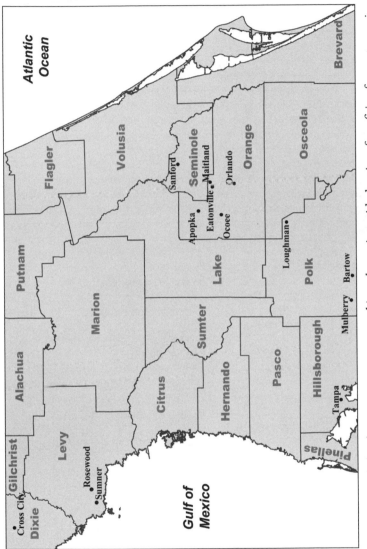

Map of central Florida. Many investors moved into the region with the aim of profiting from economic opportunities in the New South.
Credit: Courtesy of ESRI, Binghamton University, GIS Core Facility.

Mattie Clark, the eldest daughter of Joseph Clark and Julie Hightower. She often spoke to her granddaughters, Olga and Gloria, about her Blackfoot Indian mother: "My mother had the most beautiful hair you have ever seen. It was so long that she could sit on it."
Credit: Courtesy of Mrs. Olga Mitchell.

Mr. and Mrs. Larkin Franklin. Larkin Franklin, a Mohawk Indian who married a black woman, moved to Eatonville in the 1920s and worked his way up in the citrus groves until he was able to purchase his own grove.
Credit: Courtesy of Ms. Louise M. Franklin.

Turpentine industry workers.
Credit: Courtesy of the Photographic Collection of the Florida State Archives.

The porch of Joe Clark's store in Eatonville.
Credit: Courtesy of Ms. Louise M. Franklin.

Calhoun Dining Hall of the Robert Hungerford Normal and Industrial School in Eatonville. The school, an all-black private boarding and day school, was the first of its kind in the South.
Credit: Courtesy of Ms. Louise M. Franklin.

Second structure of St. Lawrence A.M.E. Church in Eatonville.
Credit: Courtesy of Ms. Louise M. Franklin.

Wedding in Eatonville.
Credit: Courtesy of Rollins College Archives.

Housing in the Negro section of Belle Glade, Florida, January 1937. Photo by Arthur Rothstein.
Credit: Library of Congress, Prints and Photographs Division, FSA/OWI Collection, LC-USF33-T01-002365-M5.

Jook joint for Negroes near Belle Glade, Florida, January 1939. Photo by Marion Post Wolcott.
Credit: Library of Congress, Prints and Photographs Division, FSA/OWI Collection, LC-USF34-051170-D.

Color and gender were often bound together in the fabric of black culture. In chapter twelve of *Dust Tracks on a Road*, Hurston confronted the gendered dimensions of color consciousness. In discussing the contradictions between race pride and race contempt in African American culture, she pointed out that dark-skinned black people were rarely represented positively. "I found the Negro, and always the blackest Negro, being made the butt of all jokes,—particularly black women." Black women

brought bad luck for a week if they came to your house on a Monday morning. They were evil. They slept with their fists balled up ready to fight and squabble even while they were asleep. They even had evil dreams. White, yellow or brown girls dreamed about roses and perfume and kisses. Black gals dreamed about guns, razors, ice picks, hatchets and hot lye. I heard men swear they had seen women dreaming and knew these things to be true.

"Oh, gwan!" somebody would chide, laughing. You know dat ain't so."

"Oh, now, he ain't lying," somebody else would take up the theme. "I know for my own self. I done slept wid yaller women and I done slept wid black ones. They *is* evil. You marry a yaller or a brown woman and wake her up in de night and she will sort of stretch herself and say, 'I know what I was dreaming when you woke me up. I was dreaming I had done baked you a chicken and cooked you a great big old cake, and we was at de table eating our dinner out of de same plate, and I was sitting on your lap and we was enjoying ourselves to death!' Then she will kiss you more times than you ask her to, and go on back to sleep. But you take and wake up a black gal, now! First thing she been sleeping wid her fists balled up, and you shake her, she'll lam you five or six times before you can get her awake. Then when she do git wake she'll have off and ast you, 'Nigger, what you wake me up for? Know what I was dreaming when you woke me up? I dreamt dat you shook your old rusty black fist under my nose and I split your head open wid a axe.' Then she'll kick your feets away from hers, snatch de covers all over on her side, ball up her fists agin, and gwan back to sleep. You can't tell me nothing. I know."[31]

Such exchanges elicited the predictable laughter. But for Hurston these exchanges suggested something twisted about race pride. "I listened to this talk and became more and more confused. If it was so honorable and glorious to be black, why was it the yellow-skinned people among us had so much prestige? Sensitivity to color ran deep in the culture, so much so, that children learned to distinguish on the basis of color. Even a child in the first grade could see that this was so from what happened in the classroom and on school programs. The light-skinned children were always the angels, fairies and queens of school plays. The lighter the girl, the more money and prestige she was apt to marry."[32] Color, for women, marked degrees of femininity and womanly softness. But it also may have suggested male resentment toward women who refused to be cowed and were willing to challenge male dominance. Even light-skinned women could be considered "black gals" if they chose to be confrontational.

The exchanges between Gene and Gold were also very much about gender. After Gold tells the humorous story about how black people became black, Gene comments, "Now Gold call herself gettin' even wid me—tellin' dat lie. 'Tain't no such a story nowhere. She jus' made dat one up herself."[33] Armetta and Shoopie confirm that the story has been around for years, to which a man named George Thomas responds:

> "Don't you know you can't get best of no woman in de talkin' game? Her tongue is all de weapon a woman got. She could have had mo' sense, but she told God no, she'd ruther take it out in hips. So God give her ruthers. She got plenty hips, plenty mouf and no brains." Mathilda Moseley opined, "Oh, yes, womens is got sense too. But they got too much sense to go 'round braggin about it like y'all do. De lady people always got de advantage of mens because God fixed it dat way." "Whut ole black advantage is y'all got?" said B. Moseley… "We got all the strength and all de law and all de money and you can't git a thing but whut we jes' take pity on you and give you."
>
> "And dat's jus de point. You *do* give it to us, but how come you do it?" said Mathilda.

Mathilda responds with a story about how once upon a time men and women were completely equal, and even though they fussed and fought, one could not get the best of the other. The man got tired of this equality and went to heaven to ask God for enough strength to subordinate the woman. After putting his request in proper form, God granted his desire. The man ran home to inform his wife, "Woman! Here's yo' boss. God done tole me to handle you in which ever way Ah please. Ah'm yo' boss." The woman flew into a rage and fought her husband, but she could not defeat him. After her third attempt failed, she went to heaven and asked God for her strength back. God informed her that she had the same strength she'd always had. "Why is it then, dat de man kin beat me now and he useter couldn't do it?"

"He got mo' strength than he useter have. He come and ast me for it and Ah give it t'im. Ah gives to them that ast, and you ain't never ast me for no mo' power." The woman asks for more but God denies her request, explaining that it is too late. The man would always have more power.

Fighting mad, the woman goes straight to the devil, who sends her back to heaven to ask God for the keys by the mantlepiece. God grants her request and she returns to the devil for instructions:

> "See dese three keys? They got mo' power in 'em than all de strength de man kin ever git if you handle 'em right. Now dis first big key is to de do' of the de kitchen, and you know a man always favors his stomach. Dis second one is de key to de bedroom and they don't like to be shut out from dat neither and dis last key to de cradle and eh don't want to be cut off from his generations at all. So now you take dese keys and go lock up everything and wait till he come to you. Then don't you unlock nothin' until he use his strength for yo' benefit and yo' desires... Jus' one mo' thing: don't go home braggin' 'bout you' keys. Jus' lock up everything and say nothin until you git asked. And then don't talk too much."

When the man learns that the doors are locked against him and that the woman has the keys, he returns to heaven, only to learn from God that she has the keys and he has his strength. The man returns to earth and attempts to trade some of his strength for her keys. The "woman wouldn't trade wid 'im and de man had to mortgage his strength to her to live. And dat's why de man makes and de woman takes. You men is still braggin' 'bout yo' strength and de women is sittin' on de keys and lettin' you blow off till she git ready to put de bridle on you," Mathildah crowed. B. Moseley, her husband, said, "You just like a hen in de barnyard. You cackle so much you give de rooster de blues."[34]

This tale embodies a view of gender that some may interpret as conservative and passive, but in the 1920s and 1930s it was nothing of the kind. A rural woman who ruled her roost and kept her mate bridled was considered powerful, as the stories above suggest. From where we sit today, such notions of gender difference would not satisfy the desire for female equality. Nor would they have satisfied women of a higher socioeconomic class in an earlier time. But in the rural black South of that era, women had their own notions of their power just as men had theirs. Hurston's ethnographic work gives us some idea of how gender patterns evolved in Eatonville. *Their Eyes Were Watching God* refines the question of gender and explores the idea of gender equality more deeply. Let us now turn to that novel.

The Novel as Historical Source

If we treat a novel written in the past as we would an archaeological site, what do we find? We find what people thought about such intangibles as gender boundaries, sex, the social markers of class, the value of land, and wealth. We discover their assumptions about freedom, relationships, skin color, and power. We learn how rural dwellers used language to defend their individual and community integrity, and how language both captures and manipulates reality. We meet characters—crapshooters and dancers, gamblers and transients—who were distorted into stereotypes and ugly caricatures by whites, but who were drawn by Hurston as complicated human beings. To evaluate these finds, let us examine in turn three locales—Killicks's farm, Joe's town, and the "Muck."

Hurston's story of Janie in *Their Eyes Were Watching God* is well known and beautifully told. It is the story of a young girl looking for love and her own identity. When her grandmother, Nanny, catches sight of Janie "sparkin'" with a local boy, Johnny Taylor, she realizes that her granddaughter is blossoming into woman-hood and fears for her future. Nanny was born into slavery and Janie's mother was the product of a rape by her white "massuh." When the mistress of the plantation discovered a near-white child in Nanny's cabin, "she begin tuh slap mah jaws ever which a'way. Ah never felt the fust ones 'cause Ah wuz too busy gittin' de kivver back over mah chile. But dem last lick burnt me lak fire." The mis-tress, typically, blamed Nanny for her husband's infidelity. Nanny explains to Janie how the mistress "kept on astin me how come mah baby look white. She asted me dat maybe twenty-five or thirty times, lak she got tuh sayin' dat and couldn't help herself. So Ah told her, 'Ah don't know nothin' but what Ah'm told tuh do, 'cause Ah ain't nothin' but uh nigger and uh slave.'"[35] The mistress bru-talized Nanny rather than understanding her helplessness:

> Ah wouldn't dirty mah hands on yuh. But first thing in de mornin' de overseer will take you to de whippin' post and tie you down on yo' knees and cut de hide offa yo' yaller back. One hundred lashes wid a raw-hide on yo' bare back. Ah'll have you whipped till de blood run down to yo' heels! Ah mean to count de licks mahself. And if it kills you Ah'll stand de loss. Anyhow, as soon as dat brat is a month old Ah'm going to sell it offa dis place. (34)

Nanny bundled up her baby and ran for her life. Critics have treated the novel as ahistorical, set in an unspecified past. Its historical markers are quite evident, however, if read carefully. From her hid-ing place Nanny sees men on the landing near the river and hears "people say Sherman was comin' to meet de boats in Savannah, and all of us slaves was free," which sets the date at about 1864. Nanny moves from Atlanta to west Florida to raise her child. The post-Emancipation world she enters presents few options to a sin-gle woman with a baby, so Nanny takes employment with white people named Washburn and lives on their plantation in west Flor-ida, an undeveloped and violent frontier. There she raises her child, Leafy, to be a teacher. But Leafy is raped by a black male teacher and Janie is the result. Leafy is only seventeen when Janie is born around 1881. After bearing the child, Leafy is swallowed up by a life of guilt, shame, and anguish. Nanny works hard and saves enough to buy a piece of land. "Ah raked and scraped and bought dis lil piece uh land so you wouldn't have to stay in de white folks' yard and tuck yo' head befo' other chillun at school," she tells Janie (37). But only marriage to a landowner can bring Janie real protection, as far as Nanny is concerned. The "white man is de ruler of everything as fur as Ah been able tuh find out... De nigger woman is de mule uh de world so fur as Ah can see" (29). She forces Janie to marry old Logan Killicks, even though he looks to sixteen-year-old Janie "like some ole skull-head in de grave yard" (28). For Nanny, love in marriage takes second place to protection.[36] Only the property and wealth that come with a good marriage can protect her granddaughter from being a "spit cup" for white folks and for men of whatever color.

With Killicks Janie lives a lonely, loveless existence shaped by work and worry. He takes her away from people to an isolated location where she has no other human connections. In a few months he stops "talking rhymes to her," stops marveling at her long, luxurious hair, and begins complaining that she is spoiled. She has become a mere investment to him, stripped of human dignity and individuality.

Logan Killicks has land, the cornerstone of freedom in the Reconstruction South. But the protection Nanny seeks for Janie cannot be achieved through land alone. Nor can Killicks be allowed to exercise manhood in the larger society. He chooses a solitary existence and views Janie as little more than a slave, someone he literally hitches to his plow. He has no "political" manhood because he has no political rights, in the Jim Crow South, to protect his land or his wife. In the post-Reconstruction rural South, black people sought autonomy and dignity in community, not in solitary existence. Killicks misses this point, adopting a solution to Jim Crow that is destructive to the spirit. He endows the idea of land ownership with a power it cannot sustain, in the process damaging Janie's soul and destroying his own. In the fate of Killicks we see the dangers in investing too heavily in land ownership as a panacea. Janie is one of the casualties of Killicks's misplaced values.

Janie's arrival on Logan's farm has been preceded by a childhood of uncertain identity as both female and black. At sixteen, she has no more concept of love than what she has seen in the bees and flowers. She doesn't even become aware of her racial identity until she is six. As a child she lived on the Washburn place, where her grandmother worked, and played with the Washburn grandchildren. She confesses to her friend Pheoby, "Ah was wid dem white chillun so much till Ah didn't know Ah wuzn't white till Ah was round six years old" (21). She is barely even conscious of her own name. "Dey all useter call me Alphabet 'cause so many people had done named me different names" (21).

In her autobiography, Hurston suggests that awareness of her own racial identity was late in arriving. Only when she was sent to school in Jacksonville did she realize that she was different from the other students. Such stories are not uncommon in African American narratives. In *Incidents in the Life of a Slave Girl*, Harriet Jacobs made a similar confession of late racial awareness, as did Frederick Douglass and W.E.B. DuBois.[37] In Janie's relationship to her skin color Hurston depicts a process of identity formation that undermines the notion of race as biology and instead underscores the social, political, and cultural character of race.

In her loneliness with Killicks, Janie yearns for the feelings that had blossomed in her before her marriage. Within a year Jody Starks, a tall, handsome, seal-brown man with a big voice and fine city clothes, appears on the horizon. She runs off with Starks, who founds a town (Eatonville) and becomes mayor. Jody's town epitomizes the entrepreneurial solution of Booker T. Washington's era and reveals the class and color hierarchies that were then emerging in African American life. Eatonville is communal in the sense that Killicks's farm was not, but the power relations rest on property, color, and status.

For a time Janie finds the love of her dreams with Jody, but this blossoming love and attention turn to possessiveness, as she comes to fulfill her social role as the pretty mulatto wife of the mayor. We see their marriage slowly sour as Jody becomes drunk on an inflated sense of his own power and prestige, which Janie deflates in the time-honored manner of the women on Joe Clark's porch. One afternoon, several porch-sitters decide to have some fun by attacking Matt Bonner's yellow mule, a starved and overworked animal. Janie is upset over the treatment of the mule, and Jody decides to free the animal. Janie comments acidly, "Freein' dat mule makes uh mighty big man outa you. Something like George Washington and Lincoln. Abraham Lincoln, he had de whole United States tuh rule so he freed de Negroes. You got uh town so you freed uh mule. You have tuh have power tuh free things and dat makes you lak a king uh something" (91–92).

Language is central to resistance in the narrative of Janie's marriage to Jody, not as an art but as the politics of a people.[38] The passion and energy of oppressed black people, "tongueless, earless, eyeless conveniences all day long," is unleashed at night, when they become "lords of sounds and lesser things"; they "passed nations through their mouths" (9–10). Janie learns to out-talk Jody. In one scene, Jody lashes out at her after she has failed to cut a plug of tobacco properly for a customer: "I god amighty! A woman stay round uh store till she get old as Methusalem and still can't cut a little thing like a plug of tobacco! Don't stand dere rollin' yo' pop eyes at me wid yo' rump hangin' nearly to yo' knees!" (121). Jody's assault brings the predictable laughter from the onlookers on the porch, but Janie strikes back and the two squabble. Finally Janie delivers a final blow:

> Ah ain't no young gal no mo' but den Ah ain't no old woman neither. Ah reckon Ah looks mah age too. But Ah'm uh woman every inch of me, and Ah know it. Dat's uh whole lot more'n *you* kin say. You big-bellies round here and put out a lot of brag, but 'tain't nothin' to it but yo' big voice. Humph! Talkin' 'bout *me* lookin' old! When you pull down yo' briches, you look lak de change uh life. (122–23)

Janie strips Jody of his male superiority in front of the town. She "had cast down his empty armor before men and they had laughed" (123).

Evidence of such domestic power struggles is difficult to find in traditional sources. African American women who left letters and diaries rarely discuss sexuality and selfhood. Love and sex were represented in formal terms, encoded (in part, at least) because of white America's voyeuristic lies about black women's supposedly loose morals.[39] Hurston used fiction to present issues that could not be discussed directly, not even in her own autobiography.

Janie is allowed her voice in the end, and she uses it deftly as Jody lies dying:

> You wouldn't listen. You done lived wid me for twenty years and don't half know me atall. And you could have but you was so busy worshippin' de works of yo' own hands, and cuffin' folks around in their minds till you didn't see uh whole heap uh things yuh could have... Ah knowed you wasn't gointuh lissen tuh me. You changes everything but nothin' don't change you—not even death... Naw, you gointuh listen tuh me one time befo' you die. Have yo' way all yo' life, trample and mash down and then die ruther than tuh let yo'self heah 'bout it... you ain't de Jody ah run off down de road wid. You'se whut's left after he died. Ah run off tuh keep house wid you in uh wonderful way. But you wasn't satisfied wid me de way Ah was. Naw! Mah own mind had tuh be squeezed and crowded out tuh make room for yours in me... And now you got tuh die tuh find out dat you got tuh pacify somebody besides yo'self if you wants any love and any sympaty in dis world. You ain't tried tuh pacify *nobody* but yo'self. Too busy listening tuh yo' own big voice. (132–33)

As she studies Jody's face in death, Janie understands that they were both oppressed, but that he took it out on her. "She was full of pity for the first time in years," Hurston writes. "Jody had been hard on her and others, but life had mishandled him too" (134).

Jody dies a wealthy man, but imprisoned by his position and property. The year is around 1918, the end of World War I and a time of migration and movement for many southern blacks seeking to escape racial violence and discrimination. But Janie, like the residents of Eatonville, stays behind.[40]

Widowed, wealthy, and free at last, Janie spurns all her male suitors until she meets Vergible "Tea Cake" Woods, a dark, penniless ne'er-do-well who is younger than she. With him she finds the love and freedom missing in her other marriages. She finds the space to be herself. He owns no land and dominates no one. Instead, they run away to the "muck" near Lake Ocheekobee in the Everglades, a place with huge agricultural camps of migrant workers who work in Florida during the season and as migrants up the Atlantic Coast in the off season. They become part of an international community of African Americans, West Indians, and Native Americans. Though all are transients, the residents create a community based on laboring on the land and living and working in a communal environment.[41] Life on the "muck" shows people in motion—singing, talking, playing—with concern for their community as well as their individual welfare. Here Janie can live without pretensions and experience love without restrictions. This idyllic existence comes to an end when Tea Cake is bitten by a rabid dog during a hurricane. In his crazed state he threatens Janie, and she is forced to kill him in self-defense. She is tried for murder, is acquitted, and returns to Eatonville to tell her story to her best friend, Pheoby.

The event of the mayor's widow, a middle-class, near-white woman, running off with a very black drifter sends shock waves through the town. But Janie cares little for wealth, only for love and being herself. Eatonville's notions of propriety do not impress her.

Far from the spacious two-story home in Eatonville, Janie finds happiness with Tea Cake in a small clapboard house in an agricultural camp. In this modest setting she finds a warmth she never knew in the refined and well-decorated rooms of the mayor's house. People come to gamble, tell stories, dance, and eat at Janie and Tea Cake's house on the muck, and Janie for once is able to participate in the gaiety. "Clerkin' in dat store wuz hard," she says, "but heah, we ain't got nothin' tuh do but do our work an come home and love" (199). Janie "got so she could tell big stories from listening to the rest. Because she loved to hear it, and the men loved to hear themselves, they would 'woof' and 'boogerboo' around the games to the limit. No matter how rough it was, people seldom got mad, because everything was done for a laugh" (200).

The lighthearted fun and games of the muck present a stark contrast to the gender politics of Jody Stark's storefront porch. But the muck is not without tensions. Jealousy, domestic violence, color prejudice, and death figure in the muck as everywhere else. Janie and Tea Cake find their marriage tested by jealousy when a woman named Nunkie begins to flirt in the fields with Tea Cake. One afternoon Janie discovers the pair struggling in the cane field and flies into a rage. Tea Cake tries to explain that they were squabbling over his work tickets and that she has misunderstood, but Janie will have none of it. She pursues Nunkie, who is too swift for her and escapes. She returns to their quarters, where Tea Cake again tries to calm her and explain that his encounter with Nunkie was innocent. Janie attacks him with violent anger. "She cut him short with a blow and they fought from one room to the other, Janie trying to beat him, and Tea Cake kept holding her wrists and wherever he could to keep her from going too far" (205). In spite of her rage, Janie is no match for Tea Cake. He holds her until they collapse in the heat of passion. "They wrestled on until they were doped with their own fumes and emanations; till their clothes had been torn away; till he hurled her to the floor and held her there melting her resistance with the heat of his body, doing things with their bodies to express the inexpressible" (205). In this sexual scene, Hurston defies the prohibition against sex on the printed page.

Next it is Tea Cake's turn to be jealous. Mrs. Turner, a light-skinned woman who manages a store in the camp, resents Janie's being married to a man as black as Tea Cake. She tries to interest Janie in her light-complected brother, and this man, unlike other camp dwellers who have flirted with Janie in the past, provokes deep fear and anger in Tea Cake. Seized with jealousy, he gives Janie a whipping that the whole community becomes aware of. The whipping "relieved the awful fear inside him" (218). In this depiction of a dark black man beating an almost white middle-class woman, Hurston breached a taboo that held in her day and still holds in our own.

That this incident troubles readers now, as it did then, does not however warrant the conclusion that its significance is the same today as it was in 1937. In literature, at least in good literature, whatever seems general and universal across time and space is also specific and particular. We may be tempted to view Janie through the lens of twenty-first-century feminism, but this would be a mistake. We must separate our own aspirations from Hurston's. The more we conflate our time with hers, the less we stand to learn about her world.

We do indeed experience a connection between Hurston's (and Janie's) present and our own, and that is the essence of good literature. But we have no warrant for going further, as some critics have in their objections to the scene in which Tea Cake whips Janie. In judging Hurston's vision by today's standards such critics are guilty of anachronism. The judgment that Janie is not so radically independent after all, that Tea Cake is not in fact a "new kind of man," that Hurston is not consistently feminist, may be legitimate for some purposes. But it cannot serve a historical investigation that strives to avoid the fallacy of reading present attitudes into the past. Hurston's subject in the whipping scene is not "domestic violence." The scene, rather, is a full-scale exploration of sexual jealousy as it arises in the marriage of a very black man and a nearly white woman who love each other intensely and who are trying to make a life for themselves in the Jim Crow South of the 1920s. If we forget our feminist and postmodernist agendas and enter imaginatively into the time and place, we can see the fear, Janie's as well as Tea Cake's, alongside the violence—and the violence is Janie's also, as well as Tea Cake's. In their objections to Tea Cake's violent expression of jealousy, critics have conveniently failed to comment on Janie's jealously and her violent response to perceived infidelity. But to withhold judgment on these aspects of Tea Cake's character, and to explore analogous aspects of Janie's, is not to justify their actions. It is to recognize, and learn from, Hurston's attempt to put a real world on the page.

It is a mistake not to read the violent tone of the novel as the result of the transgression in which a nearly white woman and very dark black man openly come together in love. Visually and morally, Janie and Tea Cake are at the hot core of what is most forbidden in the Jim Crow South. Sexuality is race-clotted in the South, yet Logan Killicks and Jody Starks both reach across the boundary for a near-white woman on the frontier. She is the portal through which Killicks establishes his manhood; she is the trophy that seals Starks's lordly position as mayor. The race-clotted nature of sexuality is salient at every turn for Janie and Tea Cake. They are the almost quintessential forbidden couple. They epitomize the wrong sort of marriage in both class and color terms. Outside the town and the muck, they, and especially he, are in physical danger. Hurston offers a richly textured portrait of the ways in which sexuality is bound up with race in the South. Black men were castrated, and white women cast out, for the kind of sexual transgression of which Janie and Tea Cake are guilty.

Not surprisingly, the violence that permeates the novel forecasts an unhappy end to the marriage. Indeed, Janie's genealogy suggests that such an ending is all but inevitable. Nanny, a black slave, is raped by her white master and gives birth to Leafy, a nearly white baby with soft hair. Leafy is desired for her light skin and soft hair by a very dark black man, who rapes her. She gives birth to another nearly white child with soft hair named Janie. Janie is desired for her light skin and soft hair by three black men. She is forced into a loveless marriage with one of them, marries another who turns out to be a possessive, power-drunk brute, and finally finds true love with the third, only to see it destroyed by violence. This genealogy recapitulates the history of Jim Crow in microcosm.

Tea Cake's life ends in a natural disaster. A devastating hurricane hits the Everglades, trapping Janie and Tea Cake in their quarters.[42] Tea Cake ignores the many warnings of the coming storm. Janie wants to heed the warnings of the Indians and the animals that are taking cover, but Tea Cake scoffs at them. He watches only the white folks; if they aren't leaving, then everything must be all right.

Janie and Tea Cake are caught in the storm and find themselves waist deep in water. Janie is suddenly threatened by a rabid dog. Tea Cake kills the dog with his knife, but not before he is bitten. He refuses treatment and he becomes infected with rabies. In his subsequent madness, he becomes irrational and dangerously jealous. Finally, out of his mind with rage and jealously, Tea Cake threatens to kill Janie; in self-defense she shoots and kills him. He manages to bite her before he dies. Janie is tried for murder and the whole community turns against her. The white women come to her defense, however, and on the testimony of the doctor she is acquitted.

The novel's conclusion has bothered many critics. Robert Hass has argued that most people today have no experience with rabies and therefore are confused by the ending. Michael Cooke views it as one more example of the violence that permeates the story. Hemenway thinks the ending poorly plotted. Lillie Howard describes it as without justification. Carla Kaplan and Alice Walker suggest that Janie's killing of Tea Cake in self-defense is revenge for the beating he gave her.[43] Once again we confront legitimate but ultimately unresolvable disputes about what Hurston had in mind and about the quality of her writing.

HURSTON HAS BROUGHT us far indeed from where Wright left us in the opening epigraph to Chapter 2, in which Wright speaks of black Americans' thin traditions, hollow memories, and lack of passion. Baldwin criticized Wright for depicting a South where blacks were only "shot, hanged, maimed, lynched, and generally hounded until they are either dead or their spirits broken."[44] Hurston did not find it easy to offer her very different portrait. During the 1930s, while working on the WPA Guide for Florida, she found herself caught between two camps. One wanted to incorporate "certain material about race relations, segregation, lynching, poll tax—that sort of thing. Health conditions among blacks, education… all crucial to life in Florida at the time… This was the essence of life, black and white: the economics of it," as Stetson Kennedy put it. Another group wanted a portrait that would appeal to tourists. Hurston was thought to belong to the latter group. She was chosen, along with Max Hunter, to attend a meeting in Washington, D.C., with W.E.B. DuBois and Sterling Brown, director of Negro Affairs in the Federal Writers' Project. Naturally, Hurston disagreed with DuBois and Brown, writing of the meeting, "We had a conference, Dr. DuBois, Sterling Brown and I, and with all knives and razors out."[45]

Hurston presented a portrait that kept the Jim Crow world of racial discrimination and oppression in view but not center stage, and she thus avoided the one-sidedness of which Baldwin complained in Wright's work. But if she refused to depict the South as black activists of the day saw it, she rejected the romanticized version as well. She exploded the caricatures of black people as crap shooters, gamblers, jook dancers, and drunks, by showing the artistic potential of these characters, by making them fully dimensional human beings, with all their virtues and vices, their beauty and ugliness, in all their love and fear and hatred and joy. Hurston's South is both violent and life affirming. She does not neglect white violence against blacks, but neither does she ignore the violence within black society. The all-black enclaves of the New South were familial spaces where social relations were carried on far from the view of the white world. The labor camps were rough and unpredictable, as we shall see in the next chapter. But they were also rich in cultural creativity. In short, life was there too.

5

A Transient World of Labor

> We stole words from the grudging lips of the Lords of
> the Land, who did not want us to know too many of
> them or their meaning. And we charged this meager
> horde of stolen sounds with all the emotions and long-
> ings we had; we proceeded to build our language in
> inflections of voice, through tonal variety, by hurried
> speech, in honeyed drawls, by rolling our eyes, by flour-
> ishing our hands, by assigning to common, simple words
> new meanings, meanings which enabled us to speak of
> revolt in the actual presence of the Lords of the Land
> without their being aware! Our secret language
> extended our understanding of what slavery meant and
> gave us the freedom to speak to our brothers in captiv-
> ity; we polished our new words, caressed them, gave
> them new shape and color, a new order and tempo,
> until, though they were the words of the Lords of the
> Land, they became our words, our language.
>
> —Richard Wright, *Twelve Million Black Voices*, 40

WHEN ZORA NEALE HURSTON arrived in Polk County,
Florida, in 1928 to collect folklore in the turpentine and sawmill
camps, the population was more than 90 percent black and com-
posed of transient labor from all over the South. The phosphate
mining camps were also heavily black. Records of the Everglades
Cypress Company, which managed the turpentine and sawmill
camps, are not available. The *Peonage Files of the U.S. Department
of Justice* offer only partial clues. Other records are sketchy and
provide only fleeting references to the life of the workers or labor

128

tensions in Polk County. For the rest of the state, records are also sparse. From debt peonage cases across the South, including Florida, however, we know that life was extremely violent.[1]

One way to reconstruct the history of people in this area is through oral history, Hurston's method in her 1928 ethnographic study of Polk County, contained in *Mules and Men* and in the play she wrote in 1944, *Polk County*. To undertake an oral history project today is to travel down the road to the abandoned lands of the sawmill side of the camp.[2] I made such a journey in 1999 to visit former residents of the camp named Harry and Mary Grant. Harry Grant dramatized for me the extreme violence of the place, which Hurston took for granted. Grant took me and my companion on a tour of a former camp in Loughman, Florida, owned by the Everglades Cypress Company. As we traveled down the road, we came to a spot with almost no vegetation in an otherwise lush and green locale. There was a large mound of chalk-white earth that was unlike any dirt I had seen before. Although the surrounding area has returned to forest, nothing grew in this barren clearing. Grant told us that many people believe that bodies are buried there. I ask the reader to keep the mound in mind. In 1928 the bodies were recently dead and the memories of their dying fresh, and undoubtedly commented on privately. Today the mound sits as a silent witness to the violence of the former Loughman camp, a place Hurston calls Lofton in *Polk County*.

The passage from Richard Wright's *Twelve Million Black Voices* quoted above highlights the irony of the conflict between Wright and Hurston discussed in Chapter 2. Wright's passage, notes Farah Griffin, "marks one of the rare instances where Wright concedes that black Southerners were capable of *creating* culture."[3] The passage also registers the "dissident political culture" embodied in the language of rural workers and migrants in the South in the 1920s and 1930s. That language did indeed allow them "to speak of revolt in the actual presence of the Lords of the Land without their being aware." These are the hidden transcripts that Robin D. G. Kelley has argued must be uncovered by historians, transcripts that lie "beneath the veil of consent" and constitute a "hidden history of unorganized everyday conflict waged by African-American working people."[4] A further irony of the conflict between Wright and Hurston is that it fell to her and not to him to document not only the language of rural dwellers but also the "consciousness of existence" of these rural people.

When Hurston left Eatonville after months of collecting folklore, she turned her shiny new Chevrolet toward Polk County and headed for a world where violence was never far removed from everyday life, a world starkly different from the sleepy little community of her childhood, where blacks held political power and experienced economic mobility and cultural autonomy. But Polk County was also a place "where dey makes up all de songs" and "de water drink lak cherry wine."[5] The sawmill and turpentine camps managed by the Everglades Cypress Company were much like the camps that flourished in north and central Florida after the Civil War. Here migrants from all over the South and immigrants from Europe worked for a wage in a restricted, almost prison-like environment.[6] Straw bosses and overseers kept a watchful eye on workers even during their leisure hours, controlled accounts at the company store (ensuring the perpetual debt of workers), and herded workers into the woods at daybreak. Yet Hurston found that the camps nevertheless were home to a diverse community of honest workers, family men, fugitive murderers, knife-wielding good-time girls, Christian mothers (also sometimes wielding knives), hard-living gamblers, jackleg preachers, and hoodoo charlatans. Together they created a rich folk tradition of stories, songs, folktales, and jokes.[7]

Hurston used the material she collected in these camps to explore the social questions that concerned members of these communities. Like the material collected in Eatonville, the folklore in these camps addressed gender tensions and sexual matters, sensitivities about color, the moral vision of workers, religious belief systems, and violence among community members. It also registered the dreams of the poorest of the poor and the dissident political culture that sustained an exploited people.

Within the camps resistance was risky business and required subterfuge, outright rebellion, or flight. Punishment for this kind of resistance was severe and could even include death. Yet workers and their families found methods and language by which to resist the cruelty and exploitation of the camps. They moved between coercion and their own small spaces of autonomy.

The culture of the camps produced the raw material upon which African American culture drew in its creation of the art forms, recognized as uniquely black and American, of blues and jazz. Hurston brings this culture to life and gives us a glimpse of the way people looked and sounded as they went through the ordinary business of daily life and extraordinary moments of crisis.

The Loughman Camps

Census data show that migrants to Polk County had come from Georgia, the Carolinas, Tennessee, and Alabama.[8] Many acres of pine forests had been exhausted by the time Hurston arrived there in 1928. Although the industry as a whole was in decline, she found a substantial community working the remaining forests. Small numbers of European immigrants and poor whites had worked in these camps previously, but by 1928 most of them had managed to move on, leaving primarily African Americans, who had always been in the majority.[9] The work was hard and unhealthy, the living conditions abysmal. As Charlotte Todes described it, "To cut cypress, the workers must wade in humid swamps, often up to their hips in water, and must live with their families in house boats built over the swamps."[10] On top of the dangerous and unhealthy conditions, black workers usually experienced discriminatory labor practices and segregation, working the most menial jobs and receiving lower wages than whites. Segregated from white workers, they lived in shacks the size of box cars and were rarely provided schooling for their children.[11]

In 1906 the Bartow *Courier-Informant* announced the construction of one of the largest lumber mills to be built at Loughman,

Florida.[12] By 1910, almost two decades before Hurston arrived at the camps, Loughman was an important industrial center with a population of 721, located five miles east of Davenport and eleven miles west of Kissimmee, according to the city directory of 1928.[13] It was the site, first, of the Chase and Co. Pine Mill and Crate Factory, and later of four different lumber companies that manufactured cypress—Carter and Weeks, Everglade Cypress Lumber Co., Everglade Cypress Co., and the Everglade Cypress Co., Inc. The first Everglade Cypress Lumber Co. was founded in 1905 and the company built the first town, which contained two white churches—Methodist and Baptist—and three black churches, also Methodist and Baptist.

During its most productive period, early in the twentieth century, the company employed 300 men and was divided into two areas, the Cypress Quarters and the Pine Mill Quarters. Workers turned out 200,000 feet of lumber a day, which was transported along the twenty-one miles of railroad track in the company's yard, connecting with rail lines throughout the state. The company built a segregated town of identical houses made from local cypress for the workers. A company commissary supplied them with goods of all sorts, and the company employed a doctor who tended to their medical needs.[14]

The sawmill operation used the most modern techniques. Steam engines did the mechanical work and hoisting machinery was used to handle many tons of lumber with ease.[15] The other side of the operation, the turpentine still, used antiquated methods of extraction that hadn't changed since antebellum days. By 1912 the Loughman operations were some of the most successful in Florida and the company had the largest payroll in the state. In 1913, however, a steam engine exploded and the sawmill was engulfed in flames. The Everglades Cypress Lumber Company burned to the ground, for a loss of $200,000. The same year the Everglades Cypress Company bought out what was left of the old company and re-created the lumber and logging portion of the business.[16] In 1918 a section of the company was converted to a canning factory. By 1928, when Hurston arrived, the whole operation was in decline and the company was on the verge of closing its doors for good.

Hurston had been passionate about developing a black theater since her collaboration with Langston Hughes on the play *Mule Bone* in 1930. She and Hughes worked for the better part of a year to write and produce this play, but they had a falling out over it and *Mule Bone* never saw the light of day until 1991, when it was finally produced in New York.[17] The failure to produce *Mule Bone* was a bitter disappointment for Hurston, and the quarrel with Hughes destroyed their friendship. For a decade and a half she continued to write plays, but only a few of them were produced. *Polk County* (1944), co-authored with Dorothy Waring, was never produced in her lifetime.

Several of these plays were set in turpentine and sawmill camps. Another play, *A Negro Lysistrata*, now lost, is set among workers in a canning factory who decide to demand higher wages. John Houseman, head of the Negro Unit of the WPA's Federal Theater Project in the 1930s, complained of a shortage of plays and thought he had found one to produce in *A Negro Lysistrata*. According to Houseman, the play was "located in a Florida fishing community, where the men's wives refused them intercourse until they won their fight with the canning company for a living wage." Houseman wanted to produce the play but could not drum up enough support to put it on. The WPA community disliked the play intensely; its right-wing members found the characters too salty and the plot too risqué for their conservative tastes. The WPA leftists complained that the workers in the play lacked a radical enough political perspective to suit them. Houseman, bowing to these criticisms, wrote, "I had to give this up," even though he considered *A Negro Lysistrata* much better than the play that was produced in its place, a play called *Turpentine*, by a forgotten pair of collaborators, full of "leftist clichés." One review of *Turpentine* described it as a drama that "creaks and in its last few moments collapses like a punctured tire."[18]

The Everglades Cypress Company closed its doors in 1928, shortly after Hurston's arrival, and the Wilson Toomer Fertilizer

Company bought the land. Wilson Toomer built a citrus canning company there that failed in the 1930s.[19] Hurston would have known all of this, for she continued to collect material well into the thirties. The canning company featured in *A Negro Lysistrata* may have been modeled on the one built in 1918 or on the Wilson Toomer cannery. After the canning factory shut down, most of the population moved away; all of the homes in the Cypress Quarters have disappeared. But descendents of workers continue to live in the Pine Quarters, where I found Harry Grant. Hurston's plays and folklore are all that we have of a world that history has erased.

Recall the tale in the previous chapter about women appealing to God for their lost power, a request God denies them because they asked too late. They seek help from the devil, who instructs them to lock their menfolk out of the kitchen, the bedroom, and the nursery until the men do the women's bidding. One reading of this tale sees women's power as limited to the personal sphere and used only for personal matters. But African American history demonstrates that politics were defined in the private sphere, that public matters were decided in the private realm among men, women, and children, even though it was the men who presented those decisions in public, particularly in the immediate years after Emancipation. For example, after the passage of the Fifteenth Amendment, women claimed the one vote allowed for men as also their own vote and that of their family and community. Put another way, women had no choice but to exercise their power in the so-called private sphere.[20] While the relative power of black women to influence how men presented their political views was more complex by the 1920s, women had their own political voices by this time with the passage of the Nineteenth Amendment. As discussed in Chapter 3, black women's vote was a cause for concern in the 1920 elections in Florida because their entrance into the electoral process could alter the outcome of the election. This is not to suggest political equality between black men and women but merely to argue that black women were never completely silenced by male prerogatives.

Polk County is informed by this context. It depicts a world that operated outside the view of bosses and company owners. The white community was afraid of black people's struggle for political power, but they saw this struggle enacted only in such public forums as the campaign for the vote. Hurston's play gives us a fuller picture of that struggle.

Polk County begins with a detailed picture of the setting of the Loughman camps (she renames the Everglades Cypress Company the "Lofton Company" in the play). "The Lofton Lumber Company has its big mill and quarters deep in the primeval woods of South Central Florida. Huge live oaks, pines, magnolia, cypress, 'sweet gum' (maple) and the like grow lush. Spanish moss drapes the trees. Tall cabbage palms tilt their crowns in clusters above the surrounding trees. Scrubby palmettos make a dense undergrowth."[21]

> The woods surround everything. Bull alligators can be heard booming like huge bass drums from the lake at night. Variegated chorus of frogs, big owls, and now and then the cry of the panther. Within this forest teeming with animal life were quarters built by the company which lacked the imagination of nature.
>
> There are a hundred or more houses in the quarters. They are laid out in straight rows like streets...
>
> The streets of the quarters are unpaved, sandy places. There are trees that have been left standing here and there...
>
> The houses are of raw, second grade lumber, unpainted, each with a porch and two or three rooms. Each man with a "family" is allotted a house for which he is docked about fifty cents a week. The single men live with others or room at the rooming house next door to the cafe. No fenced in yards, few flowers, and those poorly tended. Few attempts at any kind of decoration or relief of ugliness. (1–2)

The company provides other buildings for community use:

> There is a main street, wider than the others, called "The Square." On it were the public places like the Jook, or pleasure houses furnished by the management. There is a piano in it (sometimes a victrola also) tables for card games made of unpainted lumber, and a big table with a trip-string for dice. This is the life of the camp after work hours. There is a sort of cafe where soft drinks, tobacco,

> dried fish, chitterlings, etc. are sold. It is the second place in pop-
> ularity. (1)

Migration between camps ensured that a kind of instability was
built into the culture of these workers. After a while they got used
to this.

> Everyone lives temporary. They go from job to job, or from job
> to jail and from jail to job. Working, loving temporarily and often
> without thought of permanence in anything, wearing their switch-
> blade knives and guns as a habit like the men of the Old West,
> fighting, cutting and being cut, such a camp where there is little
> law, and the peace officers of state and county barred by manage-
> ment, these refugees from life see nothing unlovely in the sordid
> camp. They love it and when they leave there, will seek another
> place like it. (2)

The transient, unstable nature of life in these camps did not prevent a sense of community from developing. In his study of European immigrants who worked as migrant laborers, Gunther Peck
has argued that "while transient workers rarely found enduring
working-class institutions in one place, they succeeded in creating vibrant working-class communities. They were built, out of
necessity, across local, regional, and national boundaries rather
than within a single place or neighborhood. Village societies and
less formal kin networks functioned to bring coherence to an otherwise atomized life."[22] The sense of community in a transient
world is supported by Harry Grant, the former resident of the
sawmill camp at Loughman. Grant grew up in Loughman and
was a boy when Hurston visited the camp. He recalled some of
the names of those who lived in the camp, though few remained
there longer than three or four years. Even so, some connections
survived several decades.[23]

The violence of the camp bosses, designed to discipline and
control labor, has been well documented. Violence was also a feature within the workers' community, where it was understood and
tolerated. There was criminal violence and vigilante justice for
wrongs both real and imagined. None of this violence was of concern to the authorities unless it interfered with work. As Hurston

put it, matter-of-factly, violent incidents "are ephemeral in every way. The murderous fight of today is forgotten tomorrow and the opponents work together in utmost friendship inside of twenty-four hours" (2).

Just as violence was an accepted feature of camp life, casual relationships were the norm.

> The woman of today may be forgotten tomorrow. Certainly it is remarkable for a love affair to survive a change of scene. There will be more women where they are going, and they say, "Let every town furnish its own. It's a damn poor town that can't furnish its own. Take no woman anywhere." Here and there an attachment becomes permanent, and they settle down together, or travel together from camp to camp. (2)

According to Hurston, the women who attached themselves to these camps had little to offer in the way of beauty, intelligence, or commitment. They were the refuse society had cast off:

> The women are misfits from the outside. Seldom good looking, intelligent, or adjustable. They have drifted down to their level, unable to meet the competition outside. Many have made time in prisons also. Usually for fighting over men. They too pack knives. No stigma attaches to them for prison terms. In fact, their prestige is increased if they have made time for a serious cutting. It passes for bravery—something to give themselves a rating in their small world, where no intellectual activities exist. Hence the boastful song: I'm going to make me a graveyard of my own. (2–3)

The workers in these camps, men and women alike, must have at times felt the need for spiritual redemption and sought a connection with their gods: "Rough, fighting, drinking, loving, reckless, but at times a flash of religion comes to the top when they are troubled or scared. Then for a short while, a Spiritual will well up out of them and be much-felt for the moment. Small churches have a hit-and-miss existence on the camps. They feel the need of a preacher for funerals. He is more often a man of the same stripe who reformed" (3).

A good deal of the rough side of this life took place in the jook joints. "Such a place is the cradle of the Blues and work song," says Hurston. "There they are made and go from mouth to mouth of itinerant workers from one camp to the other." These "people have given the world the blues, Work Songs, guitar picking in the Negro manner, and the type of piano playing which made Fats Waller famous, and is now being taken up by the world. Because it is typical, they call that type of piano playing 'jooking'" (3). In "Characteristics of Negro Expression," Hurston defined a jook as "a Negro pleasure house." A jook joint was sometimes a bawdy house, sometimes a place "set apart on public works where the men and women dance, drink and gamble. Often it is a combination of all of these."[24] Jooks were an integral part of the camps and community life.

Hurston's description of Loughman is consistent with descriptions of other camps in Florida. Studies of the lumber industry, both contemporary and more recent ones, provide good accounts of the politics, economics, and social impact of this industry. Few, however, focus on the everyday concerns of the workers in these camps.[25]

Life, Labor, and Culture

When Hurston arrived in Loughman, she realized instantly that she was not going to be accepted as easily as she had been in Eatonville. In transient communities, outsiders are quickly sized up and judged friendly or suspect. Hurston's shiny new car and expensive dress set her apart, so she spun a yarn of her own and convinced the workers that she was a bootlegger on the lam, thereby gaining the acceptance and respect of the camp residents. They agreed to take her to the swamp gang to get the best stories. Hurston had seen the workers in the swamp and marveled at their skill:

> Having watched some members of the swamp crew handle axes, I didn't doubt for a moment that they could do all that they said. Not only do they chop rhythmically, but they do a beautiful double twirl above their heads with the ascending axe before it begins that accurate and bird-like descent. They can hurl their axes great

distances and behead moccasins or sink the blade into an alliga-
tor's skull. In fact, they seem to be able to do everything with their
instrument that a blade can do. It is a magnificent sight to watch
the marvelous co-ordination between the handsome black torsos
and the twirling axes.[26]

Passages such as this have been criticized as romanticizing rural
life. But the harshness of a system cannot prevent people from
crafting their own value and beauty or others from seeing that
beauty. DuBois found beauty and value among workers in the
Black Belt. Charles Joyner found pride in work among slaves in
South Carolina, as did Deborah Gray White in her work on women
slaves.[27] This pride in one's work could not be taken away even
by the harshness of the working conditions, and Hurston was
there to record it.

In the introduction to *Mules and Men*, Hurston wrote that black
people concealed their true thoughts from outsiders and sought
to meet the expectations of those outsiders without revealing
their true selves. "We smile and tell him or her something that satisfies the white person because, knowing so little about us, he
doesn't know what he is missing." Hurston understood that African Americans often counted on the ignorance of whites to provide camouflage for their thoughts. Underprivileged rural
dwellers were the "most reluctant at times to reveal that which
the soul lives by. And the Negro, in spite of his open-faced laughter, his seeming acquiescence, is particularly evasive." "The
Negro," Hurston wrote, "offers a feather-bed resistance. That is,
we let the probe enter, but it never comes out. It gets smothered
under a lot of laughter and pleasantries" (4).[28] Outsiders saw only
darkies smiling, unconscious of their condition.[29]

African American workers in the camps had no illusions about
their relationship to the company. Hurston records in *Mules and
Men* a revealing exchange between a man named Jim Allen and his
wife, Bertha. When Bertha sees that the men have a day off, she
fetches the rake so that her husband can help clear the yard. Jim
refuses and suggests that his grandson do the raking. This grandson, Cliffert Ulmer, retorts, "Grandma, you worries mo' 'bout dis

place than de man dat owns it. You ain't de Everglades Cypress Lumber Comp'ny sho nuff. Youse just shacking in one of their shanties. Leave de weeds go, Somebody'll come chop 'em some day" (101). Jim and Bertha continue to argue about the raking, and although their spat is couched in gender terms, the lived experience of mutual exploitation is visible underneath. For Jim Allen (and his grandson), work is done only for the boss, and he is willing to do only what he must. Bertha bears the burden of domestic responsibilities and desires some relief. At the same time, she wants a place of her own, with a neatly kept yard, even if "ownership" is an illusion.

The instability and transience of labor camps gave women a certain freedom, and a relationship to their men, that women on Joe Clarke's porch had to negotiate. Consider Hurston's first encounter upon arriving in Polk County. As she drove into the quarters, she met a woman named "Babe Hill," Bertha Allen's daughter. Hurston inquired about a place to stay and was directed to the boarding house run by Mrs. Allen under the patronage of the company. She learned later that "Babe" (whom she described as sullen), had killed her husband during the Christmas holidays in 1926 and had fled to evade capture. Living in Tampa, she changed her appearance, but she was eventually traced through letters to her mother. Extradited from Tampa, she was lodged in the Bartow jail for several months before she was allowed to come home, her case forgotten. In fact, it is surprising that Babe was arrested at all. Hurston commented dryly that "Negro women are punished in these parts for killing men, but only if they exceed the quota. I don't remember what the quota is. Perhaps I did hear but I forgot." The law was not overly concerned with such killings. "One woman," Hurston continued, "had killed five when I left the turpentine still where she lived. The sheriff was thinking of calling on her and scolding her severely" (65).

The frontier-like conditions of the camps leveled the playing field between men and women, as did the culture of the jook. In the jook women lived outside the boundaries of traditional marriage, the constraints of ladylike behavior, and the authority of the church. They were able to create new identities for themselves, but at a price. In many camps, boundaries were sometimes dissolved by the sexual exploitation facilitated by the owners and straw bosses, who often forced women into prostitution. Even married women were not free from this threat.[30] The company at the very least provided women on weekends for the men in the jook joints. W. Alston Brown, for example, encouraged both gambling and the sex trade at Cross City. He made it impossible for women to refuse when called upon to provide their bodies for the entertainment of workers.[31] According to Harry Grant, on Saturday night trains arrived from Jacksonville loaded with women. Their presence, plenty of liquor, seductive music, and paychecks, even in scrip, were a lethal combination that produced acts of violence, including sometimes murder, in which women were as likely as men to be the culprits.

In *Mules and Men* Hurston introduces one female member of the community, Big Sweet, whose doings exemplify the ways in which women created selfhood on their own terms. Big Sweet was larger than life, and her space was the jook—the incubator of the blues. Her name signified the duality she possessed—power and sexuality.[32]

Hurston reveals Big Sweet's story through the conversations that take place in *Mules and Men*. As we saw in Chapter 4, storytelling was typically the preserve of men, and the tales they told usually presented women in an unflattering light. But women contested these characterizations and sometimes told stories of their own on the men.

Hurston first encountered Big Sweet as she was challenging a male opponent before an audience in a session of playing the dozens. Big Sweet announced "in one of her mildest bulletins that his pa was a double-humped camel and his ma was a grass-gut cow."[33] The two women became friends, and Big Sweet escorted Hurston into the community. She even saved Hurston's life when Hurston once got caught in the crossfire during an outbreak of violence in one of the jook joints (190).

Hurston shows us Big Sweet fighting with her lover, Joe Willard, in the jook. In another episode, by the lake, she goes after Joe for his cheating ways. "'And speakin' 'bout hams,... if Joe Willard don't stay out of dat bunk he was in last night, Ah'm gointer sprinkle some salt down his back and sugar-cure *his* hams.'" Hurston records the exchange, in which Joe tries in vain to save face.

> "Aw, woman, quit tryin' to signify."
> "Ah kin signify all Ah please, Mr. Nappy-chin, so long as Ah know what Ah'm talkin' about.

Their banter continues.

> "See dat?" Joe appealed to the other men. "We git a day off and figger we kin ketch some fish and enjoy ourselves, but naw, some wimmins got to drag behind us, even to de lake."
> "You didn't figger Ah was draggin' behind you when you was bringin' dat Sears and Roebuck catalogue over to my house and beggin' me to choose my ruthers. Lemme tell *you* something, *any* time Ah shack up wid any man Ah gives myself de privilege to go wherever he might be, night or day. Ah got de law in my mouth."
> (133–34)

This frontier variation on marriage ignored or rejected the prevailing cultural expectations for women in respectable or settled society. Big Sweet openly acknowledged her sexual relationship and demanded the respect of both her lover and the other men. This was her declaration of authority. Her statement, "Ah got de law in my mouth," signaled her ownership of herself. She moved between feminine (sweet) and masculine (big) discourses, as the occasion dictated.[34]

Big Sweet's independence was asserted most forcefully in a dramatic incident in the jook between herself and her rival for Joe's affection, Ella Wall. On this occasion Wall entered the jook with a noisy crowd from Mulberry, the phosphate-mining town. "Ella Wall flung a loud laugh back over her shoulder as she flourished in. Everybody looked at her, then they looked at Big Sweet. Big Sweet looked at Ella, but she seemed not to mind. The air was as tight as a fiddle string. Ella wrung her hips to the Florida-flip game. Big Sweet stayed on at the skin game but didn't play. Joe Willard, knowing the imminence of forthright action, suddenly got deep into the crap game." Lucy, another of the jook women, entered "with a bright gloat in her eyes and went straight to Ella." Lucy had been a friend of Big Sweet's but apparently her loyalties had changed. Finally Big Sweet exploded: "'Dat li'l narrer contracted piece uh meatskin gointer make me stomp her right now! De two-faced heifer! Been hangin' 'round me so she kin tote news to Ella. If she don't look out she'll have on her last clean dress befo' de crack of day.'"

When Hurston expressed her surprise at Lucy's behavior, she learned that Lucy was jealous of her but that Big Sweet had told Lucy to leave Hurston alone. The object of Lucy's affection, a man named Slim from whom Hurston had been collecting folktales, was another bone of contention. Big Sweet assured Hurston, "'Neb' mind 'bout ole Lucy. She know Ah backs yo' fallin'. She know if she scratch yo' skin Ah'll kill her so dead till she can't fall. They'll have to push her over'" (158).

Ella Wall took delight in the public display of her sexuality. Someone began singing a tribute to her, a song that Hurston claimed was sung on every job in south Florida:

> Go to Ella Wall
> Oh, go to Ella Wall
> If you want good boody
> Oh, go to Ella Wall
>
> Oh, she's long and tall
> Oh, she's long and tall
> And she rocks her rider
> From uh wall to wall
>
> Oh, go to Ella Wall
> Take yo' trunk and all—

Wall enhanced the song and the emphasis on her sexual assets: "'Tell 'em 'bout me,'... 'I'm raggedy, but right; patchey but tight; stringy, but I *will* hang on.'" As she presented these challenges she "snapped her fingers and revolved her hips with her hands" (159). Big Sweet observed Ella's performance with a wry expression that Hurston knew meant trouble: "I knew that Big Sweet didn't mind fighting; didn't mind killing and didn't too much mind dying." Hurston urged her to leave. "Nope," said Big Sweet, "Ah aint got to do nothin' but die and stay black. Ah stays right here till de jook close if anybody else stay." A cold philosophy, to be sure, but one born of the material realities of life. Death was never far from the minds of many southern blacks of this era, and most understood that it could visit them at any time. But Big Sweet's philosophy was also a way, perhaps for her the only way, not to live in fear.

Wall finally sent for Big Sweet's lover, knowing full well that this kind of challenge could not be ignored. As she began throwing insults, Big Sweet warned Hurston to run if trouble started, for they meant to harm her, too. Loudly Wall ordered Lucy to "go tell Mr. Lots-of-Papa Joe Willard Ah say come here. Jus' tell 'im his weakness want 'im. He know who dat is." As Hurston wrote later, "I thought of all I had to live for and turned cold at the thought of dying in a violent manner in a sordid saw-mill camp. But for my very life I knew I couldn't leave Big Sweet even if the fight came. She had been too faithful to me." When she heard the click of Big Sweet's spring-blade knife, she knew that her "only weapons were my teeth and toe-nails."

Big Sweet blocked Lucy's way. "Stop right where you is, Lucy,... lessen you want to see yo' Jesus," Big Sweet bellowed. Wall demanded, "Gwan Lucy... tain't nothin' stoppin' yuh. See nothin', say nothin'." Hot and dangerous words flew between the women. The fight stopped when the white quarters boss stepped into the jook, "a .45 in his hand and another on his hip." He took Ella's weapon and sent her away but was challenged by Big Sweet:

> "What's the matter here, y'all? Big Sweet, what you mean tuh do wid that knife?"
>
> "Ahm jus' 'bout tuh send God two niggers. Come in here bull-dozin' me."...

"You ain't gonna kill nobody right under mah nose," the Quarters Boss snorted. "Gimme that knife you got dere, Big Sweet."

Hurston's account does not give us the all powerful gun-toting white authority of Jim Crow. Instead, events took a turn that must have surprised her readers at the time:

"Naw suh! Nobody gits *mah* knife. Ahd bought it for dat storm-buzzard over dere and Ah means tuh use it on her, too. As long as uh mule go bareheaded she better not part her lips tuh me. Do Ah'll kill her, law or no law. Don't you touch me, white folks!" (161)

Joe Willard gave voice to the group's admiration: "'You wuz noble!... You wuz uh whole woman and half uh man. You made dat cracker stand offa *you*'" (162). Big Sweet had defeated the white man in the only place where this could have happened, the jook joint, where the white boss was vastly outnumbered. Big Sweet was allowed to keep her knife. After all, her target was another black woman, and the company may not have cared much about that, as long as too many workers weren't killed. Although workers in these camps were managed like slaves, no one owned them, and so, paradoxically, their lives were less valuable to whites than they had been during slavery. Individual women's lives were even less important, from the company's standpoint. It fell to individuals to define and defend themselves. The willingness to resort to violence to protect what was hers earned Big Sweet Joe Willard's praise and established her courage. He was proud to escort her home.

Hurston commented on this episode years later in her autobiography. "Primitive minds are quick to sunshine and quick to anger." Workers in these circumstances understood the precariousness of life. "Some little word, look or gesture can move them either to love or to sticking a knife between your ribs. You just have to sense the delicate balance and maintain it," she wrote. There was nothing personal in these attacks, for "the killer wishes to establish a reputation as a killer, and you'll do as a sample." The music carried this view of life from one generation to another:

I'm going to make me a graveyard of my own,
I'm going to make me a graveyard of my own,

Oh, carried me down on de smoky road,
Brought me back on de coolin' board
But I'm going to make me a graveyard of my own.

Hurston is aware that Big Sweet, this abrasive, knife-toting, smart-talking woman, was not approved of outside the camp. A club woman who heard her talk or saw her knife might not have noticed that her lover had given her what she wanted from the Sears and Roebuck catalogue, that she was a wife in a certain way, presented with gifts that marital norms required. Polite society in Big Sweet's time was trying to erase such scenes from the general understanding of black southerners. Hurston's comment about the sordidness of the camps captured an aspect of this life that many in the black elite preferred to deny or ignore. Hurston's task, as noted by Cheryl Wall "was to legitimize Big Sweet's conduct without apologizing or positing sociological explanations for it."[35]

I have been unable to identify Big Sweet's real name either through census documents or interviews. But Ella Wall has been identified through the census for 1920 and 1930. The evidence suggests that she was a landowner from Apopka, Florida, in Seminole County. She was not a worker but spent her leisure time in the jook culture of Seminole, Orange, and Polk counties, where she bought and sold a significant amount of property for many years, renting some of it to agricultural workers around Apopka. Her story suggests that there was a fluid or at least permeable boundary between migrant workers and residents of settled communities.[36]

Mules and Men also reveals how humor and entertainment gave workers an opportunity to release the stress and pain of their work. On Saturday nights, particularly on pay nights, which came every other Saturday, there was at least one dance at the Pine Mill Camp and a couple of others at the Cypress Mill Camp. The dances were marked by huge bonfires in front of the houses where the dances were held. Refreshments were roasted over these fires—peanuts, fried rabbit, fish, chicken, and chitterlings, washed down with a great deal of a home brew, popularly called *coon dick*, that the workers drank as they told jokes and made music or just sat after a week's hard work (66).

"The brother in black puts a laugh in every vacant place in his mind," Hurston wrote of these parties. "His laugh has a hundred meanings. It may mean amusement, anger, grief, bewilderment, chagrin, curiosity, simple pleasure or any other of the known or undefined emotions" (67). One woman told Hurston that she had to laugh when her husband dumped her for another woman: "Clardia Thornton of Magazine Point, Alabama, was telling me about another woman taking her husband way from her. When the show-down came and he told Clardia in the presence of the other woman that he didn't want her—could never use her again, she told me 'Den, Zora, Ah wuz so outdone, Ah just opened mah mouf and laffed.'" Hurston observed, "The folks around the fire laughed and boisterously shoved each other about, but I knew they were not tickled" (68).

The morning after these parties, everyone returned to work. The shack-rouser, a man hired to ensure that no one overslept, was about before daybreak. Dick Willie sang the wake-up call, "Wake up, bullies, and git on de rock. 'Tain't quite daylight but it's four o'clock... Wake up, Jacob, day's a breakin'. Git yo' 'hoe-cake a baking and yo' shirt tail shakin'" (72). Then Dick Willie went to the jook, where he roused the pimps and rounders.

> About that time you see a light in every shack. Every kitchen is scorching up fat-back and hoe-cake. Nearly every skillet is full of corn-bread. But some like biscuit-bread better. Break your hoe-cake half in two. Half on the plate, half in the dinner-bucket. Throw in your black-eyed peas and fat meat left from supper and your bucket is fixed. Pour meat grease in your plate with plenty of cane syrup. Mix it and sop it with your bread. A big bowl of coffee, a drink of water from the tin dipper in the pail. Grab your dinner-bucket and hit the grit. Don't keep the straw-boss waiting. (72–73)

Hurston published in *Mules and Men* only a representative selection of the stories she collected, but she drew on these stories in the writing of *Polk County*, one of her most powerful works. Though the play has been described as a musical comedy, I would argue that it is also serious examination of the daily concerns of exploited workers.

By the time Hurston wrote *Polk County*, in the mid-1940s, her displeasure with the right and left had solidified and she felt more confident in asserting her own political views. Dorothy Waring, co-author of the play, urged Hurston to inject a "sort of Gershwinesque feeling" into their musical comedy, to which Zora replied, "You don't know what the hell you're talking about."[37] It was not a comedy or a musical Hurston had in mind.

The play confronts head on the questions of gender, color, and black-on-black violence. Many of the main characters also appear in the folktales and in some of her fictional works, and some of them are given the names of the actual people on whom they are based. Big Sweet, the heroine of the story and the leader of the community, is "a handsome Negro woman around thirty," who is strong, quick-tempered, and courageous, but also "generous and kind, and loyal to her friends." Dicey Long is "a homely narrow-contracted little black woman, who has been slighted by Nature and feels 'evil' about it. Suffers from the 'black ass.' Her strongest emotion is envy. What she passes off as a deep love is merely the determination not to be outdone by handsomer women. Yearns to gain a reputation as bad (the fame of a sawmill camp) to compensate for her lack of success with men. She is extremely jealous of Big Sweet. Being short, scrawny and black, Leafy, a pretty yellow girl, arouses violent envy in her."

Lonnie is Big Sweet's lover. He is "a soft spoken man with a baritone voice. He loves and relies on BIG SWEET because she is his opposite. He is loyal and kind. Tall, brown and well made." Two outsiders stir up trouble in the camp. One is Leafy Lee, "a slim mulatto girl, who wants to be a Blues singer. Frustrated in her hopes of a career in the music halls, she takes to wandering aimlessly, and perhaps subconsciously comes to Lofton Lumber Mills in Polk County where Blues are not only sung in the real manner, but are made. Simple, kindly and timid of life" (4). The other outsider is Nunkie, "a no-good gambler—shifty and irresponsible. His soul is as black as his face and his face is as black as the sins he commits. Any place with a dice table is his home." A third character, Ella Wall, "though primitive and pagan, has the air of a conqueror. She is strutting and self assured and accustomed to the favors of men which she in return grants freely. She practices Voodoo and feels she leads a charmed life" (5–6).

The other characters are the assortment of camp residents found throughout Florida: My Honey, a good-looking young man who loves to pick his "box"; Stew Beef, "portly, witty and good humored"; Sop-the-Bottom, a gambler with a big appetite; Laura B., "just the average woman found on saw mill, turpentine and railroad camps. No looks to speak of. Just taking what life has to offer one who has no more to offer life than she has. Not bitter nor looking for anything particular"; Do-Dirty, Box Car, and Few Clothes, the "usual type found on such 'jobs,' the kind of men who would be mis-fits in other places. Rough, cheerful, careless of human life, including their own, used to prison, hard work, and danger. Come day, go day, God send Sunday" (5).

The story centers on Big Sweet's love for Lonnie and her position and leadership in the community. It also involves Dicey Long's desire for My Honey, who rejects her and falls in love with Leafy Lee. Lonnie is the love of Big Sweet's life. He is kind and philosophical, and he dreams of beauty, heaven, and a better place to live. He adores Big Sweet. The story opens with Big Sweet searching for Nunkie, who has cheated Lonnie out of his earnings. When she finds him she retrieves Lonnie's money and gives Nunkie a good beating. Dicey Long throws herself at My Honey, who publicly rejects her, but she determines that she is going to have him at any cost. When Leafy Lee arrives in the camp, however, Dicey's chances evaporate. She flies into a rage, convinced she has been rejected because of her dark black skin, and determines to have revenge on Leafy and Big Sweet. First, with the help of Ella Wall, she sends a letter to Lonnie accusing Big Sweet of being unfaithful to him and nearly destroys their relationship. She then tells the Quarters Boss that Big Sweet is responsible for all the trouble in the camp and he decides to throw her out.

Big Sweet is devastated, for she believes she has found a community where she can put down roots. She also begins to believe, with the help of Leafy Lee and My Honey, that the community could become a different place if only people would marry and make a home there instead of living a transient life. She believes that the community needs her leadership and will fall apart without her. When the other camp residents hear that she is being evicted, they resolve to leave as well. Backed into a corner, the company bosses back down. Dicey, thwarted in her effort to get rid of Big Sweet, schemes to get even through Ella Wall's alleged skill with hoodoo.

Ella convinces Dicey that she can put a spell on the entire community, rendering everyone immobile and handing Dicey the opportunity to slice up her enemies. They choose an evening on which the community has planned a party in the woods away from the camp. When Wall's hoodoo talents fail, she and Dicey are driven from the camp. The play ends on a hopeful note with the marriage of Lonnie and Big Sweet.

The play opens with barnyard creatures singing about love and shoes, as Lonnie wakes the camp for work:

HEN: Ground cold to my feet this morning. I wish I had some shoes.

ROOSTER: What did the rooster say to the hen? Ain't had no loving in the Lord knows when.

HEN (*uninterested*): These Polk County roosters! They want plenty loving, but they don't buy no shoes.

ROOSTER: How about a lil' kiss?

HEN (*evading him*): I want some shoes!

ROOSTER: Oh, gimme a lil kiss.

ALL HENS: Well, I lay all the eggs, and I go barefooted!

ROOSTER (*trying to evade the issue*): T'aint a man in Tennessee can make a shoe to fit your foot!

HENS (*chanting in imitation of cackle*): Well, I lay all the eggs and I go barefooted!

ROOSTER: T'aint a man in Tennessee can make a shoe to fit your foot!

ROOSTER (*at end of dance*): Aw, cutta-cut cut! You Polk County hens always hollering for shoes! Why I have to buy you shoes to love you. You get just as much out of it as I do. Aw, cutta-cut cut! (*He leads them off between the houses clucking disgustedly.*) (I, i)

This scene conveys not only the workers' poverty but also the tensions that arise between men and women over sex and economic support. The women in these camps, like women everywhere, are looking for love, support, and commitment. The men are transient, discouraged from making long-term commitments to either their work or their women by the debt-peonage system and the cultural values that arise from it. The men lack the economic resources to maintain long-term relationships and the women have few economic options for self-sufficiency.

In one of her first conversations with Leafy, Big Sweet tells of her relationships with other men and discovers that Leafy has never been with a man, a fact Leafy confesses with embarrassment.[38]

BIG SWEET: I never expected to find nothing like that sure enough. (*She leans her head against the bedpost with a far-off bitter look on her face and thinks.*)

I'm glad for you, Leafy. Cause you done won the battle that I lost.
LEAFY: What do you mean by that?
BIG SWEET: I wanted to be a virgin my ownself. I always said that I was going to be one till I got married, when I was growing up, and I meant to, too. That was my firm determination. Course I didn't know what his name was going to be, but I knowed that I was going to find Lonnie some time or other. And I often wish that I could have come to him like you is now. (*A deep, long sigh.*) No use wishing now. Them years is behind the mountains. I think that I would have made it too, but you see Papa died when I was fifteen, and times got mighty hard. It was too expensive for somebody in the fix I was. I couldn't afford to be a virgin. (*Pause.*) Then, after that, I got to knocking around, and found out what folks mean by careless love. You mean good, and think maybe it will lead to something permanent. But he hits you a love-lick and be gone! So when you get through thinking and feeling, you try another one. Pretty soon, you be feeling again like you been drug through Hell on a buzzard gut. You find out it's a lot of bulldozing, imposing and biggity folks in the world that loves to take advantage. They looks fine from the top of their heads down, but if you see 'em from the foot up, they's another kind of people. They sings and says that the water in Polk County taste like cherry wine. So I come pulling here like a heap more girls done done. (*A bitter laugh.*) Well, after while, I met up with Lonnie, and then things was all right. But by that time, I had done got my craw

full of folks doing they bullying and bulldozing and trompling on everything and everybody they could git they foot upon.

LEAFY: (*Rushes across to Big Sweet and flings her arms about her.*) You make me feel so little. Just being a virgin aint a thing besides what you are, honey. (I,iii)

This exchange not only locates sexuality within the material struggles that shape the lives of these transient women, it suggests that a person's character is more important than "proper" notions of female behavior. It also sets the stage for Big Sweet's leadership to develop as the plot unfolds. "Bulldozing" was what white southerners did to freedmen and women in the years after Emancipation to terrorize them into remaining on the plantations. Nightriders beat and harassed blacks into submission in the years after the Civil War. Big Sweet uses the term in reference to relations between men and women. The conversation continues:

BIG SWEET: you don't know a thing about this world, but I aim to put my wisdom tooth in your head. I mean to be your fore-runner like John the Baptist. Fight everything from graybeard to battle height.

LEAFY: You mean you really fights?

BIG SWEET: Yeah, I has to sometimes. Some folks aint going to do right unlessen you do. I don't mean no harm, but one day about six years ago, me and God got to sort of controversing on the subject of how some folks loves to take advantage of everybody else. He said that sure was the truth, and He never had meant it to be that a'way. Preaching and teaching didn't do some of 'em no good. Jailing 'em didn't help 'em none, and hanging was too good for 'em. They just needed they behinds kicked.

LEAFY: Did God tell you to kick 'em?

BIG SWEET: Well, he didn't exactly *tell* me to kick 'em, but He looked down at my big feets and smiled.

LEAFY: So you been kicking 'em, eh? (*Laughing*)

BIG SWEET: Sure is, and its done a heap of 'em good. I done made over this place more nearly like Lonnie say it ought to be. No need in all this fighting and carrying on every pay night. Pole cats trying to make out they' lions! (I, iii)

As noted above, Big Sweet has already beaten the no-good Nunkie for cheating Lonnie out of his pay. Her violence against Nunkie, who has been known to steal from others as well, is commonplace in the camps, and it is sanctioned by the others, who do nothing to rescue Nunkie when he is caught in Big Sweet's clutches. The community serves up its own brand of justice, and Big Sweet is admired for her gumption. "I know I don't aim to get hurt trying to hold Big Sweet off you," Sop-the-Bottom tells Nunkie. "When she start to finish you Big Sweet is two whole women and a gang of men" (I, i).

Big Sweet exemplifies the powerful women who do not hesitate to resort to violence to protect themselves and their own. One can well imagine characters like this, whether male or female, emerging of necessity in frontier communities of this type. What Hurston gives us is a realistic account of how internal policing was done, and how restitution was achieved without recourse to formal judicial institutions. It is the essence of transient communities and frontiers that rules of conduct have to be created and enforced by private means. What we learn from Hurston helps us imagine what these southerners carried with them when they moved on to the north or the west—in this case, reliance on private justice rather than on police.

When the Quarters Boss hears the ruckus and Nunkie accuses Big Sweet of robbing him, he initially blames Big Sweet. Only when the boss learns that Nunkie is an outsider does he offer any defense of the black workers in his camp:

DO DIRTY: He don't belong on this job, Mr. Pringle.
QUARTERS BOSS (*Turning unfriendly eyes on Nunkie*):
He don't? Then what is he doing in these quarters?
SOP-THE-BOTTOM: Come in here last night to gamble. Bothering Big Sweet about Lonnie's money.
QUARTERS BOSS (*A great light*): Oh, he did, did he? She ought to have kilt him dead. Bulldozing the place and stealing, eh?
(*Begins to frisk Nunkie roughly. Finds the knife and a greasy deck of cards*)
Toting knives and weapons.
Stealing honest people's money too! Up to all kinds of meanness, too.
Unhunh! And toting concealed cards, highway shuffling, and attempt to gamble! (*Grabs Nunkie roughly*) You going down to Bartow to the big jail. Lets go!
NUNKIE: Don't take me to jail. Please, Cap'n! Lemme go this one time and I—

QUARTERS BOSS: Well, I'm going to let you go this time. But you know no outside folks aint allowed in these quarters. If I ever catch you on these premises again, I'll git you ninety-nine years and a jump-back jail. Hit the grit! (I, iii)

Nunkie steals and cheats his own people, and his actions are rejected even by the oppressive white overlords. Leafy is also an outsider, but she brings refinement to the camp and a sweetness not found in other camp women. She is also a light-skinned woman who is accordingly considered a real prize.[39] Hurston embodies good and evil in light and dark in these two characters, Dicey and Leafy Lee, in much the same way that the folktales she collected value women according to their skin color. The absurdity of this practice shows how the stain of racism has penetrated the consciousness of black people. Men are not marked by color in the same way that women are, a fact of racial gendering that is both internal and external to the black community. Hurston also exposes the depth of the pain caused by the color rating system. Dicey's monologue registers the pain and anger of this kind of rejection:

DICEY: How come I got to look like I do? Why couldn't I have that long straight hair like—like—Big Sweet got, and that Leafy? They own looks like horse's mane, and mine looks like drops of rain.
(*Feels disgust, self-pity, then resentment*)
And these mens is so crazy! They aint got no sense! Always pulling after hair and looks. And these womens that got it is so grasping, and griping, and mean. They wants EVERYTHING—and they gits it too. Look like they would be satisfied with *some*. Naw, they wants it all. Takes pleasure in making other folks feel bad.
(*Hurls mirror into bag face down*)
How come I got to be a swill barrel to take they leavings? (*In utter revolt*) Things ought not to be that way. What do they do more'n me? I wish they all was dead! Wish I could cut 'em and mark 'em in they faces, till they all looks worser than me! They acts like they thinks the world is made for them to strut around and brag on they selves in. (III, i)

Even today the question of color embodies so much of the human corruption of racism, and in such concentrated form, that it is hard to look upon. Hurston frequently alludes to it in descriptions of her characters, especially female ones, though usually only in passing. But Dicey's monologue is so tortured and so heartbreaking that it is hard to imagine any audience, black or white, then or now, enduring it easily.

Such color prejudice is not just a matter of unequal treatment but of the terrible damage done to the human soul. Hurston puts the rest of Dicey's monologue (which I have quoted here only in part) into verse:

> I often curse the day that I was born.
> I build some lovely dreams at night
> Then see them killed in broad daylight
> And all my tender feelings laughed to scorn.
> I sure cant help the way I'm made
> And so, when all is done and said
> I'm just a victim of relentless fate.
> I got big love, that I cant give.
> I got life, still, I cant live.
> Just all damned up and turning into hate.
> I hate the women through and through
> Who get the things that I want, too.
> I wouldn't like 'em, even if I could!
> And women thwarted, just like me
> Thought up those fires in Hell, in GLEE.
> So come on, Evil! Be thou now my good!
> (*Takes her knife out of her pocket, feels the edge*
> *carefully, and begins to whet it grimly on the edge*
> *of the stove. Stops and tests it on her thumb, and*
> *whets again vigorously*)
> Get your razor cause I got mine
> Feel mistreated and I don't mind dying—— (III, i)

The question of how dark-skinned women like Dicey handled the issue of color was rarely explored in literary works of the era and never in scholarly ones. Color was a subject whispered about over kitchen tables and joked about or fought over in jook joints. The poor often spoke of this matter openly, but the elite hid their feelings about color while teaching their children, through subtle and not so subtle cues, which colors were desirable and which ones were not. Men of the black upper class took their sexual pleasure from dark-skinned women in brothels or back rooms while marrying lighter-skinned ones. Of course, if a darker woman came from "good people," she could transcend the color code through her class affiliation. Color was important to the black elite but class was more so. Then as now, among African Americans in general, north and south, color prejudice was an open secret.

Color was such an important and powerful force that not even hoodoo could always trump it. When Dicey and Nunkie are plotting their hoodoo revenge on Big Sweet and the others, Nunkie expresses doubts about whether the black magic will work on the light-skinned, straight-haired Big Sweet: "Voodoo don't take on some folks. Specially if they got this straight hair. It aint got nothing to tangle in. Us better dash in and do what we got to do, and light out" (III, i).

When the quarters boss decides to banish Big Sweet for killing too many men, the community is finally given a unifying cause that transcends their color and other divisions. Hurston depicts in this scene the endurance of community ties even in transient frontier communities like the camp, and their need and respect for the leadership of their own.

LONNIE: But you cant go!

BOX CAR: Nobody here want you to go no where, do us?

(*A general protest against her leaving*)

BIG SWEET: But the man done told me that the Company would rather have my room than my company. (Sighs heavily)

(*General desperation and gloom*)

LEAFY (*Almost in tears*): I'm the cause of it all.

BIG SWEET: In a way you is, and then again you aint. All you done was come here and put words to the feeling I already had. I ever wanted things to be nicer than what they was. Ever since I been with Lonnie, more especial.

STEW BEEF: But My Honey and Leafy is gitting married. We going to cut Big Jim by the acre when that come off. Big woods picnic and everything. Who is going to general our business for us if you aint here?

BUNCH: Nobody can't do nothing right on this place without you. What will us do if you aint here?

BIG SWEET: Do like the folks over the creek, I reckon. Do without.

LONNIE (*Pulls out a chair and drops down in it backwards and sits in gloomy thought*): I reckon you all know that if Big Sweet has to go, I don't aim to be here another minute. Taint nothing bad about Big Sweet at all. She got plenty good friending in her if you let her be.

BUNCH: We all knows that.

LONNIE (*Face hard*): Something is wrong round here if somebody like Big Sweet can be told to go. Somebody trying to drive her.

SOP-THE-BOTTOM: And it sure aint clean.

MY HONEY (*Most dejected*): Everything was going along so good. Big Sweet doing the best she could to make everything nice——

LONNIE: What is we? We aint nothing. We didn't come from nothing. We aint got nothing but the little wages we make. Look like then us ought not to be bothered with trouble. That's for big, rich folks, that got their many pleasures. Why we got to have troubles too?

(*A harmonic, vocal chant whispers under him and gets a little stronger as he talks*)

Where is these quarters nohow? Wild woods all around and the mill in the middle. (*As if sudden discovery*) We'se in a cage! Like a mule-lot down in a swamp.

BIG SWEET (*Takes a lead in chant and puts softly sung words to chant and the others follow her*):

(*Humming*) I got my hands in my Jesus hands. (*With Chorus*) I got my hands in my Jesus hands.

LONNIE: Panthers in the swamp. Moccasins round your feet all day. Standing in water.

(*Chant grows intense but not loud. More fervent.*)

Trees falling on men and killing 'em. Saw liable to cut you in two. Sundown, nothing but these quarters to come to and keep on like that until you die!

(*Chant dominates the pause with repetition of Jesus, Jesus, Jesus, Jesus, Jesus*)

Its something wrong. But what can we do? You don't know and I don't know, so I cant tell you. Just moving around in the cage.

(*The chant comes out in the open, while Lonnie sits and looks off into space*)

BIG SWEET: Sawdust, even if it do shine sometime.

LONNIE (*Smiling and chuckling*): What make me talk so disencouraged like? Old John de Conquer would know how to beat the thing. (*Chuckles broadly*) Shucks High John could git out of things don't care how bad they was and finish it off with a laugh.

… (*Chorus of "and we're going when you go"*)

STEW BEEF: One day after you leave, there won't be a soul in the quarters.

LONNIE: And I'm going to be the one to tell the Big Boss my ownself. The man can wait till he git the straight of things, or else we all can go. If the Boss ruther for him listen to lies than for us to do his work, then we still can go. (*A great cheer goes up.*)

Tomorrow will tell the tale. (*The prayer-chant for victory takes up again.*)

LONNIE (*Getting to his feet dramatically*): Something ought to be like we want it. We aint got nothing. We aint never had nothing. Our folks aint left us nothing. (*Chant dominates for a moment*)

Six feet of earth when the deal goes down. And we aint never asked for much. (II, iii)

Black intellectuals in the 1920s professed to cherish black folk culture, but most believed that the kind of people Hurston depicted in her plays, fiction, and folklore were a primitive embarrassment to the ethic of Negro uplift. Hurston, in representing their culture faithfully, depicted both the sordid and the uplifting, the desperation and the hope. Lonnie expressed a sense of hope in the future that can only be seen as a great achievement given the conditions in which these people lived and worked. What Steinbeck did for poor white Okies, Hurston did for these southern blacks.

Scholars have paid more attention to Janie and *Their Eyes Were Watching God* than to Big Sweet and *Polk County*, and I would suggest that this is because Janie is identifiably proto-middle class and fits more easily into the feminist framework. In addition, novels and poetry are generally considered superior to folk art such as *Polk County*, and, apart from *Mules and Men*, very little attention has been paid to Hurston's folklore. The folk are interesting as a category, but not as real people.[40]

Hurston nevertheless documented the lives, art, and human dignity of these common folk. She saw it as her mission as a writer to preserve and document their culture, and we owe her an enormous debt of gratitude for that. But she was not self-sustaining in the creation of her art; she had to depend on the support of others, as did her peers in the Harlem Renaissance. It is to their predicament that we now turn.

6

Patronage

Anatomy of a Predicament

> Why was it that the Renaissance of literature, which
> began among Negroes ten years ago, has never taken
> real and lasting root? It was because it was a trans-
> planted and exotic thing. It was literature written for the
> benefit of white people and at the behest of white read-
> ers, and started out privately from the white point of
> view. It never had a real Negro constituency, and it did
> not grow out of the inmost heart and frank experiences
> of Negroes; on such an artificial basis no real literature
> can grow.
>
> —W.E.B. DuBois

W.E.B. DuBois posed the classic question about the
Harlem Renaissance, why it did not last. He also gave the classic
answer, that the black American literary artist could not be supported by the black American public of the time. The audience
for the art and its producers were both different from and socially
distant from each other. African American artists thus depended
on white patrons rather than on "a real Negro constituency."
Those patrons guided the art according to their own ideals, and
they dropped it when their interests changed. White support for
the work also distorted it, by cultivating it "privately from the
white point of view." DuBois summed up the predicament of the
Harlem Renaissance: White patronage enabled African American
artists to produce their work, but it guaranteed that they could

not produce that work authentically. Without patrons, there would have been no Harlem Renaissance; with patrons, there was a short-lived uptown Renaissance, brilliant and beautiful, but more or less on order from New York's white downtown.

One approach to studying the Harlem Renaissance is to examine the network of white people whose wealth and interest brought talented black people into print. But there is more to the story than that. If we want to know why African American literary art was so dependent on the largesse of a privileged group of northern white women and men, we must go beyond the elites, both black and white, who created the Harlem Renaissance.

Zora Neale Hurston wrote about patronage with the same style and sharpness she brought to her writing on the life of ordinary black people of the South in the 1920s and 1930s. Her writing on the Harlem Renaissance and its white patrons is the exceptionally rich firsthand view of an articulate insider, and it situates the institution of patronage both within and beyond the Harlem Renaissance.

BEFORE THE READER has finished the first chapter of *Dust Tracks on a Road*, he or she has been reminded that white patronage of black American writers and artists did not begin with the Harlem Renaissance, for Hurston reveals its unsettling kinship with a feature of slavery's successor regimes in the South. Indeed, if what we mean by "patronage" is a settled relationship of unequal exchange between a patron and a client, or protégé, in which the very acts of giving and receiving mark the participants as superior and subordinate, then this kinship extends to slavery itself, and to another word that shares the same Latin root as "patronage": paternalism. The ideology of mutual obligation and protection softened for the masters the contradictions of a system that brutally exploited slaves but that at the same time (the theory of the slave as an *instrumentum vocale* notwithstanding) could not reduce slaves to the same category as nonhuman property. It promoted the image of slaves as "acquiescent human beings" carrying out their obligations and receiving benefits.[1]

Inherent in this system was the notion of a protector, a kind of patron who cleared the way for deserving subordinates. Patron-client relationships were as southern as grits and blackstrap molasses, but also as American as apple pie. Hurston named the post-slavery variation on this theme "the pet Negro system."

In her autobiography Hurston presents herself as one of the handpicked few to whom the benefits of patronage flowed. As she tells the story, a white patron assisted with her very entrance into the world. When her mother went into labor, there were no adults around to help her, and she was too weak to help herself. The baby Zora "rushed out," and her mother lay there, exhausted, unable to cut the umbilical cord. To the rescue came "a white man of many acres," a friend of the family who, knowing of John Hurston's absence, had driven over to leave meat and vegetables. Arriving shortly after her birth, it was he who cut Zora's cord and prepared her for her sojourn in this world.[2]

This good southern white man was to become Hurston's first mentor. "[T]here is nothing to make you like other human beings so much as doing things for them," Hurston wrote in *Dust Tracks on a Road* (30). Human connections can sometimes thrive in spite racial divisions, and this appeared to be the case between Zora and the white man.

> [T]he man who grannied me was back next day to see how I was coming along... He remarked that I was a God damned fine baby, fat and plenty of lung-power. As time went on, he came infrequently, but somehow kept a pinch of interest in my welfare. It seemed that I was spying noble, growing like a gourd vine, and yelling bass like a gator. He was the kind of a man that had no use for puny things. (30–31)

Zora became the little person he affectionately called "Snidlits." As she grew, he instructed her on the proper behavior for a colored child. "'Snidlits, don't be a nigger,' he would say to me over and over. 'Niggers lie and lie! Any time you catch folks lying, they are skeered of something. Lying is dodging. People with guts don't lie. They tell the truth and then if they have to, they fight it out. You lay yourself open by lying... Truth is a letter from courage'" (31).

Hurston commented on this condescending advice, "I knew without being told that he was not talking about my race when he advised me not to be a nigger. He was talking about class rather than race. He frequently gave money to Negro schools" (43).

The white benefactor's contributions to Negro schools was not unusual; other white patrons supported black churches. For twenty years, Zora's father served as pastor of Zion Hope Baptist Church in Sanford, a church that owed its existence to General Henry Shelton Sanford. Lewis Lawrence and Josiah Eaton backed the founding of Eatonville. Some white philanthropists were southerners; others were northern carpetbaggers in an era when social Darwinism inspired white people to fund Negro schools and other worthy causes.[3]

In the early pages of *Dust Tracks*, we also meet northern whites who saw young Zora as someone deserving of help. For example, two Minnesota ladies who came to the South looking for a worthy cause to support visited Zora's school and noticed her quick mind. According to Hurston, northern whites visited Negro schools so often that these schools were practically a tourist attraction (46–47). When Mrs. Johnson and Miss Hurd noticed her, they invited her to their hotel room, where they treated her to stuffed dates and preserved ginger. They asked her to read for them, showed her Japanese dolls and other fancy items, took her picture, and gave her a present of shiny pennies, a hymnbook, an English novel, and a book of fairy tales (51–52). Whatever else might be said of that encounter, there is no doubt that Zora's brilliant individuality had begun to blossom, and the two northern ladies were astute enough to recognize and nourish it. Stuffed dates were exotic fruits for an Eatonville child, and being the recipient of such delicacies set Zora apart from her peers. The two ladies later sent her a box of good used clothes, along with more books, which were to become Hurston's real treasure.

Hurston's account of these interactions with white do-gooders leaves readers free to form their own judgments. Her own comment on one of the Minnesotans is subtle and dryly humorous: "She patted my head, and was lucky enough not to get sandspurs in her hand" (50). Readers familiar with the southern superstition that rubbing a Negro's head brought luck would see more in the woman's gesture than readers who were not. Hurston's irony, her skillful balancing of individuality and racial stereotype, is subtle enough in such anecdotes to allow readers to draw their own conclusions.

Hurston seems to offer these accounts with a straight face, but surely she wrote with tongue in cheek, knowing that they would deeply irritate some members of the black elite, who could not get around the awkward fact that they too depended on white benefactors. But whereas Hurston's stories were told, as it were, in the raw, and made no attempt to save face, her peers typically labored to salvage their pride before leaving the subject of their dependence on white patronage.

If their criticisms and real discomfiture were seldom made explicit, their need to create a mirage of equality was never far from view. Hurston's comment about the ladies' risking sandspurs in their gentle hands evoked the possibility that a snake lay amid the gifts of fruit but neither hammered the point home nor let it overwhelm the real compliment that the gift of fruit conveyed.

Hurston does not leave the subject of patronage before mentioning a would-be black patron. Several years after her mother's death, she was still without a permanent home. Her brother, Bob, who had graduated from medical school, wrote offering her continued schooling and a permanent home, but when Zora arrived, it turned out that he was offering her a job—as a maid for her sister-in-law (128).[4] It was in the context of this disappointment that Hurston began her gradual migration north, making many detours along the way. She first joined a theater company that was traveling along the East Coast. Settling after a time in Washington, D.C., and Baltimore, she took time to complete the B.A. she desperately wanted.

Along the way she met other patrons, colored ones but patrons just the same. They offered a helping hand and escorted her into the world of privilege enjoyed by the black elite. As a small-town black woman from the South, she felt no less different from them than from the white elite she encountered in New York.

Her talent and intellectual brilliance brought her notice, and in due course she traveled to New York City to accept a prize for one of her short stories. In 1925 she began to meet northern philanthropists, among them Fannie Hurst, the successful writer. Hurst, who had southern roots and was only five years Hurston's senior, became Hurston's first white friend. She hired her as a secretary (although she could not type), introduced her to members of New York's literary elite, and (once Hurston had ceased working as Hurst's secretary) invited her to be a regular companion and occasionally tided her over with cash. In that last relationship, Hurston as companion, they flashed in and out of fancy places, sometimes with the bubbling complicity of girlfriends, as we learned in the vignette with which I began the prologue.

But this was not to last. Even though virtually all of the ingredients for a friendship were present, there was no leavening agent to give rise to the thing. Despite all the two women had in common and the sense of fun they apparently shared, they were often burdened by the inevitable awkwardness of going places and doing things to which Hurst had access by right and Hurston only by subterfuge. When all was said and done, they had no real common ground, a fact that emerges poignantly from the telling detail of how they addressed each other in their letters. Hurston's letters begin "Dear Miss Hurst" or "Dear Fannie Hurst," while Hurst addressed her as "Dear Zora."[5] This appears to be a clear reminder that the patron-client relationship, with its defining norms of intimate inequality, was not easily breached, though it is possible that the discrepancy in these salutations was Hurston's doing, her way of subtly reminding Hurst of the differential in power and privilege that Hurst may have tried to erase.

Making a living at art was no more feasible in the 1920s than it is today. In 1921 Henry Seidel Canby, professor of American literature at Yale University and editor of the *Saturday Review of Literature*, suggested a patronage system not unlike the medieval feudal version. Without patrons, he wrote, "much admirable literature would have remained unwritten or unpublished, since the time provided no sure sustenance for most men of letters." Canby assumed that patronage could be modernized and shorn of the trappings of feudalism. "Art is the greediest of mistresses. Time she does not nibble at; she devours," he wrote. Artists would not have the time and freedom to create if they had to worry about providing for themselves and their families.

But Canby also argued that just as the artist needed the patron, the patron needed the artist. Contrary to popular views, he suggested, the patron did not simply seek praise but "desired, as we all desire, a more interesting life. They [artists] made life more interesting for him by giving it beauty, vividness, and significance—the service of literature. Education is one way of making life more valuable; literature is another."[6]

Canby's vision had been realized in Harlem by the mid-1920s, but it was complicated by the racial environment of the time. Although patronage is by definition based on inequality regardless of historical particularities, white patronage of black artists in America compounded inequality with incivility. The patronage of the Harlem Renaissance took shape in a society in which slavery, abolished scarcely two generations earlier, had been justified for three centuries in terms of alleged racial difference. And the parent of that patronage was paternalism, the thinnest of masks for brutal exploitation.

In her autobiography Hurston writes about several women whose patronage helped her succeed as an artist and anthropologist. In addition to Fannie Hurst, notable among them were Annie Nathan Meyer, who secured a scholarship for Hurston and helped her adjust to Barnard, and Charlotte Osgood Mason, a wealthy Fifth Avenue heiress and Hurston's primary patron. These women introduced Hurston to the white liberal intelligentsia. Within a short time, this "big-boned, good-boned young woman, handsome and light yellow," with a "dialect as deep as the deep south," as Fannie Hurst described Hurston, was moving among the wealthy, cultured members of the white world.[7] From these people Hurston learned how to use different "forks, who entered a room first, sat down first, and who offered to shake hands" (167). She attended their weddings, lunched with "the girls," and embraced the advantage this access gave her. "I had the same feeling at Barnard that I did at Howard, only more so. I felt that I was highly privileged and determined to make the most of it. I did not resolve to be a grind, however, to show the white folks that I had brains. I took for granted that they knew that. Else, why was I at Barnard?" (169). But things were never that simple for Hurston, and she adds ironically, "I have no lurid tales to tell of race discrimination at Barnard... The Social Register crowd at Barnard soon took me up, and I became Barnard's sacred black cow" (169).

Hurston, like all black students at overwhelmingly white universities in that era, undoubtedly experienced racial discrimination at Barnard. In addition to her race, Hurston's country persona and dialect provoked many reactions, including mocking laughter. Even upper-class white students who enjoyed her company felt the need to make her over, to improve her manners, dress, and the like. Hurston appears to have relished this attention. Why does her depiction of this environment contrast so sharply with the rest of America in 1925? Was her retrospective account shaped by the perspective of 1942, when she wrote *Dust Tracks*, after a successful career as scholar and artist? Does it reflect a desire to appeal to both a black and a white audience, one that included her own patrons? Is Hurston's point of view at odds with the realities of racist society, or does she merely present the "race problem" in genteel form? The answers to these questions lie in the particular contours of white patronage during the Harlem Renaissance and in Hurston's own relationships with her white patrons. Fannie Hurst and Charlotte Osgood Mason are the most complicated and intriguing of these.

Fannie Hurst

Hurston's account of her friendship with Fannie Hurst comes in a chapter of *Dust Tracks* that her publisher failed to print during her lifetime. In it, Hurston marvels at the way Hurst displayed "Princess Zora" at social engagements. "Behold her phoning to a swanky hotel for reservations for herself and the Princess Zora *and* parading me in there all dressed up as an Asiatic person of royal blood and keeping a straight face while the attendants goggled at me and bowed low!" (310).

Hurston was fascinated by the pleasure Hurst took in her new playmate and by the public excitement generated by Hurst's display of her exotic friend:

> Like a little girl, I have known her in the joy of a compelling new gown to take me to tea in some exclusive spot in New York. I would be the press agent for her dress, for everybody was sure to look if *they* saw somebody like me strolling into the Astor or the Biltmore. She can wear clothes, and who knows it is her? She has been my good friend for many years, and I love her. (310)

Hurst's background bore some similarities to Hurston's, at least superficially. She was born in 1889 into a middle-class German-Jewish family in St. Louis. She was a precocious, intelligent, lonely child given to writing stories and reading voraciously. Her parents saved enough money to put her in a private school, but she dropped out, feeling too different from the others. Early on, Hurst was pained by her second-class status as a Jew. When her mother took her to an interview at an upper-class school, inquiries about their background brought her religious difference from the girls of the St. Louis aristocracy to the surface, which upset her mother and created considerable discomfort for young Fannie. She was accepted to the school but her stay there was brief. Her mother dressed her as she thought the St. Louis upper crust expected, in fancy clothes, but Fannie stood out like a clown among the more modestly dressed gentile students. She begged to be allowed to attend public school among the "masses."[8] She finished high school and attended Washington University in St. Louis. When she began publishing her stories in *Reedy's Magazine*, she took the first step into gentile society.[9]

After moving to New York, Hurst won success quickly as a popular fiction writer. In this heady world of artists and celebrities, she remade herself by successfully hiding her real identity from reporters.[10] Clippings in her papers give contradictory information regarding her background; she is sometimes said to come from a middle-class midwestern family and at others portrayed as a rags-to-riches child of rural America. As Cynthia Ann Brandimerte puts it, "It was said of Hurst that after she was discovered her history 'seemed to have ended.'"[11] Perhaps her best-known work, *Imitation of Life*, twice made into a movie, depicts the drama of the very light-skinned child of a black woman who decides to pass as white, a plot line that suggests Hurst's view that turning her back on her past was the best route to success in the mainstream white world.

Hurst's veiled identity may have been partially expressed in her exploration of the "other" America. In full view of the press, she wandered through ethnic neighborhoods to see how the poor lived. Her wanderings sparked the imagination of reporters, who praised her for courageously living and working in the different ghettoes of New York.[12] Like other liberals of her day, Hurst became involved in civil rights causes and took a particular interest in "all those overburdened and poor women," as well as in women domestics and menial laborers.[13] Hurst was a dedicated Negrotarian, to borrow Hurston's term, who worked actively for organizations like the National Health Circle for Colored People. The letters she wrote on behalf of this organization, to raise money for its programs, sometimes exposed deeply rooted racial stereotypes. One letter aimed at a white audience referred to black people as a "languid-minded" people. Another, which sought help for a child, remarked that he was a "nice little chap with a happy friendly nature which is the heritage of a happy friendly race." And when Hurst wrote in support of her friend's application for a grant from the Guggenheim Foundation, the "languid-minded" people became Zora herself, whom she described as brilliant but unable to carry out the proposed research without supervision.[14]

Hurst was fascinated by the underprivileged but, needless to say, was never really a part of them herself. Hurston, though well educated and privileged in comparison to most African Americans, belonged to the other America. Hurst's friendship with her was, in some respects at least, an extension of her excursions into the netherworld of "colored" peoples, just as *Imitation of Life* was a literary excursion into that world. Hurst could never shed her privileged position in terms of both race and class, nor did she want to. Hurst enriched Hurston's life, and she introduced her to important celebrities in the world of letters. She was also willing to fight hard to ensure that her protégé's works came to light. When Hurston sold *Jonah's Gourd Vine* to J. P. Lippincott, Hurst agreed to write the preface and pestered Lippincott to treat Zora with special care. She even urged Jonathan Cape, her British publisher, to buy the rights to Hurston's book.[15]

But Hurst set Zora apart from her usual circle of friends, and though Zora was indeed a friend, she was never treated as a peer. Hurst often had Hurston to her apartment for personal dinners, but not to large cocktail parties and dinners. Although only five years separated Hurst and Hurston in age, Hurston was always the child in relation to Hurst. As Brooke Kroeger notes, "They always related to each other as if a generation separated them, in the manner of adored teacher and beloved student, older protector and brilliant younger protégé."[16] Still more telling is the different way they were treated in the world of letters. Even after Hurston's success as a writer put her on par with Hurst, her finances never reflected that professional equality. The advances Hurston received from her publisher were a tenth of what Hurst could command.[17] Even as a well-known author of novels, plays, short stories, and journalistic pieces, Zora Neale Hurston never became Fannie Hurst's peer. Hurst remained always a patron and sometimes a friend.

Their relationship demonstrates their similarity as women as well the chasm that lay between them as a result of race and class. Hurst lived inside the racist ideology of her day and therefore was as ambivalent about Hurston as she was about her own identity as a Jew. That ambivalence emerged in her writing as well as in her personal relationship with Hurston.

Hurston was not so enamored of the glittering world of New York high society that she accepted white patronage uncritically. In a letter to Constance Sheen she assured her friend and future sister-in-law that the attention had not swollen her head. "They are often insincere," she wrote of the white liberals she knew, "their show of friendship mere patronage." Zora also understood that the attention was temporary, that her novelty would soon wear off. "I know it won't last always, so I am playing with my toy while I may," she wrote to Sheen.[18] Fifteen years later Hurston would look back on this period with bitterness and criticize herself for having accepted the "cheap coin of patronage."[19] But before she could reach that conclusion she would enter into another patronage relationship of profound significance, one that simultaneously promoted and limited her work.

Charlotte Osgood Mason, "Godmother"

Charlotte Osgood Mason was born Charlotte Louise Van der Veer Quick on 18 May 1854, the daughter of Peter Quick of Princeton, New Jersey.[20] Little is known about Charlotte until her marriage at age thirty-two to Rufus Osgood Mason.[21] Her husband, who appears in the *National Encyclopedia of American Biography*, was born in 1830 in Sullivan, New Hampshire, a descendant of Hugh Mason, who had settled in America in 1634. After studying for the ministry he turned to medicine, gaining recognition as a physician and surgeon and following his passionate interest in psychology and psychic phenomena. His biography suggests that he was interested in the study of hypnotism and built on the pioneering work of Elliotson, Esdaile, and Braid in England and of Bertrand in France.[22] Charlotte Osgood Mason found comfort and wealth in this world, becoming a cultivated member of New York's upper crust and entering into patronage arrangements with artists to whom she was a "godmother."

Hurston was probably introduced to Mason by Alain Locke, one of Mason's "godchildren." A psychic bond quickly developed between the two women, according to Hurston, and Mason became enraptured with "the Negro farthest down." The primitive was her obsession and she had already pursued her interest in Native Americans and their art, which she loved for its "purity." She required that her charges be heavily dependent on her, so when Hurston signed a contract with Mason in 1927, Mason demanded complete control over all her research.[23]

Mason had an awe-inspiring presence that impressed and intimidated those around her. "Godmother" liked to hold court from a throne-like chair while the godchildren occupied low stools at her feet. Part of this ritual called for lush cascades of flattery and self-deprecation from her Negroes. Whatever was in Mason's heart, and this plainly included racist presumptions and paternalistic condescension, it also included a sincere interest in black culture and an avid collector's zeal. As Hurston wrote in her autobiography, "There she was sitting up there at the table over capon, caviar and gleaming silver, eager to hear every word on every phase life on a sawmill 'job.' I must tell the tales, sing the songs, do the dances, and report the raucous sayings and doings of the Negro farthest down. She is altogether in sympathy with them, because she says truthfully they are utterly sincere in living" (177).

Mason, unlike many white patrons, seemed to appreciate African Americans just as they were, without any of the pretensions of "uplift," which naturally endeared her to Hurston. Yet this intellectual common ground was also the means of Mason's power over Hurston. Hurston's letters to "Godmother" express a dependency that contrasts starkly with Hurston's fierce claim to independence. A woman who could not be humbled by second place,[24] Hurston apparently stood in awe of this white matriarch and paid mystical tribute to her: "Flowers to you—the true conceptual mother—not just a biological accident. To you—the true immaculate conception where everything is conceived in beauty and every child is covered in truth."[25] Having no money of her own, Hurston was indeed dependent on Mason for virtually everything but her brains and talent. Given that Hurston's odes to her godmother are so out of character, it is hard not to suspect that the two women invented a sort of game of patronage in which Hurston's tributes were deliberately sycophantic—the more formal, ritualized, and extravagant, the better. A poetic tribute to Mason that Hurston wrote in 1931 echoes the letter quoted above and seems to suggest such a possibility:

> Out of the essence of my Godmother
> Out the True one
> Out the Wise one I am made to be
> From her breath I am born
> Yes, as the world is made new by the breath of Spring
> And is strengthened by the winds of Summer
> The Sea is stirred by its passion
> Thus, I have taken form from the breath of your mouth
> From the vapor of your soul I am made to be
> By the warmth of your love I am made to stand erect
> You are the Spring and Summer of my existence.
> You, who permits me to call you Godmother.[26]

These servile words cannot be understood in isolation. Written in 1931, they must be understood from the vantage point of 1927, the year the two signed a contract and two years before the onset of the Depression. That contract was an exercise in control and established the power relationship that shaped their interactions from then on. As Mary Helen Washington has argued, Hurston's need for money is very important in understanding her relations with Mason. In 1927 Hurston was on the threshold of a career as a folklorist and badly needed funding, which Mason provided. The contract allowed Zora $200 per month, a car, and a camera for a year. Hurston was employed as an agent *for* Mrs. Mason. She was, according to the contract, to collect the folklore that Mason was "unable [to collect] because of the pressure of other matters to undertake the collecting of this information in person." The tightly drawn contract gave Mason exclusive rights over all that Hurston collected, binding her "faithfully to perform the task" and "to return and lay before" Mason "all of said information, data, transcripts of music, etc which she shall have obtained."[27] As Hemenway observes, "Mrs. Mason was going to preserve proprietary rights over the results of Hurston's labor. Having made an investment of capital, she wanted an exclusive, unique product in return." Hurston's folklore collections would be exclusively the property of her patron—not because Mrs. Mason wanted to steal the material, but because she felt certain that Zora Neale Hurston could not be trusted to know best what to with it.[28] She was to be, in effect, Mason's research assistant, rather than a scholar in her own right, an indignity not lost on Hurston.

This contract shaped the relationship between Mason and Hurston for the next five years. Mason thought it gave her absolute control over Hurston's creative output. Yet the contract does not explicitly say that Hurston could not publish her own work, only that she could not publish material she collected for Mason. Within a year of signing, Hurston learned how much control this document gave Mason and how arrogant and acerbic Mason could be. Hurston's first taste of Mason's wrath came in 1928, when Mason solicited her criticism of a new collection called *Negro Workaday Songs* by Howard Odum and Guy Johnson, two well-known white collectors. Hurston thought poorly of the work, to put it mildly. She wrote to Alain Locke that after reading the book she no longer feared that someone might scoop her own folklore collection. "They have done the book just about like Nicholas Murray Butler, president of Columbia University, would do the black-bottom." The book missed "the point in many places" and much of the material had been collected off phonograph records, a contaminated source in Hurston's view.[29] She sent Mason a short critique saying that "white people could not be trusted to collect the lore of others, and that the Indians were right."[30] Mason was livid, and Hurston had to explain quickly that she did not include her in that category, that she was only using Mason's own words. Hurston described Mason's anger in her autobiography: "Her tongue was a knout, cutting off your pretenses, and bleeding your vanity like a rusty nail" (177). Evidently the two women's common ground was shaky at best.

Meanwhile, the power relations between them came more and more to the fore. With relations barely smoothed over after this offense, Hurston stumbled again. She had submitted an essay entitled "How It Feels to Be Colored Me" to the *World Tomorrow* in the fall of 1927. The article was intended to defray the costs of the long-defunct magazine *Fire!!* that Hurston, Hughes, and Wallace Thurman had published before meeting Mason. Mason was incensed, believing that the contract gave her the right to control

Hurston's publications and that Hurston could not publish even her own creative work without Mason's approval. If Hurston could make her own money by writing independently, where did that leave Mason's control? Hurston objected that Mason did not understand that she did not have any money, but Mason may have understood that very well. Rather than risk losing her funding by challenging Mason, Hurston solicited Locke's help in convincing Mason that she had made no money for herself from the essay, and that all the proceeds had gone to pay the debts incurred by *Fire!!* [31] Hurston soon realized that Mason's continued financial support carried a high price. In another incident, Mason dismissed Hurston's desire for a Negro theater, which Hurston had discussed with Hughes, as a "hazy dream" that must be abandoned "until the gods decree that they shall materialize."[32] Apparently Mason was the god who would issue the decree.

Toward the end of their relationship, Hurston was reduced to begging for money for simple necessities. In 1932 she wrote: "I really need a pair of shoes. You remember that we discussed the matter in the fall and agreed that I should own only one pair at a time. I bought a pair in mid-December and they have held up until now. My big toe is about to burst out of my right shoe and so I must do something about it."[33] She was required to itemize and account for every dime she spent, including carfare and medicine; even a box of Kotex is listed.

In light of all this, it is most surprising to read Hurston's affectionate descriptions of her "godmother," written ten years later in *Dust Tracks*, when she was free of the relationship. Hurston herself seems to explain away this apparent discrepancy by alluding to a psychic bond between the two women: "the thing that delighted her [Mason] was the fact that I was her only Godchild who could read her thoughts at a distance." The telepathy was mutual; Hurston was convinced that Mason could read her mind even from far away: "a letter would find me in Alabama, or Florida, or in the Bahama Islands and lay me by the heels for what I was *thinking*. 'You have broken the law,' it would accuse sternly. 'You are dissipating your powers in things that have no real meaning,' and go on to lacerate me. 'Keep silent. Does a child in the womb speak?'" (176).

Hurston recounts humiliating episodes in Mason's sanctuary with a strange mixture of affection and oppression.

> Sometimes, I would feel like a rabbit at a dog convention. She would invite me to dinner at her apartment, 399 Park Avenue, and then she, Cornelia Chapin, and Miss Chapin's sister, Mrs. Katherine Garrison Biddle, would all hem me up and give me what for. When they had given me a proper straightening, and they felt that I saw the light, all the sternness would vanish, and I would be wrapped in love. A present of money from Godmother, a coat from Miss Chapin, a dress from Mrs. Biddle. We had a great deal to talk about because Cornelia Chapin was a sculptor, Katherine Biddle, a poet, and Godmother, an earnest patron of the arts. (176–77)

Such episodes have the character of an abusive parental relationship—browbeat the child into submission, convince her of her unworthiness, and then shower her with love for acquiescing submissively. Hurston was not unaware of this, and she also knew that a great deal of performance was required, which she clearly had decided was worth the effort. One must also consider the historical tensions surrounding the question of identity for black people in this era, tensions shaped and mediated by the psychic push toward racial wholeness for black people and the pull toward the American mainstream, the price of which was the integrity of one's racial identity.[34]

The genteel expressions of racism characteristic of upper-class white liberals like Fannie Hurst and Charlotte Osgood Mason went along with their power to usher Hurston into their world as well as to control her movements in that world. This power flowed from both their class and their race; one kind of privilege without the other would not have produced the same result. Despite her aspirations, Hurston was bound by the class realities of her time. She needed the material support of these women in order to survive as a writer. Yet she had to find a way to maintain a measure of psychic independence within the confines of her material dependence. The effort to do so often led to behavior that appeared to concede the very independence she sought to maintain. It also earned her the opprobrium of her peers, who called her an opportunist and a "perfect darkie." Her patrons—Hurst and Mason—always maintained their racial and class privilege relative to Zora. She was never even remotely imagined to be their equal. Her struggle for psychic independence in this context may partially explain why she abhorred the "race problem," for in a sense she carried the full weight of that problem within herself. Notice the desperation of her statement, "I would feel like a rabbit at a dog convention." Even so, she did not feel compelled to make that problem the center of her art.

It goes without saying, then, that Hurston's dealings with her patrons were complex. It is not the case that Hurston was merely manipulating Mason for gain or that Mason was dense enough to be manipulated in that way. Both were very bright, strong-willed women. White patrons were a diverse lot, and their motives for helping black artists varied. Most genuinely wanted to assist young artists. All, at some level, were interested in the work they supported. But their thinking about this kind of patronage was inevitably shaped by constructions of race in a racist society. Mason's position as a white matriarch depended as much on Hurston's identity as a poor southern black girl as it did on Mason's wealth. Having a well-kept, well-dressed, trusted "darkie" was one of the symbolic trappings of class and of an older paternalist social order.

It may well be that Hurston not only tired of her role as flatterer in Osgood's court but also found the intellectual demands of producing art in that setting intolerable. What we know for certain is that her most productive creative period came after her relations with Mason ended. Perhaps the idea that creative work could not have been accomplished without the support of patrons needs to be reconsidered.

In one important instance, Hurston managed to prevail on Mason to go along with an initiative of her own that had nothing to do with Mason's agenda. On 10 January 1932, Hurston staged a Negro folk concert at the John Golden Theater in New York. The concert was to be a dramatization of a workday on a Florida railroad camp that ended with a dramatic fire dance. Hurston turned to Hall Johnson, who initially agreed to help, and she imported Bahamian dancers for the fire dance sequence, but Johnson backed out. Locke, who had opposed the venture, had to be won over, because Hurston needed Locke to persuade Mason to withdraw her own opposition to the depiction of northern Negroes ridiculing West Indians as "monkey chasers." Despite all those obstacles, Hurston prevailed, and the production opened to a full house. Locke escorted Mason to the concert, which was a tremendous success. Hurston had proved her point that real Negro music, heard for the first time in this northern outpost, would win over a white audience. To the sound of thunderous applause, Hurston was pushed out onto the stage, an honor Mason had planned for Locke alone. Hurston explained to her audience why she had done the concert: "That music without motion was unnatural with Negroes, and what I had tried to do was to present Negro singing in a natural way—with action."[35] Though Mason was peeved because Locke had not been showcased, she finally bestowed her approval on Hurston in this case.

One Good White Publisher, J. P. Lippincott

Hurston intended to include the concert episode in *Dust Tracks*, but her publisher, J. P. Lippincott, censored it. I include Lippincott as one of Hurston's patrons, for his relationship with Hurston is similar to the others and certainly shares their intimate deployment of unequal power. Publishers exercised an unusual level of control over their clients, above all their black clients. They determined what writers were exposed and which of their works would see the light of day. Lippincott decided that Hurston should publish an autobiography, and he commissioned it and gave her deadlines. She was reluctant to write such a book but did as she was told. Having asked her to write, Lippincott freely censored what she wrote, according to his own standards, editing out some of her more controversial views. Although these excised sections have been restored by Hurston's biographer, Robert Hemenway, and Cheryl Wall in an appendix to the Library of America reissue of *Dust Tracks*, few scholars have bothered to examine the restored sections. But these censored portions of Hurston's autobiography provide a glimpse of how patronage affected the content of an artist's work, revealing, in the process, the content of what DuBois called the "white point of view."

Hurston set forth an analysis of racism in a chapter of the autobiography that Lippincott refused to print. A Lippincott editor, writing across the bottom of a page of the original manuscript, advised "eliminating international opinions as irrelevant to autobiography."[36] Hurston heeded the advice. Carefully examined alongside an essay published in *Negro Digest* in 1954, this deleted chapter reveals Hurston's race consciousness and her understanding of the complexity of American racism, while at the same time it informs us indirectly about the American reading public.

Hurston uncovers the capitalist motivations of the West and their impact on the third world:

> As I see it, the doctrines of democracy deal with the aspirations of men's souls, but the application deals with things. One hand in somebody else's pocket and one on your gun, and you are highly civilized. Your heart is where it belongs—in your pocketbook. Put it in your bosom and you are backward. Desire enough for your own use only, and you are a heathen. Civilized people have things to show their neighbors.[37]

Hurston's understanding of capitalism also informs her comments on Hitler and World War II. The passage bears repeating at length, as it was censored completely and virtually forgotten:

> All around me, bitter tears are being shed over the fate of Holland, Belgium, France, and England. I must confess to being a little dry around the eyes. I hear people shaking with shudders at the thought of Germany collecting taxes in Holland. I have not heard a word against Holland collecting one twelfth of poor people's wages in Asia. Hitler's crime is that he is actually doing a thing like that to his own kind. That is international cannibalism and should

be stopped. He is a bandit. That is true, but that is not what is held against him. He is muscling in on well-established mobs. Give him credit. He cased some joints away off in Africa and Asia, but the big mobs already had them paying protection money and warned him to stay away. The only way to climb out of the punk class is to high-jack the load and that is just what he is doing.[38]

Such writing was risky business in the middle of the war, a fact that cannot have escaped Hurston, who deliberately chose to include it in her autobiography. She followed it with a bitingly ironic criticism of President Roosevelt, who she said should consider applying his Four Freedoms at home—except of course that doing so would not cover the United States in glory the way his crusade abroad did.[39] Hurston's caving in to the publisher's requests is not surprising; what is surprising is that she included these passages in the first place. Perhaps Hurston was testing Lippincott. The "perfect darkie" of the past, though still alive and well in the passages on Charlotte Osgood Mason, was beginning to act up, to reveal a quite imperfect and awkward black political mind.

Hurston continued her attack on the hypocrisy of American democracy by parodying FDR's description of America as the arsenal of democracy. Deliberately mispronouncing arsenal as "arse and all" and "ass and all," Hurston leveled a broadside at U.S. support for colonialism in a piece published in *Negro Digest*: "Our weapons, money, and the blood of millions of our men have been used to carry the English, French and Dutch and lead them back on the millions of unwilling Asiatics. The Ass-and-all-he-has been very useful."[40] With penetrating insight Hurston commented on the Vietnamese conflict that would ultimately divide the United States after her death:

The Indo-Chinese are fighting the French now in Indo-China to keep the freedom that they have enjoyed for five or six years now. The Indonesians are trying to stay free from the Dutch, and the Burmese and Malayans from the British.

But American soldiers and sailors are fighting along with the French, Dutch and English to rivet these chains back on their former slaves. How can we so admire the fire and determination of Toussaint Louverture to resist the orders of Napoleon to "Rip the

gold braids off those Haitian slaves and put them back to work"
after four years of freedom, and be indifferent to these Asiatics for
the same feelings under the same circumstances?[41]

Most of Hurston's critics, who relied solely on the published version of *Dust Tracks* and did not question its reliability, concluded
that Hurston had no race consciousness. Yet when the censored
passages are restored, we hear a different voice, one that is all too
aware of racial oppression and victimization and has plenty to say
about it—and that most acerbically. In fact Hurston's statements
on the hypocrisy of the West, including such larger-than-life
heroes as FDR, are downright radical. Of the defenders of Western democracy, she wrote:

> Have we not noted that not one word has been uttered about the
> freedom of the Africans? On the contrary, there have been mut-
> terings in undertones about being fair and giving different nations
> sources of raw materials there? The Ass-and-All Democracy has
> shouldered the load of subjugating the dark world completely.[42]

If we relied only on Lippincott's censored version of Hurston's
autobiography, we might conclude that Hurston saved her radi-
calism for black audiences alone. In fact, however, she offered
them first to him and his predominantly white readership. The
Negro Digest was courageously willing to print what mainstream
white publications would not in the mid-1940s. By then, Hurston
seemed sufficiently disillusioned and cynical to make no bones
about her radical views. As it is unlikely that such views suddenly
materialized in the 1940s, they were probably longer-standing
beliefs that Hurston repressed in her seeming complacency with
her white patrons.

I have suggested that Hurston took the advice of her publishers and acquiesced in their censorship of her work. But it may be
more likely that Hurston bristled under this censorship and had
no choice but to consent to it if her work was to be published, a
reading of the matter that is suggested by a close look at the original manuscript, with the excised passages and the editorial mar-
ginalia. As Claudine Raynaud has noted, because the published

text is ambiguous, even when the deleted chapters are restored, "the first draft might be precisely the place where self-construction is less embroiled in tactics of delusion."[43] The omitted sections of *Dust Tracks* clarify the "complexity of Hurston's resistance to the white publishing world, and the ways in which she eventually complied."[44]

Hurston was well aware of the control exercised by her publisher/patron. Invoking the paternalistic structure she had known intimately all her life, she even referred to Lippincott as "the *Colonel*." The comments Hurston's editor scribbled across her manuscript suggest more than the usual editorial intrusion. Hurston's interpretation of world events was being contested, and the interaction between writer and censor was anything but equal.

HURSTON SAID in her autobiography that she was thoroughly sick of the "race problem." "My interest lies in what makes a man or woman do such-and-so, regardless of his color." This sentiment was partially a response to pressure from white publishers, patrons, and audiences, as well as from the "Niggerati," to restrict African American artists to writing only about the race problem. But it is also a response to the conception of blackness solely as a problem. Neither Hurston nor her contemporaries thought of black people as other than a problem, whether to be solved or transcended. The problem of race in its more overt manifestations was difficult for Zora to address if she was also to maintain her links with the world of her patrons. Yet her writings reveal that the race problem was always a factor, sometimes concealed by class, in her thinking. Being wealthy and white meant having the privilege to invite a "poor, colored primitive" into the world of wealth and patronage, at least for a temporary stay. Hurston's reaction to this experience embodied all the contradictions characteristic of a patron-client or master-slave relationship: the desire for acceptance by the master and belief in his sincerity; the need to cultivate a sense of freedom and independence in spite of dependency; and the nagging and painful recognition of one's difference. Within these conflicting responses, Zora had also to define and protect her own self. The struggle that her life and canon embody is the struggle of all black intellectuals of her time. How she resolved that struggle or coped with its contradictions is what set her apart from many of her contemporaries and what in part explains the hostility of her critics. Hurston was willing to do openly what others did only covertly.

Hurston's obsequious behavior toward her "godmother" and her other patrons was one way she coped with the humiliation of having to play the primitive for the master. If a thing had to be done, then it was well to take charge of the doing. I believe that such an attitude explains the extravagant praise with which Zora wrote to Charlotte.

A smoldering anger flares up at times, only to disappear again beneath the image that Hurston created so carefully. She appears to have lived with a dual pride in black culture and rejection of the northern white view of that culture. Their view of black culture was also, inevitably, their view of her. To affiliate herself with such people in pursuit of artistic freedom was to live with the daily experience of personal constraint and entrapment.

The predicament of black artists was that in exchange for one kind of freedom, they had to relinquish another. The freedom that black artists experienced through white patronage during the Harlem Renaissance belongs to the larger story of African Americans' passage from slavery to freedom. They had the freedom to do artistic work, but not to live their own lives with dignity.

Epilogue

THE TESTIMONIES recorded in Zora Neale Hurston's writing take us beyond traditional sources and help us understand a particular place and time. Traditional sources allow us to know the external world that I have described in Chapter 3; Hurston's work, both fiction and nonfiction, takes us beyond that world to the inner lives of the human beings that inhabited it.

It has often been said that history repeats itself. When Hurston's play *Mule Bone* was performed on Broadway in 1991, it met with the hostility of an audience unprepared for the "Negro farthest down." Viewers of *Mule Bone* disliked its brand of humor, felt uneasy about the predicaments its characters faced, and were embarrassed by the earthy language in which these characters spoke. They might as well have been George Schuyler's contemporaries, echoing Schuyler's prescriptions for the proper sentiments, appearance, and language through which the "best-foot-forward Negroes" could present their most respectable selves. It is surprising, in a way, how little things have changed. But it is the central premise of every historian's work that things do change, in spite of seeming likenesses between past and present.

In Zora Neale Hurston's day, the "Negro farthest down" was not considered a fit subject for literature. What has changed today is that this view, while it survives in some quarters, as the *Mule Bone* audience shows, is no longer at the core of a life-and-death political struggle against disenfranchisement, segregation, and violence.

Today black people in America enjoy a freedom that Hurston's contemporaries did not—the freedom to engage with her characters without embarrassment.

Subjects once considered unsuitable for literature were once also thought unsuitable for historical inquiry—not because racism continued to brand them as subhuman but because prevailing historical practices mistrusted the kind of sources that bring such subjects into view. This study has tested the ability of Zora Neale Hurston's work to take historical understanding beyond the limits of conventionally accepted source material.

One of the most stubborn difficulties in all historical inquiry is that of placing our own assumptions and biases to the side in order to see historical subjects in their own terms. The risk of anachronism is always present, despite our best efforts to ward it off. It is difficult for even the best of historians to avoid at all times the pitfall of viewing the past as prologue, of interpreting the past in light of the present. I have tried to avoid this pitfall by allowing Zora Neale Hurston and her characters to speak for themselves, in the hope that we can thereby catch a glimpse, at least, of what was to them the present.

Notes

Prologue

1. Zora Neale Hurston, *Dust Tracks on a Road* (1942; repr., Urbana: University of Illinois Press, 1984), 242.

2. Fannie Hurst was born into a middle-class Jewish family in Missouri. She apparently reconstructed her identity as gentile when she entered the world of letters in New York. Her ability to pass puts her surprise at Hurston in context. See Cynthia Ann Brandimerte, "Fannie Hurst and Her Fiction: Prescriptions for American Working Women" (Ph.D. diss., University of Texas at Austin, 1980), 84; Zora Neale Hurston, "Fannie Hurst: By Her Ex-Amanuensis," *Saturday Review* (9 Oct. 1937).

3. Fannie Hurst, "Zora Neale Hurston: A Personality Sketch," *Yale University Library Gazette* 35 (July 1960): 20.

4. Brandimerte, "Fannie Hurst and Her Fiction," 84.

5. Quoted in Hurst, "Zora Neale Hurston," 20.

Introduction

1. Toni Morrison, "Rootedness: The Ancestor as Foundation," in *Black Women Writers, 1950–1980,* ed. Mari Evans (New York: Anchor/Doubleday Books, 1983), 342.

2. Wallace Thurman's satirical novel *The Blacker the Berry* (1929) certainly exposed the absurdity of color prejudice in black communities. Jessie Fauset's novels *Plum Bun* (1929) and *Chinaberry Tree* (1931) explored the phenomenon of passing and its conflicts for women. Before Fauset, Charles W. Chestnutt and Nella Larsen had examined these questions. Only Wallace Thurman specifically addressed color prejudice from the perspective of a "dark-skinned" woman and the impact of color prejudice

within the race on dark-skinned persons, particularly women that elite men and women tried to keep a secret that was supposed to remain within the racial family.

3. For a discussion of the male writers who were unwilling to discuss these divisions, see David Levering Lewis, *When Harlem Was in Vogue* (New York: Knopf, 1981); Steven Watson, *The Harlem Renaissance: Hub of African-American Culture, 1920–1930* (New York: Pantheon, 1995); and Nathan I. Huggins, *Harlem Renaissance* (New York: Oxford University Press, 1971).

4. See W.E.B. DuBois, "Review of Claude McKay's *Home to Harlem*," in *Book Reviews by W.E.B. DuBois*, comp. and ed. Herbert Aptheker (Millwood, N.Y.: KTO Press, 1977), 113. DuBois described McKay's *Home to Harlem* as a book that "for the most part nauseates me, and after the dirtier parts of its filth I feel distinctly like taking a bath." The subject of McKay's novel was the Harlem poor.

5. Morrison, "Rootedness," 342. Emphasis added.

6. Zora Neale Hurston, "Race Cannot Become Great until It Recognizes Its Talent" *Washington Tribune* (29 Dec. 1934), 3.

7. Deborah G. Plant, *"Every Tub Must Sit on Its Own Bottom": The Philosophy and Politics of Zora Neale Hurston* (Urbana: University of Illinois Press, 1995), 5.

8. Plant argues throughout her study that Hurston adhered to a philosophy of individualism. This philosophy, according to Plant, informs much of Hurston's work. My argument is different. Hurston was an individualist but she did not accept individualism as her path. Plant conflates two terms—individualist and individualism—which I believe carry distinct meanings. Plant's own evidence supports my position. She states that Hurston engaged in community organizing, even organizing and developing a "block mothers plan" which resembled current day-care programs. In Hurston's words, "It's the old idea, trite but true, of helping people to help themselves that will be the only salvation of the Negro in this country" (ibid., 196–97). See also Robert Hemenway, *Zora Neale Hurston: A Literary Biography* (Urbana: University of Illinois Press, 1977), 303.

9. Hurston, *Dust Tracks on a Road*, 13–14.

10. Anna Lillios, "Excursions into Zora Neale Hurston's Eatonville," in *Zora in Florida*, ed. Steve Glassman and Kathryn Lee Seidel (Orlando: University of Central Florida Press, 1991), 13–27. The interviews in this article are of Eatonville residents, several of whom discuss the pattern of domestic work for the women in Eatonville during Hurston's lifetime.

11. Frank M. Otey, *Eatonville, Florida: A Brief History* (Winter Park, Fla.: Four-G Pub., 1989), 17.

12. See both Hurston's autobiography, *Dust Tracks on a Road*, and Hemenway's biography.

13. Hemenway, *Zora Neale Hurston*, 16. She was around thirteen when her mother died, not nine, as she reported in her autobiography.

14. Ibid., 17.

15. David M. Katzman, *Seven Days a Week: Women and Domestic Service in Industrializing America* (New York: Oxford University Press, 1978), 184.

16. Hemenway, *Zora Neale Hurston*, 16.

17. Ibid., 17.

18. For a discussion of Boasian anthropology, see George W. Stocking Jr., ed., *A Franz Boas Reader: The Shaping of American Anthropology, 1883–1911* (Chicago: University of Chicago Press, 1974), particularly the essays entitled "The Basic Assumptions of Boasian Anthropology," "Human Faculty as Determined by Race," and "The Boas Plan for American Anthropology." See also the important collection of essays in Marc Manganaro, ed., *Modernist Anthropology: From Fieldwork to Text* (Princeton: Princeton University Press, 1990), particularly Marc Manganaro, "Textual Play, Power, and Cultural Critique: An Orientation to Modernist Anthropology"; Arnold Krupat, "Irony in Anthropology: The Work of Franz Boas"; Deborah Gordon, "The Politics of Ethnographic Authority: Race and Writing in the Ethnography of Margaret Mead and Zora Neale Hurston"; and Francesco Loriggio, "Anthropology, Literary Theory, and the Traditions of Modernism."

Chapter One

1. Hurston, *Dust Tracks on a Road*, 3.

2. Ibid., 13–14.

3. There is a disjunction between the "real present" of others and our own "real past." Our past is the present of Hurston's subjects. It is the world that they can take for granted in a way that we cannot. The producers of these documents lived in a past in which certain events had not yet occurred. We return to our past from a present in which those events have occurred and we take our knowledge of those events with us and seek a past that makes sense of our present. We must take care neither to romanticize our past nor to exaggerate its horrors. We cannot take our past for granted, for it is a place that is both foreign and familiar. See David Lowenthal, *The Past Is a Foreign Country* (Cambridge: Cambridge University Press, 1985), esp. 185–262; Roy Rosenzweig and David Thelen, *The Presence of the Past: Popular Uses of History in American Life* (New York: Columbia University Press, 1998).

4. The literature on the Great Migration is extensive and includes studies of back-and-forth movement between North and South, the gendered aspects of migration, and the class dynamics of the migration and the formation of northern communities. See Nell Irvin Painter, *Exodusters: Black Migration to Kansas after Reconstruction* (New York: Knopf, 1976; repr., Lawrence: University of Kansas Press, 1986); James R. Grossman, *Land of Hope: Chicago, Black Southerners and the Great Migration* (Chicago: University of Chicago Press, 1989); Peter Gottlieb, *Making Their Own Way: Southern Blacks' Migration to Pittsburgh, 1916–30* (Urbana: University of Illinois Press, 1997); Carole Marks, *Farewell—We're Good and Gone: The Great Black Migration* (Bloomington: Indiana University Press, 1989); Joe William Trotter Jr., ed., *The Great Migration in Historical Perspective: New Dimensions of Race, Class, and Gender* (Bloomington: Indiana University Press, 1991); Joe William Trotter Jr., *Black Milwaukee: The Making of an Industrial Proletariat, 1914–45* (Urbana: University of Illinois Press, 1985); Earl Lewis, *In Their Own Interests: Race, Class, and Power in Twentieth-Century Norfolk, Virginia* (Berkeley and Los Angeles: University of California Press, 1991); Joe William Trotter Jr., *Coal, Class, and Color: Blacks in Southern West Virginia, 1915–1932* (Urbana: University of Illinois Press, 1990); Richard W. Thomas, *Life for Us Is What We Make It: Building Black Community in Detroit, 1915–1945* (Bloomington: Indiana University Press, 1992); Elizabeth Clark-Lewis, *Living In, Living Out: African American Domestics in Washington, D.C., 1910–1940* (Washington, D.C.: Smithsonian Institution Press, 1994); Cindy Hahamovitch, *The Fruits of Their Labor: Atlantic Coast Farmworkers and the Making of Migrant Poverty, 1870–1945* (Chapel Hill: University of North Carolina Press, 1997); Joe William Trotter Jr., "African Americans in the City: The Industrial Era, 1900–1950," *Journal of Labor History* 21 (May 1995): 438–57; Kimberley L. Phillips, *Alabama North: African American Migrants, Community, and Working-Class Activism in Cleveland, 1915–45* (Urbana: University of Illinois Press, 1999); Virginia W. Wolcott, *Remaking Respectability: African American Women in Interwar Detroit* (Chapel Hill: University of North Carolina Press, 2001).

5. Susan Porter Benson, e-mail to the author, 23 July 2003. I thank Susan Porter Benson for pushing me to clarify this point further.

6. Jane Tompkins, *Sensational Designs: The Cultural Work of American Fiction, 1790–1860* (New York: Oxford University Press, 1985), xi.

7. Quoted in Michael Woods, "Lost Paradise," *New York Review of Books* (3 March 1994): 45.

8. In *Mules and Men*, Jim Allen chides young Arthur Hopkins for being so impertinent as to call him by his first name: "Don't you be callin' me by my first name. Ah'm old enough for you' grand paw! You respect my

gray hairs. Ah don't play wid chillun. Play wid a puppy and he'll lick yo' mouf." Zora Neale Hurston, *Mules and Men* (1935; repr., Bloomington: Indiana University Press, 1963), 104.

9. Earl Lewis, "Discourse on Class Formation: The Inner World of Black School Teachers," paper presented at the annual meeting of the Organization of American Historians, Louisville, Kentucky, 11–14 April 1991. I am grateful to Dr. Lewis for sharing his research with me.

10. The intelligentsia does not mislead or lie deliberately but by documenting the Jim Crow South, and black resistance, selectively. Thus they offer only partial truths. Between Jim Crow and black resistance lies a world of living that at times is barely visible. Hurston, too, offers partial truths, but in documenting the inner worlds of her subjects she does not neglect the oppression and degradation of racism entirely in order to put a human face on black people.

11. Lawrence W. Levine, *Black Culture and Black Consciousness: Afro-American Folk Thought from Slavery to Freedom* (New York: Oxford University Press, 1977), ix.

12. Ibid.

13. C. Vann Woodward discussed this problem long ago when he examined the problem of slave narratives. He noted that these narratives were often "[f]ull of paradox and evasions, contrasts and contradictions, lies and exaggerations, pure truth and complete fabrications" and yet were "the daily bread on which historians feed." Historians cannot therefore discard these sources as worthless, according to Woodward, "unless they are prepared to be consistent and discard most of the other sources they habitually use. Not while they still use newspapers as sources, or, for that matter, diaries and letters and politicians' speeches and the *Congressional Record* and all those neatly printed official documents and the solemnly sworn testimony of high officials." See Woodward, "History from Slave Sources," *American Historical Review* 79 (April 1974): 470–81. The critical use of sources that Woodward called for applies to Hurston's work. Hurston was not an academic historian and should not be held to such a standard. Her objectives were not the same as historians'.

14. Quoted in Lawrence W. Levine, "Imagining Freedom," *Labor History* 39 (May 1998): 179–80. Levine's essay is part of a symposium on Tera Hunter's *To 'Joy My Freedom: Southern Black Women's Lives and Labors after the Civil War* (Cambridge: Harvard University Press, 1997).

15. These debates have been settled for many scholars long ago but for many others they remain as contentious as ever. See Gertude Himmelfarb, *The New History and the Old: Critical Essays and Reapprisals, Revised Edition* (Cambridge: Belknap Press of Harvard University Press, 2004); see also the AHR Forum in the *American Historical Review* 97,

no.5 (Dec. 1992) especially T. J. Jackson Lears, "Making Fun of Popular Culture," pp. 1417–1426, and Lawrence W. Levine, "Levine Responds," pp. 1427–1430.

16. Oral traditions and memory were viewed as suspect in the writing of African history in the same manner that imaginative sources are viewed as suspect. Even after unwritten sources were acknowledged as valuable, most scholars accepted them as a supplement to written sources, which were considered the really pertinent material. Unwritten sources must be accepted as meriting inspection and yielding information on their own. I argue that written sources may in fact not tell us much about the consciousness of a people who did not leave their own written records. In these instances, imaginative works and oral traditions may be all we have. See Daniel F. McCall, *Africa in Time Perspective: A Discussion of Historical Reconstruction from Unwritten Sources* (Boston: Boston University Press, 1964), 13. See also Jan Vansina, *Oral Tradition as History* (Madison: University of Wisconsin Press, 1985). For discussions on memory and history, see Paul Connerton, *How Societies Remember* (Cambridge: Cambridge University Press, 1989), 1–40; Natalie Zemon Davis and Randolph Starn, "Introduction," *Representations* 26 (spring 1989): 1–6; Pierre Nora, "Between Memory and History: Les Lieux de Mémoire," *Representations* 26 (spring 1989): 7–24; Steven Knapp, "Collective Memory and the Actual Past," *Representations* 26 (spring 1989): 123–49; Susan A. Crane, "Writing the Individual Back into Collective Memory," *American Historical Review* 102 (Dec. 1997): 1372–85; Rosenzweig and Thelen, *Presence of the Past*.

17. Vansina, *Oral Tradition as History*, 27.

18. There is disagreement on this point. David Henige restricts the definition further by suggesting that oral traditions should be commonly or universally known in a given culture. Joseph Miller restricts traditions only to conscious historical statements. See Vansina, *Oral Tradition as History*, 28; David Henige, *Oral Historiography* (London: Longman, 1982), 2; Joseph C. Miller, "Listening for the African Past," in *The African Past Speaks: Essays on Oral Tradition and History*, ed. Joseph C. Miller (Folkestone, Eng.: Dawson, 1980), 2.

19. Heinrich Schliemann, *Troja: Results of the Latest Researches and Discoveries on the Site of Homer's Troy* (1882; repr., New York: Harper & Bros., 1967).

20. Tompkins, *Sensational Designs*, xi.

21. My thinking on this subject has been influenced by the Annales School of French historians, who were interested in the reconstruction of mentalités. Though the Annales School was interested in long-term social trends rather than individual thinkers, their approach is neverthe-

less significant for this study. See Traian Stoianovich, *French Historical Method: The Annales Paradigm* (Ithaca: Cornell University Press, 1976); Peter Burke, *The French Historical Revolution: The Annales School, 1929–1989* (Stanford: Stanford University Press, 1990). Of particular interest is the five-volume series, *A History of Private Life*, ed. Philippe Aries and Georges Duby (Cambridge: Belknap Press of Harvard University Press, 1987–91).

22. James M. McPherson et al., eds., *Blacks in America* (Garden City, N.Y.: Doubleday, 1971), 26–27.

23. Pierre Samuel Du Pont de Nemours, *The Autobiography of Dy Pont de Nemours*, trans. and with an introduction by Elizabeth Fox-Genovese (Wilmington, Del.: Scholarly Resources, 1984), 41.

24. Claude Levi-Strauss, *Structural Anthropology* (New York: Basic Books, 1963), 16–17.

25. Jean Comaroff and John Comaroff, *Ethnography and the Historical Imagination* (Boulder: Westview Press, 1992), 7–8; Talal Asad, "Two European Images of Non-European Rule," in *Anthropology and the Colonial Situation*, ed. Talal Asad (London: Ithaca Press, 1973), 103–18; Johannes Fabian, *Time and the Other: How Anthropology Makes Its Object* (New York: Columbia University Press, 1983); Edward Said, "Representing the Colonized: Anthropology's Interlocutors," *Critical Inquiry* 15 (winter 1989): 205–25.

26. See Evelyn Brooks Higginbotham, *Righteous Discontent: The Women's Movement in the Black Church* (Cambridge: Harvard University Press, 1993); Kevin K. Gaines, *Uplifting the Race: Black Leadership, Politics, and Culture in the Twentieth Century* (Chapel Hill: University of North Carolina Press, 1996); Jacqueline Anne Rouse, *Lugenia Burns Hope: Black Southern Reformer* (Athens: University of Georgia Press, 1989), esp. chap. 5; Lillian S. Williams, "And Still I Rise: Black Women and Reform, Buffalo, New York, 1900–1940," in *"We Specialize in the Wholly Impossible": A Reader in Black Women's History*, ed. Darlene Clark Hine, Wilma King, and Linda Reed (Brooklyn: Carlson Publishing, 1995), 521–42.

27. See Robert Darnton, *The Great Cat Massacre and Other Episodes in French Cultural History* (New York: Vintage Books, 1985), 6; see also Emmanuel Le Roy Ladurie, *Montaillou: The Promised Land of Error*, trans. Barbara Bray (New York: G. Braziller, 1978); Carlo Ginzburg, *The Cheese and the Worms: The Cosmos of a Sixteenth-Century Miller*, trans. John and Anne Tedeschi (Baltimore: Johns Hopkins University Press, 1980); Raphael Samuel, *Theatres of Memory* (London: Verso, 1994).

28. James Baldwin, "Many Thousands Gone," in *Notes of a Native Son* (Boston: Beacon Press, 1955), 34–35.

29. Riffaat Abou-al Haji, "How to Write the History of the Unlettered," paper in possession of author.

30. Robin D. G. Kelley, "'We Are Not What We Seem': Rethinking Black Working-Class Opposition in the Jim Crow South," *Journal of American History* 80 (June 1993): 76. See also Peter J. Rachleff, *Black Labor in the South: Richmond, Virginia, 1865–1890* (Philadelphia: Temple University Press, 1984), 109–15; Peter J. Rachleff, "Black, White, and Gray: Working-Class Activism in Richmond, Virginia, 1865–1890" (Ph.D. diss., University of Pittsburgh, 1981); Hunter, *To 'Joy My Freedom*; Elsa Barkley Brown, "Uncle Ned's Children: Negotiating Community and Freedom in Postemancipation Richmond" (Ph.D. diss., Kent State University, 1994); George Lipstiz, *A Life in the Struggle: Ivory Perry and the Culture of Opposition* (Philadelphia: Temple University Press, 1988); Michael K. Honey, *Southern Labor and Black Civil Rights: Organizing Memphis Workers* (Urbana: University of Illinois Press, 1993); Lewis, *In Their Own Interests; Trotter, Coal, Class, and Color*; Robin D. G. Kelley, *Hammer and Hoe: Alabama Communists during the Great Depression* (Chapel Hill: University of North Carolina Press, 1990).

31. Kelley, "'We Are Not What We Seem,'" 76.

32. Michel de Certeau, *The Practice of Everyday Life* (Berkeley and Los Angeles: University of California Press, 1984), 30.

33. Herbert Aptheker, *American Negro Slave Revolts* (New York: Columbia University Press, 1943).

Chapter Two

1. Eudora Welty, *Place in Fiction* (New York: House of Books, 1957).

2. Richard Wright, "Between Laughter and Tears," *New Masses* 25 (5 Oct. 1937): 25, cited in *Zora Neale Hurston: Critical Perspectives Past and Present*, ed. Henry Louis Gates and K. Anthony Appiah (New York: Amistad Press, 1993), 17.

3. See Jean Toomer, Cane (1923; repr., New York: Harper & Row, 1969); Sterling Brown, "Spirituals," in *The Book of Negro Folklore*, ed. Langston Hughes and Arna Bontemps (New York: Dodd, Mead, 1958), 279–89.

4. W.E.B. DuBois bluntly expressed the unease that many intellectuals felt in his review of Claude McKay's *Home to Harlem*, a novel that focused on the "unwashed migrants" from the South. The book "nauseated" DuBois and left him in need of a bath. The low comedy, sex, and violence that characterized the book reminded the angry DuBois of Carl Van Vechten's *Nigger Heaven*. He confided in a letter to Amy Spingarn that this kind of writing threatened to undo the hard work that educated black people were doing to achieve civil rights; there needed to be some control over the representation of black people. His own answer was

Dark Princess, a novel conceived, in the words of his biographer, as "a sort of black Comedié Humaine in the manner of Balzac," with "strong women and decisive... and sensitive, educated males." See David Levering Lewis, *W.E.B. DuBois: The Fight for Equality and the American Century, 1919–1963* (New York: Henry Holt, 2000), 214–15; W.E.B. DuBois, "Review of Claude McKay's *Home to Harlem*," *Crisis* (June 1928), in Aptheker, *Book Reviews of W.E.B. DuBois*, 113; DuBois to Amy Spingarn, 19 Jan. 1928, Joel and Amy Spingarn Collection, Schomburg Center for Research in Black Culture, New York Public Library. See also Kelley Miller, "Where Is the Negro's Heaven? Review of *Home to Harlem* by Claude McKay," *Opportunity* (Dec. 1928): 370–73.

5. Lewis, *When Harlem Was in Vogue*, 71.

6. Nathan Irvin Huggins, ed., *Voices of the Harlem Renaissance* (New York: Oxford University Press, 1976), 142.

7. As Arnold Rampersad writes, "it might be important to see the Harlem Renaissance not as the triumph of an aggressive racial confidence, but as a necessary mixture of confidence and insecurity out of which came the most important literature of the age... To turn from emphasizing racial confidence toward emphasizing racial confusion might be necessary, as I am arguing, but certainly it is also unpopular. The degree of unpopularity might be gauged from the tone of responses not long ago to Gerald Early in his position as editor of a collection of essays. The basis of this collection was responses by certain black writers today to the theory of inherent African-American double-consciousness enunciated by W.E.B. DuBois in his epochal book *The Souls of Black Folk* (1903). Apparently, few African-American artists among those approached by Professor Early would concede the idea that cultural ambivalence, along with a complex of related ambivalences, was or could be a necessary aspect of the African-American condition." Arnold Rampersad, "Racial Doubt and Racial Shame in the Harlem Renaissance," in *Temples for Tomorrow: Looking Back at the Harlem Renaissance*, ed. Genevi've Fabre and Michel Feith (Bloomington: Indiana University Press, 2001), 33.

8. Ibid., 32. See also Cornel West's sensitive but critical examination of DuBois's ambivalence toward the masses in "Black Strivings in a Twilight Civilization," in Cornel West, *The Cornel West Reader* (New York: Basic Civitas Books, 1999), 87–118.

9. Theodore Roosevelt, "Kidd's 'Social Evolution,'" *North American Review* 161 (July 1895): 109, quoted in Lee D. Baker, *From Savage to Negro: Anthropology and the Construction of Race, 1896–1964* (Berkeley and Los Angeles: University of California Press, 1998), 78.

10. Ibid., 90.

11. Quoted in Henry Louis Gates, *The Signifying Monkey: A Theory of Afro-American Literary Criticism* (New York: Oxford University Press, 1988), 173.

12. Ibid.

13. Ibid., 180.

14. Langston Hughes, "The Negro and the Racial Mountain," in *The Portable Harlem Renaissance Reader*, ed. David Levering Lewis (New York: Viking, 1994), 91–95. Hughes's statement first appeared in the Nation (16 June 1926).

15. W.E.B. DuBois, "Criteria for Negro Art," in *W.E.B. DuBois: A Reader*, ed. David Levering Lewis (New York: Henry Holt and Co., 1995), 514. Originally published in the *Crisis* (Oct. 1926).

16. See Lewis, *DuBois: The Fight for Equality*, 168, 175–77, 180.

17. George S. Schuyler, "The Negro-Art Hokum," in Lewis, *Portable Harlem Renaissance Reader*, 96–99. Originally published in the *Nation* (16 June 1926).

18. George S. Schuyler, "Instructions for Contributors," reprinted in Eugene Gordon, "Negro Fictionist in America," *Saturday Evening Quill* (April 1929): 20.

19. W.E.B. DuBois, *Darkwater: Voices from within the Veil* (1921; repr., Mineola, N.Y.: Dover Publications, 1999), 19.

20. *Outlook* 26 (15 Dec. 1920): 690.

21. "The Negro in America," *Times Literary Supplement* (London) (4 Nov. 1920): 13.

22. Richard Wright, "Blueprint for Negro Writing," in Lewis, *Portable Harlem Renaissance Reader*, 200. Originally published in the *New Challenge* 11 (1937).

23. Baldwin, "Many Thousands Gone," 34–35.

24. Ibid.

25. Richard Wright, "How 'Bigger' Was Born," Introduction to *Native Son* (New York: Harper & Row, 1940) viii, xi.

26. Zora Neale Hurston, "What White Publishers Won't Print," *Negro Digest* 8 (April 1950): 85–89, reprinted in *Zora Neale Hurston: Folklore, Memoirs, and Other Writings*, ed. Cheryl A. Wall (New York: Library of America, 1995), 954.

27. Ibid.

28. Richard Wright, *Twelve Million Black Voices: A Folk History of the Negro in the United States of America* (New York: Viking Press, 1941), 10.

29. Hurston, *Mules and Men*, 4.

30. For Wright, there were only two possibilities for blacks: to be a victim or a killer. "If you act at all," he wrote, "it is either to flee or kill; you are either a victim or a rebel." *Twelve Million Black Voices*, 57.

31. Sterling Brown, "From the Inside," *Nation* (16 April 1938): 448.

32. Zora Neale Hurston, "Stories of Conflict" (Review of *Uncle Tom's Children*), *Saturday Review* (2 April 1938): 32.

33. ZNH to William Stanley Hoole, Hurston Collection, University of Florida (hereafter HCUFLA), 7 March 1936.

34. The reception of *Mules and Men* was mixed and would characterize Hurston's reputation from then on. Some liked its purity and simplicity, while others spurned the unsophisticated portraits. See Hemenway, *Zora Neale Hurston*, 218–20.

35. Sterling Brown, review of *Mules and Men*, 25 Feb. 1936, James Weldon Johnson Collection, Beineke Library, Special Collections, Yale University. See also Hemenway, *Zora Neale Hurston*, 219.

36. Sterling Brown, Review of *Their Eyes Were Watching God, Nation* (16 Oct. 1937). Also published in Gates and Appiah, *Zora Neale Hurston*, 20–21. See also Brown's "A Negro Folk Expression," *Phylon* 21, no. 4 (1950): 318–27, an essay critical of Hurston's emphasis on black folk speech and expression.

37. Charles Scruggs, *Sweet Home: Invisible Cities in the Afro-American Novel* (Baltimore: Johns Hopkins University Press, 1993), 285.

38. Hazel Carby, "The Politics of Fiction, Anthropology, and the Folk: Zora Neale Hurston," in *New Essays on Their Eyes Were Watching God*, ed. Michael Awkward (Cambridge: Cambridge University Press, 1990), 77.

39. Ibid.

40. Farah Griffin offers a brilliant exception to the rule in *"Who Set You Flowin'?" The African American Migration Narrative* (New York: Oxford University Press, 1995).

Chapter Three

1. Maya Angelou, "Foreword," in Zora Neale Hurston, *Dust Tracks on a Road* (New York: Harper Perennial, 1991), x.

2. Hurston, *Dust Tracks* on a Road, 1. Hurston was actually born in 1891 in Notasulga, Alabama, according to census records. She always identified Eatonville as her birthplace, however, a curious fabrication that is addressed elsewhere in this study. For an excellent study of the economic and political world into which Hurston was born, see Theodore Rosengarten, *All God's Dangers: The Life of Nate Shaw* (New York: Knopf, 1974).

3. Quoted in Tony Martin, ed., *African Fundamentalism: A Literary and Cultural Anthology of Garvey's Harlem Renaissance* (Dover, Mass.: Majority Press, 1991), 196.

4. Hurston, *Dust Tracks on a Road*, 1.

5. Kristy Anderson, "The Tangled Southern Roots of Zora Neale Hurston," paper in author's possession, 6. Anderson argues that Hurston moved around the South before landing in Harlem: born in Alabama, her family moved to Eatonville; from there Hurston moved to Jacksonville and then to Nashville, Tennessee, before going north to Baltimore, Washington, and finally Harlem.

6. Zora Neale Hurston, "The Negro in Florida, 1528–1940," photocopy, Jacksonville University Library, Jacksonville, Florida. See also Zora Neale Hurston, "Communication," *Journal of Negro History* 12 (Oct. 1927): 664–67.

7. Hurston, *Dust Tracks on a Road*, 110.

8. "Muck" was the name for the sticky black soil in areas where agricultural products such as beans and celery were grown. If the soil got on the skin, it itched terribly and had to be washed off immediately, which was difficult for workers who often had no access to adequate bath facilities. I first heard the term "mucksteppers" during an interview with Rev. Jimmy Howard, the pastor of St. Lawrence A.M.E. Church, in the summer of 2002. He had been a muckstepper as a boy in Seminole County, in 1951.

9. Adam Gussow makes a distinction between what he calls disciplinary violence and intimate violence. Disciplinary violence is the violence committed by whites against blacks to maintain control of labor and racial boundaries; intimate violence took place within African American communities. For a more detailed discussion of these distinctions, see Adam Gussow, *Seems Like Murder Here: Southern Violence and the Blues Tradition* (Chicago: University of Chicago Press, 2002), chaps. 5 and 6.

10. Hurston, *Dust Tracks on a Road*, 78–80.

11. For a discussion of the changes that came to Florida and the South after the Civil War, see Jerrell H. Shofner, *Nor Is It Over Yet: Florida in the Era of Reconstruction, 1863–1877* (Gainesville: University Press of Florida, 1974), 108–58; and, by the same author, "Negro Laborers and the Forest Industries in Reconstruction Florida," *Journal of Forest History* (Oct. 1975): 180. For the South in general, see also Gavin Wright, *Old South, New South: Revolutions in the Southern Economy since the Civil War* (New York: Basic Books, 1986), 60–64; Roger L. Ransom and Richard Sutch, *One Kind of Freedom: The Economic Consequences of Emancipation* (New York: Cambridge University Press, 1977), 42–43; Dewey W. Grantham, *The South in Modern America: A Region at Odds* (New York: Harper-Collins, 1994), 24–30; C. Vann Woodward, *Origins of the New South, 1877–1913* (Baton Rouge: Louisiana State University Press, 1951), esp. 205–320; Pete Daniel, *The Shadow of Slavery: Peonage in the South, 1901–1985* (Urbana: University of Illinois Press, 1972); Julie Saville, *The Work of Reconstruc-*

tion: *From Slave to Wage Laborer in South Carolina, 1860–1870* (Cambridge, 1994); Rachleff, *Black Labor in the South;* Jacqueline Jones, *Labor of Love, Labor of Sorrow: Black Women, Work, and the Family, from Slavery to Freedom* (New York: Basic Books, 1985).

12. Michael David Tegeder, "Prisoners of the Pines: Debt Peonage in the Southern Turpentine Industry, 1900–1930" (Ph.D. diss., University of Florida, 1996), 34–35; see also Edward L. Ayers, *The Promise of the New South: Life after Reconstruction* (New York: Oxford University Press, 1992), 3–33, 55–80; Paul M. Gaston, *The New South Creed: A Study in Southern Mythmaking* (New York: Knopf, 1970). For another study of sawmill and turpentine workers, see William Powell Jones, "Cutting through Jim Crow: African American Lumber Workers in the Jim Crow South, 1919–1960" (Ph.D. diss., University of North Carolina, Chapel Hill, 2000).

13. Tegeder, "Prisoners of the Pines," 2–3.

14. Ibid. See Ayers, *Promise of the New South*, 132–59. Also see John W. Cell, *The Highest Stage of White Supremacy: The Origins of Segregation in South Africa and the American South* (Cambridge: Cambridge University Press, 1982); J. William Harris, "Etiquette, Lynching, and Racial Boundaries in Southern History: A Mississippi Example," *American Historical Review* 100 (April 1995): 387–410; George M. Frederickson, *The Arrogance of Race: Historical Perspectives on Slavery, Racism, and Social Inequality* (Middletown: Wesleyan University Press, 1988), 154–60.

15. Tegeder, 3. See Edward L. Ayers, *Vengeance and Justice: Crime and Punishment in the Nineteenth-Century American South* (New York: Oxford University Press, 1984); W. Fitzhugh Brundage, *Lynching in the New South: Georgia and Virginia, 1880–1930* (Urbana: University of Illinois Press, 1993); Stewart E. Tolnay and E. M. Beck, *A Festival of Violence: An Analysis of Southern Lynchings, 1882–1930* (Urbana: University of Illinois Press, 1995); Christopher Waldrep, *Night Riders: Defending Community in the Black Patch, 1890–1915* (Durham: Duke University Press, 1993).

16. Tegeder, 4. See Harold D. Woodman, "Class, Race, Politics, and the Modernization of the Postbellum South," *Journal of Southern History* 63 (Feb. 1997): 3–22.

17. Jerrell H. Shofner, "Forced Labor in the Florida Forests, 1880–1950," *Journal of Forest History* (Jan. 1981): 14. See also Shofner's "Negro Laborers and the Forest Industries in Deconstruction Florida," *Journal of Forest History* (Oct.1975): 180–91.

18. Tegeder, "Prisoners of the Pines," 4–7.

19. Ibid., 34–38, 72–76.

20. Ibid., 7, 35. A tree needed sixteen years of growth to yield a good supply of sap.

21. Stetson Kennedy described this process in a report on the turpentine industry at Cross City, Florida, a trip he made with Hurston. Stetson Kennedy Papers #4193, 2–4, Southern Historical Collection, Library of the University of North Carolina at Chapel Hill (hereafter Kennedy Papers).

22. Ibid., 3.

23. Tegeder, "Prisoners of the Pines," 35.

24. Kennedy Papers, 5.

25. Michael David Tegeder, drawing on the work of Harold Woodman, Roger Ransom, and Richard Sutch, notes that factorage houses declined after the war, as railroads displaced factors for cotton merchants and granted credit to local planters. This process did not work in the deep forests, where turpentine manufacturers had little collateral. See Tegeder, "Prisoners of the Pines," 7, 47–50. See also Harold D. Woodman, *King Cotton and His Retainers: Financing and Marketing the Cotton Crop of the South, 1800–1925* (Lexington: University Press of Kentucky, 1968), 269–94; and Harold D. Woodman, *New South–New Law: The Legal Foundations of Credit and Labor Relations in the Postbellum Agricultural South* (Baton Rouge: Louisiana State University Press, 1995); Ransom and Sutch, *One Kind of Freedom*, 108–15.

26. Tegeder, "Prisoners of the Pines," 48. See also A. Stewart Campbell, *The Naval Stores Industry*, rev. ed. (Gainesville: University Press of Florida, 1934), 25–27, 68–73; Douglas Fraser Martin Jr., "An Historical and Analytical Approach to the Current Problems of the American Gum Naval Stores Industry" (Ph.D. diss., University of North Carolina at Chapel Hill, 1942), 82–84, 87–99, 143–44.

27. Tegeder, "Prisoners of the Pines," 48–49.

28. Ibid., 7–12.

29. Jacqueline Jones, *Dispossessed: America's Underclass from the Civil War to the Present* (New York: Basic Books, 1992), 128. See also Frederich Arch Blackey, *The Florida Phosphate Industry: A History of the Development and Use of a Vital Mineral* (Cambridge: Harvard University Press, 1973), 36–60.

30. Jones, *Dispossessed*, 127–28.

31. N. Gordon Carper, "Slavery Revisited: Peonage in the South," *Phylon* 37, no. 1 (1976): 89.

32. Jones, *Dispossessed*, 128–29.

33. Ibid. See also Blackey, *Florida Phosphate Industry*, 61–75.

34. Carper, "Slavery Revisited," 91.

35. Ibid., 90.

36. Alex Lichtenstein, *Twice the Work of Free Labor: The Political Economy of Convict Labor in the New South* (New York: Verso, 1996). See also

Armstead Robinson, "'Plans Dat Comed from God': Institutional Building and the Emergence of Black Leadership in Reconstruction Memphis," in *Toward a New South? Studies in Post–Civil War Southern Communities*, ed. Orville Vernon Burton and Robert C. McMath Jr. (Westport, Conn.: Greenwood, 1982), 72–73. See also Armstead Robinson, "Beyond the Realm of Social Consensus: New Meanings of Reconstruction for American History," *Journal of American History* 68 (Sept. 1981): 276–97. Robinson draws on the work of E. P. Thompson and Herbert Gutman, who examined the lives of workers outside the workplace. See MARHO—The Radical Historians Organization, *Visions of History* (New York: Pantheon, 1983), 27–46, 186–216.

37. Jones, *Dispossessed*, 148–49.

38. Ibid. Mary Ellen Curtin's study, *Black Prisoners and Their World, Alabama, 1865–1900* (Charlottesville: University Press of Virginia, 2000), is one of the few that explores the lives of prisoners before, during, and after incarceration. She situates their lives within community and cultural institutions and puts faces on these prisoners from the inside.

39. Woodward, *Origins of the New South*, 215.

40. Curtin, *Black Prisoners and Their World*, 4. The best study to date of convict leasing in Florida is Noel Gordon Carper, "The Convict-Lease System in Florida, 1866–1923" (Ph.D. diss., Florida State University, 1964). See also Lichtenstein, *Twice the Work of Free Labor*, chap. 4; David M. Oshinsky, *Worse than Slavery: Parchman Farm and the Ordeal of Jim Crow Justice* (New York: Free Press, 1996); Matthew J. Mancini, *One Dies, Get Another: Convict Leasing in the American South, 1866–1928* (Columbia: University of South Carolina Press, 1996); Karin A. Shapiro, *A New South Rebellion: The Battle against Convict Labor in the Tennessee Coalfields, 1871–1896* (Chapel Hill: University of North Carolina Press, 1998); Robert Perkinson, "Between the Worst of the Past and the Worst of the Future: Reconsidering Convict Leasing in the South," *Radical History Review* 71 (spring 1998): 207–16. Though women prisoners rarely appear in histories of convict leasing, there were a few. See Anne M. Butler, *Gendered Justice in the American West: Women Prisoners in Men's Penitentiaries* (Urbana: University of Illinois Press, 1997); Nicole Hahn Rafter, *Partial Justice: Women in State Prisons* (Boston: Northeastern University Press, 1985).

41. See the sources listed in the previous note. See also Robert N. Lauriault, "From Can't to Can't: The North Florida Turpentine Camp, 1900–1950," *Florida Historical Quarterly* 67 (Jan. 1989): 310–28.

42. Shofner, "Forced Labor in the Florida Forests," 14. For a discussion of debt peonage, see Daniel, *Shadow of Slavery*, 36–40. See also Tegeder, "Prisoners of the Pines," 70–154.

43. Jerrell H. Shofner, "Postscript to the Martin Tabert Case: Peonage as Usual in the Florida Turpentine Camps," *Florida Historical Quarterly* 60 (Oct. 1981): 162.

44. James Weldon Johnson, secretary to the NAACP, wrote to the *New York World* to congratulate the paper for exposing the brutality in these camps. See James Weldon Johnson to Editor, *New York World*, Series C, Box 386, NAACP Papers, Library of Congress. See also clippings from *New York World* (15 March 1925) and *Pensacola Journal* (19 May 1925), both in C-386, NAACP Papers; Jacksonville *Florida Times-Union* (22, 24, 30 May, 2 June 1925; 29 May 1937); Tallahassee *Smith's Weekly* (29 May 1925); *New York Age* (30 May 1925); clipping from the *Nation* (21 Aug. 1937), in peonage files, Schomburg Center for Research in Black Culture, New York Public Library. The files of the Workers Defense League, located in the NAACP Papers, which worked on behalf of many of these workers, also contains much information on these cases.

45. Barbara Jeanne Fields, "The Nineteenth-Century American South: History and Theory," *Plantation Society in the Americas* 2 (April 1983): 19. See also Michael Taussig, *The Devil and Commodity Fetishism in South America* (Chapel Hill: University of North Carolina Press, 1989), 18–22.

46. Sandra M. Mohl, "Migrant Farmworkers in America: A Florida Case Study" (master's thesis, Florida Atlantic University, 1981), 3. See also Hahamovitch, *Fruits of Their Labor*, 113–38.

47. Ibid.

48. Hurston, *Their Eyes Were Watching God* (New York: J. B. Lippincott, 1937; repr., Urbana: University of Illinois Press, 1978), 196.

49. Most of the work on black towns has been in the form of articles or broadly conceived comparative studies such as Kenneth Hamilton, *Black Towns and Profit: Promotion and Development in the Trans-Appalachian West, 1877–1915* (Urbana: University of Illinois Press, 1991); Janet Sharp Hermann, *The Pursuit of a Dream* (New York: Vintage Books, 1983); Orville Vernon Burton, "The Rise and Fall of Afro-American Town Life: Town and Country in Reconstruction Edgefield, South Carolina," in Burton and McMath, *Toward a New South*, 152–92. Few towns have merited full monographs; for examples, see Juliet Walker, *Free Frank: A Black Pioneer on the Antebellum Frontier* (Lexington: University Press of Kentucky, 1983), and Sundiata Keita Cha-Jua, *America's First Black Town: Brooklyn, Illinois, 1830–1915* (Urbana: University of Illinois Press, 2000). Though Hurston thought Eatonville was the first all-black town incorporated in the United States, evidence suggests that Brooklyn, Illinois, was incorporated before the Civil War, while Fort Mose had legal sanction in eighteenth-century Spanish Florida. See Jane L. Landers, "Gracia Real de Santa Teresa de Mose: A Free Black Town in Spanish Colonial Florida,"

American Historical Review 95 (Feb. 1990): 9–30, and Jane L. Landers, *Black Society in Spanish Florida* (Urbana: University of Illinois Press, 1999).

50. Cha-Jua, *America's First Black Town*, 22n1. See also Harold M. Rose, "The All-Negro Town: Its Evolution and Function," *Geographical Review* 55 (July 1965): 362–81.

51. See Wilson Moses, *The Golden Age of Black Nationalism, 1850–1925* (New York: Oxford University Press, 1978). See also Wahneema Lubiano, "Black Nationalism and Black Common Sense: Policing Ourselves and Others," in *The House That Race Built: Black Americans, U.S. Terrain*, ed. Wahneema Lubiano (New York: Pantheon, 1997); John H. Bracey Jr., August Meier, and Elliot Rudwick, eds., *Black Nationalism in America* (Indianapolis: Bobbs-Merrill, 1970); Wahneema Lubiano, "Standing in for the State: Black Nationalism and 'Writing' the Black Subject," in *Is It Nation Time? Contemporary Essays on Black Power and Black Nationalism*, ed. Eddie S. Glaude Jr (Chicago: University of Chicago Press, 2001).

52. More research on maroons in North America is needed to fully understand the full range of organized black communities. Research from the Caribbean and Latin America suggests the possibility of other forms of political organization. The literature on maroons is extensive, but among the best works on the subject are Herbert Aptheker, "Maroons within the Present Limits of the United States," *Journal of Negro History* 24 (April 1939): 167–84; Hugo Prosper Leaming, *Hidden Americans: Maroons of Virginia and the Carolinas* (New York: Garland Press, 1995); Stuart B. Schwartz, *Slaves, Peasants, and Rebels: Reconsidering Brazilian Slavery* (Urbana: University of Illinois Press, 1992), esp. chap. 4.

53. See Leaming, *Hidden Americans*.

54. Cha-Jua, *America's First Black Town*.

55. Hamilton, *Black Towns and Profit*, 22, 4n2, quoted in Cha-Jua, *America's First Black Town*, 220.

56. Hiram Tong, "The Pioneers of Mound Bayou," *Century Illustrated Monthly Magazine* 79 (Jan. 1910): 390–98.

57. In his chapter on Mound Bayou, Kenneth Hamilton identified the railroad as the L., N., O., and T. Railroad. See *Black Towns and Profit*, 49.

58. Tong, "Pioneers of Mound Bayou."

59. Ibid., 394.

60. Ibid. This would seem to suggest that women in Boley enjoyed the level of political participation that women enjoyed after Emancipation but lost toward the end of the nineteenth century; see Elsa Barkley Brown, "Negotiating and Transforming the Public Sphere: African American Political Life in the Transition from Slavery to Freedom," *Public Culture* 7 (fall 1994), 124–25. Brown argues in this article on Richmond, Virginia, that African American women participated in consensus decision making in

the years immediately following the Civil War. This collective autonomy formed the basis on which black families were organized, communal institutions were constructed, schools were formed, and formal politics was conducted. Though women in the black community later lost this role, they fought to regain it and wove it into their emancipatory dreams.

61. Booker T. Washington, "Boley, A Negro Town in the West," *Outlook* 88 (4 Jan. 1908): 28–31; see also Washington's article, "A Town Owned by Negroes: Mound Bayou, Miss., An Example of Thrift and Self-Government," *World's Work* 14 (July 1907): 9125–34.

62. "Wonderful Mound Bayou," *Colored American Magazine* 12 (June 1907): 417.

63. Ibid., 418–20.

64. Caughey W. Roberts, "The Call to Boley, Okla.," *Colored American Magazine* 16 (June 1909): 355–61.

65. See Landers, "Gracia Real de Santa Teresa de Mose." See also Kathleen Deagan and Darcie MacMahon, *Fort Mose: Colonial America's Black Fortress of Freedom* (Gainesville: University Press of Florida, 1995).

66. Joseph A. Fry, *Henry S. Sanford: Diplomacy and Business in Nineteenth-Century America* (Reno: University of Nevada Press, 1982), 95.

67. Ibid., 104–7.

68. Altermese Smith Bentley, *Seminole County* (Charleston, S.C.: Arcadia Publishing, 2000), 9.

69. "From the early black settlements came those who laid the tracks, then fired the boilers that turned the wheels of trains on newly opened railroads. The first African-American families opened the first black-owned businesses in Central Florida and established family traditions that shaped their communities" (ibid.). The information on Georgetown and Goldsboro is taken from Bentley's *Seminole County* and her *Georgetown: The History of a Black Neighborhood*, and from Jim Robison and Mark Andrews, *Flashbacks: The Story of Central Florida's Past* (Orlando: Orange County Historical Society, 1995), 9–10.

70. Bentley, *Seminole County*, 21.

71. Sanford City Directory, 1913.

72. Zora Neale Hurston, "Goldsborough," in *Go Gator and Muddy the Water: Writings by Zora Neale Hurston and the Federal Writers' Project*, ed. Pamela Bordelon (New York: W. W. Norton, 199), 126–27.

73. Ibid., 127.

74. "Colored People of the United States Solve the Great Race Problem by Securing a Home in Eatonville, Florida, a Negro City Governed by Negroes," *Eatonville Speaker* (22 June 1889): 1.

75. U.S. Census Bureau, Eighth Census of the United States, Population, 1860; Olga Fenton Mitchell and Gloria Fenton Magbie, with Mar-

ion Civetta Elden, *Life and Times of Joseph E. Clark: From Slavery to Town Father* (Eatonville, Fla., 2003), 15.

76. U.S. Census Bureau, Seventh Census of the United States, Population, 1870, Chattanooga, Tennessee.

77. Ibid., 22.

78. For a discussion of the meaning of freedom for the newly freed slaves, see Eric Foner, *Reconstruction: America's Unfinished Revolution 1863–1877* (New York: Harper & Row, 1988), chap. 3.

79. *Eatonville Speaker* (22 June 1889): 1.

80. Scholarship on the promises and failures of Reconstruction is extensive and includes Foner, *Reconstruction*; Leon F. Litwack, *Been in the Storm So Long: The Aftermath of Slavery* (New York: Knopf, 1979); Rayford W. Logan, *Betrayal of the Negro: From Rutherford B. Hayes to Woodrow Wilson* (New York: Collier Books, 1965); Peter Kolchin, *First Freedom: The Responses of Alabama's Blacks to Emancipation and Reconstruction* (Westport, Conn.: Greenwood, 1972); Thomas Holt, *Black over White: Negro Political Leadership in South Carolina during Reconstruction* (Urbana: University of Illinois Press, 1977); Herbert G. Gutman, *The Black Family in Slavery and Freedom, 1750–1925* (New York: Pantheon, 1976); Jones, *Labor of Love*; Cell, *Highest Stage of White Supremacy*; W.E.B. DuBois, *Black Reconstruction in America* (New York: Harcourt, Brace, 1935); Barbara Jeanne Fields, *Slavery and Freedom on the Middle Ground: Maryland during the Nineteenth Century* (New Haven: Yale University Press, 1985); Ransom and Sutch, *One Kind of Freedom*. For Florida, see Shofner, *Nor Is It Over Yet*; Arnold H. Taylor, *Travail and Triumph: Black Life and Culture in the South since the Civil War* (Westport, Conn.: Greenwood, 1976); Woodward, *Origins of the New South*, and, also by Woodward, *Reunion and Reaction: The Compromise of 1877 and the End of Reconstruction*, rev. ed. (Garden City, N.Y.: Doubleday, 1956); Painter, *Exodusters*.

81. Jimmie Lewis Franklin, "Black Southerners, Shared Experience and Place: A Reflection," *Journal of Southern History* 60 (Feb. 1994): 11. For a discussion of the importance of land in framing identity and the ambivalence African Americans often feel about the South, see Chalmers Archer Jr., *Growing Up Black in Rural Mississippi: Memories of a Family, Heritage of a Place* (New York: Walker, 1992), and Willie Morris, *Homecomings* (Jackson: University Press of Mississippi, 1989).

82. Historian Jeffrey Kerr-Ritchie discusses this dual response to land among the freed people of the tobacco region of Virginia. He contends "that both landholding and exodus were the culmination of emancipation, prolonged agricultural depression, and a transformed tobacco economy. Furthermore, these two processes were twin aspects of the erosion of the older social relations. This dissolution occurred not simply

between former slaves and former masters, but also among younger and older generations of freedpeople as each pursued their freedoms in very different terms." See also Jeffrey Kerr-Richtie, *Freedpeople in the Tobacco South: Virginia 1860–1900* (Chapel Hill: University of North Carolina Press, 1999), 209.

83. Hurston, *Dust Tracks on a Road*, 10.

84. Quotations from ibid., 6–8.

85. J. M. Johnson, "Eatonville," *Federal Writers Project*, Orange County, Florida, n.d., 1.

86. Hurston, *Dust Tracks on a Road*, 9.

87. Johnson, "Eatonville," 1. Johnson depicts a much more troubled relationship between blacks and whites in Maitland than either Hurston or Otey does.

88. Hurston, *Dust Tracks on a Road*, 9–10.

89. *Eatonville Speaker* (22 June 1889): 1.

90. Johnson, "Eatonville," 2.

91. Ibid.

92. There are conflicting accounts about whether Lawrence sold or donated the land. The more plausible accounts come from one of the FWP's versions by J. M. Johnson, cited in n. 17, and the *Eatonville Speaker* (22 June 1889). See also Pearl Randolph, *Federal Writers Project*, American Guide (Negro Writers' Unit) Eatonville, Florida, ed. John A. Sims.

93. Randolph, *Federal Writers Project*, 1.

94. Petition for Incorporation, Orange County, State of Florida, Florida Historical Society, Melbourne, Florida.

95. Hurston says that Joe Clark was the first mayor but the petition for incorporation lists Boger. Otey gives 15 August as the date of incorporation, but the records indicate the 18th.

96. U.S. Census Bureau, Twelfth Census of the United States, 1900, Florida Population.

97. U S. Census Bureau, Fourteenth Census of the United States, 1920, Florida Population.

98. Otey, *Eatonville, Florida*, 22.

99. Larkin's daughter, Louise Franklin, still lives on Lake Sybelia. I conducted several interviews with Ms. Franklin and she provided me with several documents.

100. Zora Neale Hurston, "Eatonville When You Look at It," in Bordelon, *Go Gator and Muddy the Water*, 124.

101. Otey, *Eatonville, Florida*, 9–10.

102. Bordelon, *Go Gator and Muddy the Water*, 10.

103. Hungerford School Booklet, n.d., 1. See also, "Mississippi to Florida," *Ebony* (Feb. 1946): 40; Otey, *Eatonville, Florida*, 11. Different

sources give conflicting dates for the founding of the school. I have relied on the official history in the Hungerford Booklet and Otey's history of Eatonville.

104. Hungerford School Booklet, n.d., 1. The booklet claims that Dr. Hungerford died after contracting typhoid from a patient. Otey claims he died from malaria after treating some black children in the lowlands of Louisiana. Otey also claims that Mr. Hungerford gave 160 acres rather than the forty recorded in the official history. See Otey, *Eatonville, Florida*, 12–13.

105. Washington's interest in Hungerford is indicated not only by his cash contributions but by articles in the *Co-Operator*, the Hungerford School's newsletter, which Washington apparently read. See the *Co-Operator* 7 (Feb. 1912): 1, Booker T. Washington Papers, Tuskegee Institute, Reel 433. See also "A Press Release on Washington's Tour of Florida, Jacksonville, Fla., March 8, 1912," *The Booker T. Washington Papers*, vol. 11 (1911–12), ed. Geraldine McTigue (Urbana: University of Illinois Press, 1981), 482–86.

106. *Co-Operator* 7 (Feb. 1912): 13.

107. "Brown Town: Eatonville, Florida Is Oldest Negro Village in the United States," *Ebony* (Feb. 1946): 41.

108. Otey, *Eatonville, Florida*, 35.

109. Ibid., 26. One of Hurston's brothers became a pharmacist, the other a doctor.

110. Brown, "Uncle Ned's Children."

111. Painter, *Exodusters*.

112. Ida B. Wells, *Crusade for Justice: The Autobiography of Ida B. Wells*, ed. Alfreda M. Duster (Chicago: University of Chicago Press, 1970), 65–66.

113. Grace Elizabeth Hale, *Making Whiteness: The Culture of Segregation in the South, 1890–1940* (New York: Vintage Books, 1998), 199–240.

114. The account of Sam Hose's lynching is based on Leon Litwack's *Trouble in Mind: Black Southerners in the Age of Jim Crow* (New York: Knopf, 1998), 280–83, quotation on 281. His discussion is based on a story in the *Richmond Planet* (14 Oct. 1899), which reprinted the extensive investigation conducted by a detective sent by Ida B. Wells, and on articles in the *Savannah Tribune* (29 April, 6 and 13 May 1899); *Atlanta Constitution* (14–25 April 1899); *Atlanta Journal* (24 April 1899); *New York Tribune* (24 April 1899); *New York Times* (24–25 April 1899); *Boston Evening Transcript* (24 April 1899); *Kissimmee Valley (Florida) Gazette* (28 April 1899); *Springfield (Massachusetts) Weekly Republican* (28 April 1899). See also Ralph Ginzburg, ed., *One Hundred Years of Lynchings* (New York: Lancer Books, 1962), 10–21; Thomas D. Clark, *Southern Country Editor* (Indianapolis:

Bobbs-Merrill, 1948), 229–31; Brundage, *Lynching in the New South*, 82–84; Donald L. Grant, *The Way It Was in the South: The Black Experience in Georgia* (Secaucus, N.J.: Carol Publishing Group, 1993), 162–64. The *New York Times* story about an observer taking a slice of Hose's heart to the governor appeared on 25 April 1899.

115. See Maxine Jones, Larry Rivers, Thomas Dye, et al., *A Documented History of the Incident Which Occurred at Rosewood, Florida, in January 1923* (Tallahassee, Fla.: Board of Regents, 1993).

116. Zora Neale Hurston, "The Ocoee Riot," in Wall, *Hurston: Folklore, Memoirs, and Other Writings*, 897.

117. Walter White, "Election by Terror in Florida," *New Republic* (12 Jan. 1921): 195.

118. Ibid., 196.

119. See also Michael McLeod and Joy Wallace Dickinson, "Ocoee Race Riot Scars Generations" *Orlando Sentinel* (5 Feb. 2001): A8.

120. Hurston, "Ocoee Riot," 900.

121. Ibid., 901.

122. This letter was found by a researcher in the NAACP files in the Library of Congress.

123. McLeod and Dickinson, "Ocoee Race Riot Scars Generations."

124. Bordelon, *Go Gator and Muddy the Water*, 147.

Chapter Four

1. In Eudora Welty, *The Eye of the Story: Selected Essays and Reviews* (New York: Random House, 1977), 46.

2. Karen Fields, "What One Cannot Remember Mistakenly," in *History and Memory in African-American Culture*, ed. Geneviève Fabre and Robert O'Meally (New York: Oxford University Press, 1994), 150–63.

3. U.S. Census Bureau, Twelfth Census of the United States, 1900, Population, Schedule I, Eatonville, Florida, Sheet No. 11.

4. The family record page of the Hurston family Bible records the birthplace of the Hurston children as Alabama. I am grateful to Dr. Lois Hurston Gaston for sharing a copy of this page with me. See also Pam Bordelon, "New Tracks on *Dust Tracks*: Toward a Reassessment of the Life of Zora Neale Hurston," *African American Review* 31 (April 1997): 7–8.

5. Earl Lewis, "Connecting Memory, Self, and the Power of Place in African-American Urban History," paper in possession of author, Feb. 1994, 17.

6. Ibid., 18.

7. Hemenway, *Zora Neale Hurston*, 74.

8. "Black Death," Charles S. Johnson Papers, Fisk University, Special Collections, 1, hereafter cited parenthetically in the text.

9. Morrison, "Rootedness," 342.

10. A play on the name of blues singer Bo Diddley (Ellas McDaniel). "Bo diddley" is southern slang for "nothing at all," as in "he ain't bo diddley."

11. The memory of Africa was still very much alive for black people, particularly those in rural areas. WPA narratives suggest that some people remembered being born in Africa, while others believed that it was the "real" world, the one that they viewed with respect. As late as the 1930s many American blacks believed that native-born Africans could fly, having heard such stories in their childhood. James Moore of Tin City, Georgia, stated, "I seen folks disappeah right fo muh eyes. Jis go right out uh sight. Dey do say dat people brough frum Africa in slabery times could disappeah an fly right back tuh Africa. Frum duh things I see myself I blieb dat dey could do dis." Henry Gamble heard similar stories growing up near Savannah: "Wen I wuz a boy I heah lots uh stories bout people flyin. Some folks brung obuh frum Africa could fly off aw disappeah anytime dey wanted tuh." As historian Michael Gomez argues, "These people had no trouble accepting the notion that Africans could fly, for Africa was for them a mystical place and source of great wonder." See Georgia Writer's Project, *Drums and Shadows: Survival Studies among the Georgia Coastal Negroes* (Athens: University of Georgia Press, 1940), 18, 31, 48. Also quoted in Michael Gomez, *Exchanging Our Country Marks: The Transformation of African Identities in the Colonial and Antebellum South* (Chapel Hill: University of North Carolina Press, 1999), 118. The census records from 1900, 1910, and 1920 indicate that large numbers of black Floridians came from Georgia, the Carolinas, and Alabama, and that a few came from Virginia. See also George Rawick, ed., *Florida Narratives*, vol. 17 of *The American Slave: A Composite Autobiography* (Westport, Conn.: Greenwood, 1972), 3–7, for a narrative about "hants."

12. See Brenda Stevenson, *Life in Black and White: Family and Community in the Slave South* (New York: Oxford University Press, 1996), and Deborah Gray White, *Ar'n't I A Woman: Female Slaves in the Plantation South* (New York: W. W. Norton, 1985).

13. Danille Taylor-Guthrie, ed., *Conversations with Toni Morrison* (Oxford: University Press of Mississippi, 1994), 125.

14. Most of these names are listed in the 1900 and 1920 censuses; see the Twelfth Census of the United States, Schedule I, Population, Sheets 11–13; Thirteenth Census of the United States, Schedule I, Population. See also Lillios, "Excursions into Zora Neale Hurston's Eatonville," 26.

15. Hemenway, *Zora Neale Hurston*, 69.

16. Zora Neale Hurston, "The Eatonville Anthology," in Wall, *Hurston: Folklore, Memoirs, and Other Writings*, 813, hereafter cited parenthetically in the text.

17. Though Williams was probably joking, her comment was a gesture toward hoodoo revenge.

18. Lillios, "Excursions into Zora Neale Hurston's Eatonville," 19.

19. Ibid., 21.

20. John Bracey, interview by author, 18 July 2003, Library of Congress, Washington, D.C., and phone interview by author, 31 Aug. 2003.

21. Lillios, "Excursions into Zora Neale Hurston's Eatonville," 23.

22. See Higginbotham, *Righteous Discontent*; Darlene Clark Hine, "Rape and the Inner Lives of Black Women in the Middle West: Preliminary Thoughts on the Culture of Dissemblance," *Signs* 14 (summer 1989); and Deborah Gray White, *Too Heavy a Load: Black Women in Defense of Themselves, 1894–1994* (New York: W. W. Norton, 1999), chaps. 2–3.

23. Several historians have called for more research on the issue of color, but few have ventured into these waters. See Darlene Clark Hine, ed., *The State of Afro-American History* (Baton Rouge: Louisiana State University Press, 1986.

24. Hurston, *Dust Tracks on a Road*, 25. Hemenway explains the two different endings by suggesting that the version that appeared in the *Messenger* may have been missing the ending.

25. Hurston uses Joe Clark, the mayor of Eatonville, in her novels and many of her stories. But the Clarke here is obviously a representation. His name is spelled with an "e," while the real Clark's name is not. Moreover, Mattie Clarke is identified as his wife, but Mattie was actually his daughter's name. His second wife's name was Martha. Mattie was also the name of Hurston's stepmother, whom she disliked intensely.

26. This story was possibly true because Hurston returns to it again and again.

27. Cheryl A. Wall, "*Mules and Men* and Women: Zora Neale Hurston's Strategies of Narration and Visions of Female Empowerment," *Black American Literature Forum* 23 (winter 1989): 665. I am indebted to Cheryl Wall for our conversations on this subject and for sharing her work with me.

28. Ibid.

29. Hurston, *Mules and Men*, 31.

30. Ibid., 74, 85, 99.

31. Hurston, *Dust Tracks on a Road*, 225. Color could also be used to resist the racism that created divisions among black people. For example, my grandfather, who was extremely light-skinned, hated his color and insisted on blackening up his family. He refused to marry anyone

but a dark-skinned women. Many blues lyrics also suggest a complicated view of women and color. Sometimes very light-skinned women were viewed as untrustworthy.

32. Ibid., 226.

33. Hurston, *Mules and Men*, 33.

34. Ibid., 33–38.

35. Hurston, *Their Eyes Were Watching God*, 34, hereafter cited parenthetically in the text.

36. In the 1890s, when the action of the novel begins, black women's respectability was a major issue because of their ubiquitous characterization as loose, as we have seen. In 1894 Josephine St. Pierre Ruffin called a national meeting of all club women in Boston to protest the public characterizations of black women as "whores and prostitutes." This meeting resulted in the formation of a national organization of all black club women. See White, *Too Heavy a Load*, chaps. 1–2.

37. See Harriet Jacobs, *Incidents in the Life of a Slave Girl* (Cambridge: Harvard University Press, 1987), 5–8; Frederick Douglass, *The Narrative of the Life of Frederick Douglass: An American Slave* (New York: Signet, 1968), chap. 1; W.E.B. DuBois, *The Autobiography of W.E.B. DuBois* (New York: International Publishers, 1968), 61–100.

38. See Wahneema H. Lubiano, "Messing with the Machine: Four Afro-American Novels and the Nexus of Vernacular, Historical Constraint, and Narrative Strategy" (Ph.D. diss., Stanford University, 1987), 143.

39. See Hine, "Rape and the Inner Lives of Black Women," 912–20.

40. See Doris E. Saunders, ed., *Those Who Stayed: A Collection of Papers Presented in Six Public Forums, 1988–89* (Jackson: Jackson State University, Margaret Walker Alexander Research Center for the Study of African American Life, 1989). See also the U.S. Census Bureau, Twelfth, Thirteenth, and Fourteenth United States Censuses, Population, Schedule I, which show growth in Eatonville.

41. See Gunther Peck, "Mobilizing Community: Migrant Workers and the Politics of Labor Mobility in the North American West, 1900–1920," in *Labor Histories: Class, Politics, and the Working-Class Experience*, ed. Eric Arnesen, Julie Greene, and Bruce Laurie (Urbana: University of Illinois Press, 1998), 175–200.

42. An actual hurricane hit the Everglades at Belle Glade in 1928, killing more than 2,000 people.

43. Robert Haas, "Might Zora Neale Hurston's Janie Woods Be Dying of Rabies? Considerations from Historical Medicine," *Literature and Medicine* 19 (fall, 2000): 205–28; Hemenway, *Zora Neale Hurston*, 6, 355; Alice Walker, "Afterword: Looking for Zora," in Zora Neale Hurston, *I Love Myself When I Am Laughing... and Then Again When I Am Looking Mean*

and Impressive: A Zora Neale Hurston Reader, ed. Alice Walker (Old West-bury, N.Y.: Feminist Press, 1979), 297–99; Carla Kaplan, *The Erotics of Talk: Women Writing and Feminist Paradigms* (New York: Oxford University Press, 1996); Lillie Howard, *Zora Neale Hurston* (Boston: Twayne, 1980), 106.

44. Wright, "How Bigger Was Born," xi.

45. The WPA Guide to Florida: A conversation between Ann Henderson and Stetson Kennedy, Kennedy Papers, 11–12.

Chapter Five

1. See Peter Daniel, ed., *Peonage Files of the U.S. Department of Justice, 1901–1945* (Bethesda, Md.: University Publications of America, 1989). See also Tegeder, "Prisoners of the Pines," chap. 4, 155–201. Tegeder examines the violence in these camps on the part of the company and among the workers. See also Gussow, *Seems Like Murder Here.*

2. Vansina, *Oral Tradition as History.*

3. Griffin, *"Who Set you Flowin'?"* 32.

4. Kelley, "'We Are Not What We Seem,'" 76.

5. Hurston, *Mules and Men,* 60.

6. See Tegeder, "Prisoners of the Pines," chap. 3.

7. Hemenway, *Zora Neale Hurston,* 111.

8. See the Thirteenth and Fourteenth U.S. Censuses, 1910 and 1920, Schedule I, Population, Loughman, Polk County. Charlotte Todes, in *Labor and Lumber* (New York: International Publishers, 1931), suggests that logging camps were generally staffed by migrant labor.

9. Tegeder examines the racial tensions fostered by the company that pitted immigrants, particularly Jewish immigrants, against African Americans. See "Prisoners of the Pines," esp. chap. 3, 100–154. The testimony Tegeder cites is based on the debt peonage files cited in note 1 above.

10. Todes, *Labor and Lumber,* 83–84, quoted in David G. Nicholls, *Configuring the Folk: Forms of Modernity in African America* (Ann Arbor: University of Michigan Press, 2000), 50.

11. Tegeder, "Prisoners of the Pines."

12. "A Big Enterprise Establishment," (Bartow) *Courier-Informant,* 22 Feb. 1906.

13. Morris S. Addison, "Lake Locke or Loughman," *Polk County Historical Quarterly* 26 (Dec. 1999): 1. Historical data on Loughman and the Everglades Cypress Co. have been extremely difficult to find, and none of the historical societies in Florida I consulted had any of the company's records.

14. Bernice More Barber, *From Beginnings to Boom* (Haines City, Fla., Sept. 1975), 196.

15. "The Everglades Cypress Co., Loughman, Florida," *Polk County Historical Quarterly* 2 (June 1975): 1.

16. Barber, *From Beginnings to Boom*, 196, 198.

17. See "The Mule Bone Controversy," which includes accounts by Langston Hughes, Robert Hemenway, and Arnold Rampersad, as well as all the correspondence between Hurston and Hughes, in Langston Hughes and Zora Neale Hurston, *Mule Bone: A Comedy of Negro Life*, ed. Henry Louis Gates. (New York: Harper-Collins, 1991).

18. This play is apparently lost; it could not be found in John Houseman's papers at the UCLA Library Special Collections, at the Federal Writer's Theater Project at George Mason University, at the National Archives in Washington, D.C., or at the Schomburg Center for Research in Black Culture of the New York Public Library. No one seems to know the play and my only source is John Houseman's autobiography, *Run-Through: A Memoir* (New York: Simon & Schuster, 1972), which tells the story of the play on p. 205.

19. Barber, *From Beginnings to Boom*, 200.

20. See Brown, "Negotiating and Transforming the Public Sphere," 107–46. Many scholars have accepted the concept of separate spheres and the public-private dichotomy among black women, along with other groups. Brown challenges this argument, noting that much of this work revolves around the work of Jürgen Habermas, particularly *Struktur-wandel der Offenlichkeit* (1962), published in 1989 in English as *The Structural Transformation of the Public Sphere: An Inquiry into a Category of Bourgeois Society*, trans. Thomas Burger, with Frederick Lawrence (Cambridge: MIT Press, 1989).

21. Zora Neale Hurston and Dorothy Waring, "Polk County," unpublished play, HCUFLA, 1, hereafter cited parenthetically in the text.

22. Peck, "Mobilizing Community," 193.

23. Harry and Mary Grant, interview by author, Loughman, Florida, June 1997.

24. Hurston, "Characteristics of Negro Expression," in Wall, *Hurston: Folkore, Memoirs, and Other Writings*, 841.

25. Tegeder combed the peonage files for information on violence and lawlessness. See "Prisoners of the Pines," 183–201; for more information see also Nollie Hickman, *Mississippi Harvest: Lumbering in the Longleaf Pine Belt, 1840–1915* (Jackson: University Press of Mississippi, 1962); Stetson Kennedy, *Palmetto Country* (New York: Duell, Sloan, and Pearce, 1942); Gay Goodman Wright, "Turpentining: An Ethno-Historical Study of a Southern Industry and a Way of Life" (master's thesis,

University of Florida, 1979); Campbell, *Navel Stores Industry*; Elwood R. Maunder, ed., *Voices from the South: Recollections of Four Foresters* (Santa Cruz: Forest History Society, 1977); Gloria Jahoda, *The Other Florida* (New York: Charles Scribner and Sons, 1967); Gussow, *Seems Like Murder Here*.

26. Hurston, *Mules and Men*, 71, hereafter cited parenthetically in the text.

27. Charles Joyner, *Down by the Riverside: A South Carolina Community* (Urbana: University of Illinois Press, 1984); White, *Ar'n't I A Woman*; Hunter, *To 'Joy My Freedom*.

28. For a valuable study of hidden and public transcripts and of subtle cultural forms of resistance, see James C. Scott, *Domination and the Arts of Resistance* (New Haven: Yale University Press, 1990). See also Ladurie, *Montaillou*, for a wonderful account of the history of consciousness.

29. See Griffin, *"Who Set You Flowin'?"* 31–33.

30. See Shofner, "Forced Labor in the Florida Forests," 21; and Tegeder, "Prisoners of the Pines," 191–92.

31. Ibid.

32. Wall, *"Mules and Men* and Women," 667.

33. Hurston, *Dust Tracks on a Road*, 187.

34. Wall, *"Mules and Men* and Women," 668.

35. Ibid., 670. See Elizabeth Faue, who, according to Kelley, reminds us that class identities and ideologies are not simply made at work or in collective struggle against capital (Kelley, "We Are Not What We Seem," 82). Carolyn Steedman and Elizabeth Faue point out that because radical histories of working people are so invested in a materialist, workplace-centered understanding of class, they leave very little space "to discuss the development of class consciousness." Elizabeth Faue, *Community of Suffering and Struggle: Women, Men, and the Labor Movement in Minneapolis, 1915–45* (Chapel Hill: University of North Carolina Press, 1991), 15. Faue asks us to examine race, class, and gender identities long before we enter the workplace, as identities learned in childhood.

36. I have seen Ella Wall's land deeds, which are in the possession of a private collector named Carol Mundy, but they are not available for citation as yet. One of my informants, the Rev. Jimmy Howard, former pastor of St. Lawrence A.M.E. Church in Eatonville, escorted me around neighborhoods in the small towns and rural areas in Orange and Seminole counties. Jook joints dominated the social life on weekends in this area, and Rev. Howard informed me that local residents, for all of their wariness of violence, were very much a part of that world.

37. Hemenway, *Zora Neale Hurston*, 298.

38. This conversation also took place between Hurston and Big Sweet. Hurston, *Dust Tracks on a Road*, 189.

39. When I interviewed Mr. and Mrs. Harry Grant in the summer of 1997, Mrs. Grant said to me, "If you came to the camp on a Saturday night, there would be a killing for sure." When I asked what she meant, she laughed and said that my light color would cause a killing.

40. Sw. Anand Prahlad, "Guess Who's Coming to Dinner: Folklore, Folkloristics, and African American Literary Criticism," *African American Review* 33 (winter 1999): 565–75.

Chapter Six

1. See Eugene Genovese, *Roll, Jordan, Roll: The World the Slaves Made* (New York: Pantheon, 1972), 5–7, for a discussion of paternalism.

2. Hurston, *Dust Tracks on a Road*, 29, hereafter cited parenthetically in the text.

3. The history of white philanthropy is well documented. In *The Education of Blacks in the South, 1860–1935* (Chapel Hill: University of North Carolina Press, 1988), 79–109, 137–38, 276, James D. Anderson argues that northern philanthropists—through the John F. Slater Fund, the Julius Rosenwald Foundation, and the General Education Board—were willing to spend huge sums of money on the industrial and vocational education of southern Negroes because such a system of education would ensure a subservient labor force. See also Raymond Fustic, *Adventure in Giving: The Story of the General Education Board* (New York: Harper & Row, 1962), 328–35; John F. Potts Sr., *A History of South Carolina State College, 1896–1978* (Columbia: R. L. Bryan Co., 1978). For more on the ideological foundations of black education in the South, see Louis Harlan, *Booker T. Washington: The Making of a Black Leader, 1856–1901* (New York: Oxford University Press, 1972).

4. Whether this is an accurate assessment of this event we may never know; certainly her family contradicts Zora's account. For a discussion of this event from the family's point of view, see Bordelon, "New Tracks on *Dust Tracks*"; Hemenway, *Zora Neale Hurston*, 17–18. Hurston began and ended her work life as a maid. In this she shared the experience of thousands of African American women in the first half of the twentieth century. The literature on domestic work is vast and continues to grow. See Jones, *Labor of Love*; Clark-Lewis, *Living In, Living Out*; Lois Rita Helmhold, "Beyond the Family Economy: Black and White Working-Class Women in Chicago during World War I and the Great Depression," *Feminist Studies* 13 (fall 1987): 629–55; Susan Strasser, *Never Done: A History of American*

Housework (New York: Pantheon, 1982); David Katzman, *Seven Days a Week: Women and Domestic Service in Industrializing American* (New York: Oxford University Press, 1978); Ula Taylor, "From White Kitchens to White Factories: African American Working Women in Chicago during World War I," *Ufahamu* 14, no. 3 (1985): 5–51; Phyllis Palmer, *Domesticity and Dirt: Housewives and Domestic Servants in the United States, 1920–1945* (Philadelphia: Temple University Press, 1989); Harley, "For the Good of Family"; Eileen Boris, "Black Women and Paid Labor in the Home: Industrial Homework in Chicago in the 1920s," in *Homework: Historical and Contemporary Perspectives on Paid Labor at Home*, ed. Ellen Boris and Cynthia Daniels (Urbana: University of Illinois Press, 1989); Julia Kirk Blackwelder, "Women in the Workforce: Atlanta, New Orleans, and San Antonio, 1930–1940," *Journal of Urban History* 4 (May 1978): 331–58; Heidi Hartmann, "The Family as the Locus of Gender, Class, and Political Struggle: The Example of Housework," *Signs* 6 (spring 1981): 366–94; Martha E. Gimenez, "The Dialectics of Waged and Unwaged Work: Waged Work, Domestic Labor and Household Survival in the United States," in *Work without Wages: Domestic Labor and Self-Employment within Capitalism*, ed. Jane L. Collins and Martha Gimenez (Albany: State University of New York Press, 1990), 25–45.

5. Brooke Kroeger, *Fannie: The Talent for Success of Writer Fannie Hurst* (New York: Random House, 1999), 126.

6. Henry Seidel Canby, "Patrons and Patronage," in *Saturday Papers*, ed. Henry S. Canby, William Rose Benet, and Amy Loveman (New York: Macmillan, 1921), 111–12, quoted in Ardie Sue Myers, "Relations of a Godmother: Patronage during the Harlem Renaissance" (master's thesis, George Washington University, 1981), 1, 114–15.

7. Hurst, "Zora Neale Hurston," 17.

8. Fannie Hurst, *Anatomy of Me* (New York: Doubleday, 1958), 42–43.

9. Gay Wilentz, "White Patron and Black Artist: The Correspondence of Fannie Hurst and Zora Neale Hurston," *Library Chronicle of the University of Texas* 35 (1986): 22.

10. Ibid., 102.

11. Brandimerte, "Fannie Hurst and Her Fiction," 54.

12. See the *Jewish Tribune* (6 April 1928), Fannie Hurst, Vertical File 192, Hurst Papers, University of Texas at Austin.

13. Brandimerte, "Fannie Hurst and Her Fiction," 84.

14. Quoted in Kroeger, *Fannie*, 188.

15. Ibid., 190.

16. Ibid., 126.

17. Ibid.

18. ZNH to Constance Sheen, 5 Jan. 1926, HCUFLA.

19. ZNH to Countee Cullen, 5 March 1943, Countee Cullen Papers, Amistad Collection, Tulane University.

20. Myers, "Relations of a Godmother," 27.

21. Ibid., 28; Arthur Craig Quick, *A Genealogy of the Quick Family* (South Haven, Mich.: By the Author, 1941), 89, 134.

22. *National Encyclopedia of American Biography* (New York: James T. White, 1939), 27:287.

23. Hemenway, *Zora Neale Hurston*, 106.

24. Alice Walker, "On Refusing to Be Humbled by Second Place in a Contest You Did Not Design: A Tradition by Now," in Hurston, *I Love Myself When I Am Laughing*, 1.

25. ZNH to Mrs. Mason, 10 May 1931, Alain Locke Papers, Howard University.

26. Ibid.

27. Contract between Mrs. Mason and Zora Neal Hurston, 8 Dec. 1927, Zora Neale Hurston Collection, Moorland Spingarn Library, Howard University.

28. Hemenway, *Zora Neale Hurston*, 110.

29. ZNH to Alain Locke, 10 May 1928, Alain Locke Papers, Howard University.

30. ZNH to Alain Locke, 14 June 1928, ibid.

31. For a full account of the tensions between Mason and her protégés, see the new biography of Hurston by Valeria Boyd, *Wrapped in Rainbows: The Life of Zora Neale Hurston* (New York: Scribner, 2003), esp. chaps. 18 and 19. Unfortunately this biography appeared too late for me to make full use of it.

32. ZNH to Alain Locke, 16 Dec. 1928, Alain Locke Papers, Howard University.

33. ZNH to Mrs. Mason, 27 April 1932, ibid.

34. See Dickson D. Bruce, Jr., *Black Writing from the Nadir: The Evolution of a Literary Tradition 1877–1915* (Baton Rouge: Louisiana State University Press, 1989), 139.

35. Zora Neale Hurston, "Concert," in Wall, *Hurston: Folklore, Memoirs, and Other Writings*, 807.

36. ZNH, manuscript of *Dust Tracks on a Road*, 214, James Weldon Johnson Collection, Beineke Library, Special Collections, Yale University.

37. Hurston, "The World as I See It," in the Appendix of *Dust Tracks on a Road*, 343.

38. Ibid., 342.

39. Ibid.

40. Zora Neale Hurston, "Crazy for This Democracy," *Negro Digest* (Dec. 1945).

41. Ibid.

42. Ibid.

43. Claudine Raynaud, "Rubbing a Paragraph with a Soft Cloth"? Muted Voices and Editorial Constraints in *Dust Tracks on a Road*," in *De/Colonizing the Subject*, ed. Sidonie Smith and Julia Watson (Minneapolis: University of Minnesota Press, 1992), 35.

44. Ibid. Raynaud has performed a valuable task by carefully reading the original text side by side with what Lippincott published. Her findings suggest that Hurston was always well aware of the restraints to which she was subject in the white publishing world and attempted to resist.

Index

African Americans, northern states: culture, 10; dissemblance, 45; as historical agents, 45; in literature, 48–49; racism and, 8, 29, 34–35, 41, 42, 43; West Indians and, 177

African Americans, southern states: Africa and, 95–96, 207n11; behavior, 14, 53; business/economy, 14, 52, 54, 65, 66, 67, 68, 69, 77, 78, 130; churches, 14, 67, 68, 69, 77, 78, 100, 132; class and (*see under* class); color and (*see under* color); community relations, 52, 70, 77, 122, 136, 150, 156 (*see also* communities, African American); conflicts, 53, 81, 102–3, 104–5; consciousness, 7, 31, 130; culture (*see* culture, African Americans, southern states); dance, 107; debt, 57, 58; dissemblance, 28, 45, 139; domestic violence (*see* domestic violence); economic exploitation and, 52, 54; education, 35, 51, 54, 57–58, 60, 67, 69, 70, 77, 78–80, 81; elite, 8, 35, 37, 98; emotions/feeling, 34; employment, 14, 16, 58, 59, 61, 70, 74, 76, 81; entertainment, 51, 57, 80, 107, 137–38, 146–47 (*see also* jook joints); families, 9, 21, 49, 50, 52, 53, 70, 81; folklore, 7, 10, 12, 13, 17, 18, 47, 58, 91, 111, 114–16, 128, 134, 172, 173; fraternal organizations, 68, 78; freedom, conceptions of, 72; gender and (*see* gender; women, African American, southern states); government, 50, 65, 66, 67, 76, 80, 130; as

historical agents, 9, 20, 23, 29, 30, 45, 48, 49, 82, 129; honor, 96–97; historiography (*see* historiography, African American, southern states); hoodoo and, 8, 10, 95–97, 98, 150; housing, 57, 60, 81, 132, 135, 139–40; humor, 10, 11, 78, 81; hunger, 100; infidelity, 102, 104, 123; institutions, 52, 54, 65, 68, 80; intellectuals, 7, 8, 9, 10, 11, 13, 35, 36; intelligence, 58; justice, 95, 96–97, 152–54; knowledge, 9, 10, 81, 93, 94, 97; land ownership and, 71, 72–73, 74, 76, 77, 81, 118, 203n82; language, 120, 128, 129, 130; law and order, 21, 22, 51, 65, 66, 76, 78, 80; leadership, 150, 156–57; leadership, political, 14, 76, 80; in literature, 2–3, 7, 10, 11, 183; love, 92, 108, 116, 118, 119, 121, 122, 123; manhood/masculinity, 108, 109–10, 118, 120; manners, 22, 188n8; maroonage and, 12, 31, 66, 68; migration (*see* Great Migration; workers, migrant, African American); morals, 35, 48, 68, 81; music, 8, 10, 107–8, 137–38, 143, 145, 177; naming, 22, 23, 112, 141; nationalism, 6, 12, 66; newspapers, 65, 67, 68, 76; norms, 106–7; northern states and, 21, 29, 35, 37, 45; orality, 24; poetry, 10, 17; political participation, 62–63, 67, 75, 76, 80, 85–86, 89, 134; political rights, 55; privacy, 101; prostitution, 141; psychology, 33–34; public space, 78, 102, 108, 135–36; racism and, 2–3, 6, 8, 11, 29, 33, 34–35, 43;

217

TIFFANY RUBY PATTERSON teaches history and Africana studies at Hamilton College and is associate editor of *Black Women in United States History*, a sixteen-volume series.